STEPPING INTO A
MINEFIELD

A life dedicated to landmine clearance around the world

STEPPING INTO A
MINEFIELD

A life dedicated to landmine clearance around the world

BIG SKY PUBLISHING
www.bigskypublishing.com.au

Ian Mansfield

Big Sky Publishing Pty Ltd

PO Box 303, Newport, NSW 2106, Australia

Phone: 1300 364 611

Fax: (61 2) 9918 2396

Email: info@bigskypublishing.com.au

Web: www.bigskypublishing.com.au

Cover design and typesetting: Think Productions

Printed in China by Asia Pacific Offset Ltd

National Library of Australia Cataloguing-in-Publication entry (pbk.)

Author: Mansfield, Ian, author.

Title: Stepping into a minefield : a life dedicated to landmine
             clearance around the world / Ian Mansfield.

ISBN: 9781925275520 (paperback)

Notes: Includes bibliographical references.

Subjects: Mansfield, Ian.
             Land mines--Detection.
             Land mines--Safety measures.
             Land mines--International cooperation.
             Land mines--Afghanistan.

Dewey Number: 363.1798

CONTENTS

To Margaret, Zoe and Charles …
who have been with me every step of the way.

ACKNOWLEDGEMENTS

The motto of my publisher is 'Everyone has a story to tell'. I never would have believed this about my own life, until some friends said to me that I should write a book about my travels and experience over the past 20 years with landmine clearance projects around the world. Their suggestion remained in my head, but it wasn't until recently that I had the time and motivation to make the book become a reality.

I initially want to thank an ex-army colleague, Ian Gordon of Barrallier Books, who saw potential in my draft manuscript and passed it on to the Australian Army History Unit. Here, I must sincerely thank Dr Roger Lee and Dr Andrew Richardson for accepting my manuscript and including it as one of their projects. At Big Sky Publishing, my editors Denny Neave and his colleagues Sharon Evans, Sean Doyle and Jenny Scepanovic have expertly guided me through the editing and publishing process.

A number of family, friends and former colleagues have helped me with the book along the way. In particular, my brother and historian, Dr Peter Mansfield, guided and encouraged me from the start. I also wish to thank the following people who reviewed the whole draft manuscript and offered useful edits and suggestions: Sheree Bailey, Phil Bean, Christine Pahlman, John Pepper, Julie Pepper, Penny Drew and Doug McGill. Other people who provided detail and jogged my memory for various chapters include Graeme Membrey, Dave Edwards, Kefayatullah Eblagh, Faiz Paktian, Craig Egan, Paddy Johnston, John Raddatz and Irene Schiebel for Afghanistan; Jenni Rauch and Ben Lark for Laos; and JJ van der Merwe and Tim Horner for Bosnia. For assistance with the provision of photos my thanks go to Erik Tollefsen, Tim Lardner, Sean Sutton and Helene Tejerina.

Finally, I would like to thank a number of people who have influenced my life and assisted me to achieve what I have. In the Australian Army, I had the privilege to serve under Generals Mike Jeffrey and John Sanderson, both outstanding Australians who inspired me and led by personal example. I owe a special debt to my boss in Darwin, Brigadier Ian Bryant, and his wife Helen. They were our friends and later guardians for our children when they were attending boarding school while Margaret and I were overseas. Sadly, Ian Bryant passed away in 2011 – an inspirational leader and soldier of the highest integrity.

Within the United Nations system, I owe a special debt of gratitude to Martin Barber. A most unlikely role model, Martin guided me through the transition from the narrow confines of the military, to understanding the broader humanitarian world and how to engage respectfully with people from all cultures. I also wish to acknowledge two close friends who are no longer with us today, Mohammed Shakir, who accidently drowned in the Indus River in Pakistan in 1994, and Michael Creighton, who tragically died in a plane crash in Laos in 2014.

Stepping into a minefield? I could not have taken any of these steps without the love and support of my family; to my beloved wife, Margaret, who has made 22 'homes' in seven countries and has supported me in everything I have done - I could not have done it without you. And to our children, Zoe and Charles, who were with us along the way and accepted change and disruption with maturity and good humour, and grew into fine young adults. Lastly, a special thanks to their respective spouses, Craig and Rachel, and our four beautiful grandchildren Harry, Blair, Zara and Sophie, who bring joy and happiness into our lives every day.

FOREWORD

BY JODY WILLIAMS
NOBEL PEACE LAUREATE 1997

In 1997 I was awarded the Nobel Peace Prize in my capacity as the coordinator of the International Campaign to Ban Landmines (ICBL). This award was shared with the ICBL in recognition of our efforts to bring about a total ban on all anti-personnel landmines.

The official announcement from the Nobel Committee stated that; 'There are at present over one hundred million anti-personnel mines scattered over large areas on several continents. Such mines maim and kill indiscriminately and are a major threat to the civilian population and to the social and economic development of the many affected countries. The ICBL and Jody Williams started a process which in the space of a few years changed a ban on anti-personnel mines from a vision to a reality'.

The campaign was unique in every way. It grew out of the frustration of the slow pace and lack of action in the conventional weapons arms control talks held under the auspices of the United Nations. Hundreds of civil society organizations around the world started a movement calling for a ban on these inhumane and indiscriminate weapons, that were killing or wounding hundreds of people a month in countries like Afghanistan, Angola and Cambodia. The governments of several small and medium countries also took up the issue and lent their political support to the 'activist' campaign being led by the ICBL. Despite opposition from some major world powers and the militaries of almost every country, the so-called 'Ottawa Treaty' totally banning anti-personnel mines came into force in March 1999.

However, the political activism and lobbying was not the only part to this success story. While members of the Ottawa Treaty had to pledge to stop making and selling landmines, those war torn and mine affected countries that were littered with landmines had to commit 'to clear all known mined areas within 10 years'. To make the Ottawa Treaty work these countries would require more help, and this is where people like Ian Mansfield came in.

I first came into contact with Ian in 1993 when he was managing the landmine clearance program in Afghanistan for the United Nations. This was in the very early days of the campaign and we decided that we needed more evidence to support a call for a ban. I co-authored a book called 'After the Guns Fall Silent – the Enduring Legacy of Landmines' which was a series of case studies from 12 mine affected countries. I remember being impressed by the innovation, enthusiasm and achievements of the Afghan Mine Clearance program, and the leadership displayed by Ian.

The skills and equipment needed to clear mines lay with the military, but in Afghanistan the techniques and procedures were successfully being adapted to become civilian in nature, or 'humanitarian demining' as it became known. The landmine sector was becoming an unusual mix of left-wing anti-war activists through to right-wing military technical specialists (many of whom still believed landmines were a useful weapon). When I finally got to meet Ian personally a few years later, my normal anti-military scepticism was quickly allayed by his enlightened approach, positive attitude and support for the ban.

Ian went on to establish a highly successful cluster bomb clearance program in Laos and later managed another mine clearance program in Bosnia. Throughout his work Ian was able to show that the clearance of landmines was not 'mission impossible' nor would it take thousands of years, but rather with proper training, equipment and management, most countries could achieve the task in a reasonable time frame. His 10 years of strong field experience made him an ideal candidate to lead the mine action team in the headquarters of the United Nations Development Program in New York in 1998. One of his first activities in that position was to attend a small ceremony at the United Nations headquarters on 1 March 1999, when the United Nations Secretary-General Kofi Annan rang the peace bell to mark the entry into force of the Ottawa Treaty. I would regularly meet Ian at the various international meetings set up to oversee the implementation of the Treaty, and he was always a powerful advocate and voice for those people and organizations who were working in the field to clear mines.

This book by Ian Mansfield adds another dimension to the story of the successful anti-landmine campaign. This highly personal account tells of the motivation and bravery of thousands of deminers working around the world today, of the tragedy and heartache seeing landmine victims, and of the humour and friendships forged working among people of many cultures. It is also the personal journey of an ex-army officer who saw the need first-hand to ban an indiscriminate and inhumane weapon.

Vermont, USA, June 2015

PROLOGUE

The first landmine accident I ever came across was also the worst I ever experienced. It occurred in early 1992 during my initial visit to the city of Khost, located in eastern Afghanistan. While travelling with senior Afghan officials from the local mine clearance organisations we visited a site where a number of machines were being used to clear mines. We received an urgent message by radio that there had been an accident at another landmine clearance site so we left to investigate.

On arrival at the accident site an hour later we were advised that one of the Afghan men clearing mines, or a 'deminer' as they were called, was using his metal detector and had discovered a suspicious object on a dirt pathway running adjacent to a mud-walled compound. Not sure what he had found, he called for his partner to come and investigate. Still not sure, they summonsed their section leader but within moments something obviously went wrong and the device exploded.

Their colleagues found one badly damaged body 20 metres from the site, two legs from the second person were found on the other side of the mud wall, and nothing was ever found of the third man. From the initial analysis it looked like two anti-tank mines had been stacked on top of each other and then buried with some sort of anti-handling device – a type of ad hoc weapon arrangement now called an improvised explosive device, or IED. The remaining members of the demining team were given the rest of the day off as a mark of respect to their martyred team-mates. The next day the team was back at work, searching for more of the millions of landmines that littered Afghanistan.

Why was I, an Australian Army officer, in Afghanistan in 1992 and witnessing terrible events like these? The answer lay in the fact that the Soviet Union had recently withdrawn from Afghanistan, leaving behind a deadly legacy of millions of landmines. The clearing of landmines had traditionally been seen as a military responsibility, but there was no Afghan army in existence to do this. In response to this situation, the United Nations had asked a number of countries to provide advisers to train Afghan civilians in the clearance of landmines. Australia had agreed with this request, and I subsequently was posted (along with my family) to Pakistan for one year to command the Australian Army Mine Clearance Training Team, which was attached to the United Nations.

Due to a growing global awareness of the presence of landmines in other war-torn countries, such as Angola, Bosnia, Cambodia and Mozambique, the United Nations became increasingly involved with assisting these landmine-affected countries. As a result, I left the Australian Army and joined the United Nations and continued to work on the landmine issue for the next 20 years in Afghanistan, Laos, Bosnia, New York and Geneva. During these years I was literally 'stepping into minefields', but I was also walking into metaphorical minefields like politics, corruption, security threats and financial scandals.

CHAPTER 1:
A GRADUATE OF DUNTROON

My entry into the world was unremarkable. I was born in the Ararat and District Hospital on 23 November 1952, the fifth and youngest child of my parents, Fred and Annie Mansfield. My father worked for the Shell Oil Company as a sales representative, but his career had been interrupted by World War II. He had joined the Australian Militia Forces and served as a captain in a machine-gun battalion for over four years in Papua New Guinea. During the whole period of the war he only came home once for a couple of weeks leave. Dad's father, Harry, had served in the Royal Artillery of the British Army in World War I. So although my father and grandfather had served in the army, we were in no way considered a 'military family', because their service was only in response to the two world wars. Mum had been a nurse before and during the war in Mildura in northern Victoria, but like most women at that time stopped work to raise our family. My oldest brother, Alan, was born just before the war and then the rest of us – Brian, Helen, Peter and I – were born in quick succession after the war.

Ararat is a small country town in western Victoria about two hours' drive from Melbourne. The population in 1952 was less than 8000 people and the town was a centre for the surrounding 'wheat and wool' farms. We lived in town at 8 Clay Street, which was an appropriate name as our street was unsealed. As a child you are unaware of many things, but to me no-one seemed particularly rich or poor at that time. However, Dad did get a car with his job and we were one of the few homes in the street with a telephone. I can still remember our phone number – 'Ararat 750'. Neighbours would often come and ask to use the phone, or one of us kids would be sent running up the road to deliver an incoming message – usually bad news for someone in the street.

Milk was delivered by horse and cart each afternoon by the 'milko' who ran from house to house distributing the glass bottles of milk and collecting the empties – he did not have to drive the cart as the horse knew where to go. Old swagmen would ride their bicycles along the street selling rabbits they had shot, which were now strung over the cross bar of the bike. We were too far from Melbourne to receive its TV channels and it was not until April 1962 that the neighbouring town of Ballarat started broadcasting on channel BTV 6. We didn't get a TV at home for some years after that, but on hot summer nights the people who lived opposite us would put their TV out on their verandah and all the neighbourhood kids would sit on their lawn watching grainy black and white images. Life was simple and because I could go off with my older brothers, our mother's message was only 'be back before dark and don't get into trouble'.

If you mentioned the word 'mines' to me back then I would have immediately thought of goldmines. Gold had been discovered in Ararat during the gold rush period of the 1850s and the town had swelled in population with people hoping to find their fortune. Some gold mining techniques involved shallow diggings and panning for gold in rivers and creeks. Other times groups of miners would dig deep shafts hundreds of feet deep searching for the elusive seam of gold in the quartz rock. Many of these mine shafts were never filled in and they presented a hazard to people walking in the bush outside town. Sometimes logs may have been thrown over the opening of the mine shaft and then covered with dirt.

In 1957 Helen, Peter and I started at a new primary school called Ararat West. The site for the school had been carved out of bushland, and one day a student came running to the teacher and said that a mine shaft had collapsed on the sports field. The kid had a reputation for telling tales so the teacher said 'go and stand in it so I can see how deep it is'. The kid came back and said it was too deep to stand in and when we all went to look, we found a 'bottomless' mineshaft in the middle of our football oval.

In those days there were no controls on the sale of fireworks and 'bonfire night' was a big occasion. Maybe my interest in explosives started here, as I used to save up all my pocket money to buy as many 'crackers' or fireworks as I could. One year my brother Peter and I were fooling around lighting crackers in our bedroom and then throwing them out the window at the last moment before they went off. Naturally our mother came in and gave us a clip under the ear and confiscated all our fireworks. The next day the local paper came to our school and asked to take a photo of the 'best two boys' for an article on fireworks safety. My best mate Glenn Rundell and I were chosen and the following day our photo appeared in the paper with a caption saying we were both sensible boys who knew about the dangers of fireworks. Given that all our friends had seen the newspaper article, my mother had to relent and give back the fireworks to my brother and me.

In 1966 my father was transferred to Geelong, the second biggest city in Victoria and only about one hour from Melbourne. By then my oldest brother Alan had gone to university in Melbourne on a scholarship and Brian and Helen had left school and had jobs. Peter and I attended our local suburban school, Belmont High. The big excitement at that time in Australia was the changeover to the decimal system on a date well publicised by a TV jingle – 'on the 14th of February 1966'. The currency became dollars and cents and the distances kilometres. Despite all the predictions of confusion everything went smoothly and within a year no-one could remember the old system. You had to specialise in your high school studies quite early in those days and for the last two years I undertook only five subjects: English, Maths 1, Maths 2, Physics and Chemistry. I wanted to study engineering at university but the fees were prohibitive without a scholarship, which is where the army came in.

The late 1960s were a turbulent time in Australia as opposition to our involvement in the Vietnam War was growing and there were mass protests in the streets of most major Australian cities. Conscription, or compulsory military service, had been introduced for only the second time in Australia's history. The system of selecting conscripts was based on a random drawing of birth dates from a lottery barrel – if your birthdate came out you were drafted. Surprisingly, in a family of four boys, not one of my brothers' birthdates was drawn. I was too young to enter the ballot, but going against the national mood I found myself attracted to becoming an army officer. I enjoyed the outdoor life and playing sport, and officer training could also lead to an engineering degree.

In 1969 I was selected to go on a schoolboy trip to the Royal Military College, Duntroon, in Canberra as part of a recruiting campaign. The Ansett airlines flight from Melbourne to Canberra was the first time I had flown on a plane and also my first trip out of Victoria. I liked what I saw and despite a major bullying, or 'bastardisation' scandal at Duntroon hitting the national headlines the very next week, I went ahead with an application. I actually won a hard-to-get scholarship of $400 in Year 11 that was meant to help the successful applicants complete their studies in Year 12 before entering Duntroon. I saved the money and bought a car as soon as I could. I sat my major high school exams in November 1970 and then had to wait for the results. The system back then was that the results would be published in the newspaper in early January, followed up by a letter through the post to each student. It was quite an event for anxious kids to stay up all night around the back of the newspaper office, waiting to get their results when the first edition of the paper was printed.

The army moved fast. I got my letter saying I had passed my final exams on 13 January 1971 and the very next day received a yellow telegram from the army directing me to report to the army recruiting office in Melbourne three days later. Although I had applied for other university scholarships and courses this was the first 'offer' to be confirmed. As the training at Duntroon started well before the university year there was not much time to think before having to go and sign up. As attending Duntroon was still what I wanted to do, Dad drove me up to Melbourne where about 30 pimply-faced young men from all over Victoria were sworn into the army. Dad didn't normally express much emotion, but he told me he was very proud of me and as I had just turned 18, he bought me my first legal beer in a Melbourne pub. The pimply young men then boarded the overnight train for the trip to Canberra. What had happened to the airline flights, I thought to myself?

It is hard to express the emotion you go through when marching into the Royal Military College – feelings fluctuate wildly from excitement, challenge and comradeship through to fear, inadequacy and loneliness. I had signed up for an intensive four-year course involving military training and academic studies that would lead to a degree in civil engineering. The first few months of 1971 were just a blur as 108 new staff cadets from all over Australia were put through rigorous basic training with little spare time to think. The only relief was receiving mail, but that didn't always help morale when the letter contained an offer of a place at a civilian university – which would mean a much easier life and girls – because at that time there were only male cadets at Duntroon. However, most of us soon adapted and got into the routine and rhythm of college life.

The military focus was on counter-insurgency operations based on the Australian Army experience in Vietnam. I believe that we received some of the best training available in the world at that time. Our instructors were all combat-experienced sergeants and warrant officers who had just returned from tours in Vietnam, and ample logistic support was always available for our training, which included firing all types of weapons. I recall on one three-week training exercise my platoon instructor was the Victoria Cross recipient, Warrant Officer Keith Payne. Looking back I think Payne had some difficult times still serving in the army after receiving his VC, but I found him to be excellent. He was highly experienced and took the time to explain things and to correct faults without belittling you.

I also broadened my horizons at Duntroon in many ways. I had only been outside the state of Victoria once before and now I was surrounded by hundreds of officer cadets from all around Australia. In addition to the normal military training various adventure training activities were on offer. One year I went on a cross-country journey in four-wheel drive vehicles to Cameron Corner – the spot where New South Wales, Queensland and South Australia all meet. My first trip out of Australia was to Papua New Guinea, where a small group of us walked the World War II Busival Trail from Wau to Salamua. In my final year at the college I led another small group on a two-week exchange with the Indonesian Military Academy, Akabri, located in central Java. It was a fascinating experience to live and work beside Indonesian officer cadets.

It was also quite tough, as we all came down with severe diarrhoea, but had to 'soldier on' through a number of field exercises as we didn't want to appear weak to our Indonesian hosts.

While the majority of cadets were Australian, we did have some foreign students, mainly from New Zealand. However, in 1972, the Crown Prince of Thailand, Prince Maha Vajiralongkorn, started at Duntroon. To make things easy for us, he was known at the college as 'Mr Mahidol'. In his second year he was assigned to my section, so in the cadet hierarchy, I was his direct supervisor. Whenever I meet Thai people, they cannot comprehend that I was in a position to tell their Prince what to do. I actually felt sorry for him in some ways, as he had been sent to school in England and later Australia, and now he was packed off to military college – whether he wanted to go or not. He had spent more of his life in boarding schools in foreign countries, than he had in Thailand.

I got on well with Mr Mahidol and was invited to his 21st birthday party, and at the end of 1973 he invited me to Thailand as his guest. Unfortunately at the last minute he could not go, citing security concerns. However, I still went to Bangkok and enjoyed two weeks of sightseeing and VIP treatment. Some years later when I was posted to Perth, Mr Mahidol came back to Australia to undertake some training with the Australian Special Air Service regiment (SAS). My wife, Margaret, and I invited him and his bodyguard, Sammy, around to our modest apartment for a fondue dinner (which was popular at the time!). We sat on cushions around a low table and unbeknown to me the liquid fuel from the fondue burner had leaked out. When I went to light the burner, the whole table went up in flames. Sammy leapt over and dragged Mahidol away. There was no real danger, but I hate to think of the consequences if I had blown up the Crown Prince of Thailand.

Life for an army officer

The early 1970s was a turbulent time in Australian politics. Even though most troops had been pulled out of Vietnam, there was still a strong anti-war sentiment and regular protests were held in the streets of Australian cities. On our weekend leave from Duntroon we were not allowed to wear uniform, but with our short hair and conservative dress we would stand out, and we would often be the target of abuse and threats from anti-war crowds in Garema Place in Canberra. A huge change came when Gough Whitlam was elected Prime Minister in December 1972 and he officially ended Australia's involvement in Vietnam. Soon after the elections, the Whitlam government undertook a major Defence review that concluded that 'there was no foreseeable threat to Australia's security for the next 15 years'. This was greeted at the time with ridicule by the Defence community, as Australia had had troops on active service for the past 30 years. However, when we graduated from Duntroon there was no prospect of any operational service and the strategic assessment proved to be accurate.

By 10 December 1974 our class had been whittled down to 57 cadets and we graduated as officers in the Australian Army. Our parade was the first official function of the newly sworn in Governor-General, Sir John Kerr. Sir John looked resplendent in his top hat and tails, and my family members were all very excited when they got to meet him at morning tea, which was held in the gardens at Duntroon House. However, the gloss of meeting him later faded when Kerr became 'infamous' in Australian history one year later, by sacking the elected Prime Minister and the man who had nominated him, Gough Whitlam.

After four years of intense training and living in close quarters the Duntroon bond is strong and unique, and classmates keep in touch and support each other. One of our class, Peter Leahy, rose to become Chief of the Australian Army, New Zealander Lou Gardiner became Chief of their army and many other class members rose to prominence in business or government. The last year at Duntroon in 1974 was also memorable for me on a personal level as I met my future wife, Margaret. We met through mutual friends and after only a few dates we seemed to 'click'. Margaret was English and was in Australia for work. She had already booked a trip home and had signed up for work in a Swiss ski lodge over the winter. We wrote letters to each other after she left (she said mine were more like army memos!) and in one of them I suggested she come back – which happily she did in September 1975.

I was now a lieutenant in the Royal Australian Engineers and this involved another round of training courses, specialising in combat engineering. Topics included road building, bridging, water supply and so on, but the interesting subjects were demolitions and mine warfare. We were trained in the use of a wide range of explosives and became qualified to blow things up, conduct range practices and destroy certain types of unexploded ordnance. With regards to landmines, most of the emphasis was on laying them. Elaborate calculations were needed to determine the minefield density and detailed procedures dealing with mapping and marking minefields had to be followed. We also learned mine clearance drills, but the metal detectors were quite heavy and the work was boring, so we never really took it too seriously. If you accidently stood on one of the training mines they would emit a big cloud of purple smoke and stain all your clothes, but this just brought howls of laughter from your mates and the obligation to buy beer that evening. My attitude towards mine clearance certainly changed when I saw the real thing many years later.

My first posting was to an engineer unit in Perth and I liked being an army officer. As a very young man you were given great responsibility for soldiers and equipment, and had to quickly display wisdom beyond your years. Lots of real life incidents occurred that were never covered in the training manuals or exercises. I recall one evening I was just about to leave the troop office. A man telephoned and asked to speak to one of the soldiers, but when I said he had already left the man said 'tell him I am going to kill myself'. At age 22, I sat there for an hour and talked a complete stranger out of killing himself. Another soldier was in trouble for having a number of girlfriends on the go at the same time. I said to him, 'You seem to have a problem with sex.' He replied, 'I don't have a problem with sex; I just like it.' The leadership manual didn't have an answer for that one.

In late 1975 the Senate blocked the supply bill and the government was running out of money. All officers had to read a telegram from Prime Minister Whitlam to their troops that said soldiers may not get paid, but we were all expected to stand by our posts. My soldiers all started booing and jeering and I thought, 'They can't do that to the

Prime Minister.' But there was no doubt in my mind that all of them would have stood by their posts if need be.

Life for an army officer was all about a new posting and frequently moving location in order to get the necessary range of experience. This made a normal social life difficult, but Margaret and I were married in May 1976, not long after she returned from England. We were married at home by a civil marriage celebrant, which was rather bold and unusual in those days, as the first civil celebrant in Australia had only been appointed in July 1973. Shortly afterwards we headed off on a posting to Wewak in Papua New Guinea. Wewak was very remote and things were changing rapidly in post-independence Papua New Guinea.

My job was to look after the engineer services like electricity, water, sewerage and construction on three PNG Defence Force bases in Lae, Wewak and Manus Island. Again this was quite a heavy responsibility because all the services were provided by the Defence Forces on the bases. If any equipment broke down, my staff and I had to act quickly or improvise, otherwise the base would go without the essential service. There was not a lot of formal entertainment but we made our own fun and as Margaret and I both spoke 'Pidgin English' fluently, we got on well with the local community. I also was fortunate to be part of a small group that walked the famous Kokoda Track. We trained hard for the walk and completed it in five days, carrying all our own equipment.

A series of posting and moves followed, as did the birth of our daughter Zoe in 1978 and son Charles in early 1981. In late 1981 I was selected to go to the USA and Canada to undertake training in nuclear, biological and chemical warfare. Chemical weapons had been used in Yemen and during the Iran-Iraq war, and there was mounting concern in the West over the possible use of chemical weapons by terrorist groups. As the courses would last for longer than one year I was eligible to take my family, so we all set off to the US Army Chemical School in Anniston, Alabama.

The US Army has enormous resources and our training involved undertaking bomb disposal training with bombs filled with live nerve agents. The chemical is often referred to as 'nerve gas' but in weapons it is in a thick liquid form and when the bomb bursts it dissipates as droplets and then evaporates. One tiny droplet of nerve agent on a person's skin can cause instant death. During the live agent training we wore protective underclothing, rubber suits, boots, gloves and gas masks, and we had to defuse the bomb and neutralise the chemical agent. One of the symptoms of nerve agent poisoning is a headache, and as everyone had their masks fastened extremely tight because we were dealing with live agent, we all came out with headaches. This always caused great concern as to whether we had been contaminated or not.

Later, in Canada, we undertook more live agent training by having to decontaminate a vehicle covered in mustard gas – which again is delivered as a heavy liquid but then evaporates and causes blisters on the skin, or damages the lungs. I also did some training on targeting nuclear weapons and radiological defensive measures, but the US would not let foreign students undertake nuclear bomb disposal training – which didn't bother me too much, as I didn't fancy sitting on top of a nuclear bomb trying to defuse it.

On our return to Australia the Whitlam Government had long gone, but their prediction of no threat to Australia held true and the late 1980s and early 1990s were a quiet time for the Australian Defence Forces. We kept busy with training and exercises, but it didn't provide the motivation or excitement of an operational deployment. There were a number of United Nations peacekeeping missions underway, but these usually only involved a few individual Australian servicemen or women. I continued on with my career through a variety of postings which included commanding an engineer squadron and attending the Army Command and Staff College.

Next stop was Darwin where I was promoted to Lieutenant Colonel and worked at the headquarters of Northern Command. This was interesting work as it involved assisting customs, immigration and the Northern Territory police with coastal surveillance. Refugee boats were arriving in Darwin even at that time and the boats were routinely confiscated and then destroyed by blowing them up on the beach as required. With a change of focus by Defence on the north of Australia,

Margaret became heavily involved with advising the Government on Defence family issues. She was elected as a member of the National Consultative Group of Service Spouses (NCGSS), which was better known by the sceptics as the 'whingeing wives club'. The NCGSS had a very positive influence on Defence, which led to many improvements in housing and service conditions for families. Margaret also was appointed to the Northern Territory Women's Advisory Council set up to advise the Chief Minister on women's issues.

I had avoided working in a desk job at army headquarters in Canberra for as long as possible, but after three years in Darwin the 'system' finally caught up with me and I was posted to Canberra in January 1991. Canberra was a great posting location for families and we got the kids into school, Margaret found a job and we quickly settled into life in the suburbs. I was on the staff of the Chief of the Army and my job was to arrange his annual training exercise. This was meant to be a two-year posting, and then I expected the usual posting cycle to continue. It was in this context of a fairly normal army career that my subsequent involvement with the global landmine crisis was totally unexpected and unplanned.

A career opportunity presents itself

Late one Friday afternoon the duty officer walked past my office in army headquarters and casually remarked that he had a message that might interest me. He said that the United Nations had requested an engineer officer at the rank of lieutenant colonel to advise their fledgling landmine clearance program in Afghanistan. New Zealand had provided the first officer but they were unable to provide anyone else. I knew that small teams of army engineers were being sent to train Afghans in landmine clearance, but until then the highest rank to go had been a major, so I had paid little attention. My response to the duty officer was straightforward: 'Who on earth would pack up their family to go and live in Pakistan and work in war-torn Afghanistan?'

I had some recollection of the Soviet invasion of Afghanistan in late 1979 from the TV news coverage. I also recalled Australia's partial boycott of the 1980 Moscow Olympic Games over the issue, but other than that my knowledge of the country was fairly thin. The plight of the millions of Afghan refugees in Pakistan, following the withdrawal of Soviet forces from Afghanistan, was a long way from home and seemed to be dragging on forever. The whole situation was quite remote from life in Australia.

That evening I went home and discussed this possible 'career opportunity' with Margaret, and in spite of all the risks we decided that I would express interest in the job. I had served in a peacetime army for 20 years, and even though I had been fortunate to have worked in Papua New Guinea, Canada and the USA during my military career, I was always on the lookout for something more meaningful and exciting. Overseas postings were still hard to come by and this opportunity certainly presented a number of positive challenges. My major conference and exercise commitments would be over by the end of September, which coincided with the start date for this request, so I figured I was in a good position to get it.

In my favour was the fact that I had command experience, worked as an instructor at the army engineer school and had done a range of demolitions and mine warfare courses. The Australian Army had built up an excellent knowledge of mine warfare during the Vietnam War era and we were trained by highly experienced non-commissioned officers with hands-on experience in combat. One relevant experience of my own had been in 1987 when I was commanding an engineer squadron based in Brisbane. We had deployed to a cattle station near Mount Isa in outback Queensland and as part of the training we laid a live minefield. We placed a number of objects on some of the landmines, such as weighted down army boots, and then remotely fired the mines. In what has turned out to be a rather ironic twist, my photo appeared on the front page of the local newspaper, proudly showing the extensive damage inflicted on a soldier's boot by an exploding anti-personnel landmine.

After expressing my interest in the post I became extremely busy with work and the time just seemed to fly by. Margaret had a good job in Canberra and had also just been selected as a tour guide at Australia's new Parliament House. Our children's schooling was also a factor we had to consider, but when the offer came through what did we do? We chose Pakistan. As it was for most service families, moving was part of the routine; by that time we had lived in 15 different houses during our 15 years of marriage. So in September 1991 we set off to Pakistan on another new adventure.

CHAPTER 2:

'MR MINEFIELD' IN COMMAND

No matter how many briefings you attend they cannot prepare you for the heat and wave of humanity that awaits you on arrival at an airport in Pakistan. We overnighted in Pakistan's largest city, Karachi, and then flew on to Islamabad, the capital city, the next day. With our daughter Zoe, then aged 12 years old, our son Charles, who was 10, and a dozen suitcases we emerged from the airport terminal near Rawalpindi with literally thousands of Pakistanis pushing forward to meet their white-robed relatives returning from the Muslim ritual of the Haj in Mecca. Islamabad and Rawalpindi were 'twin towns', about 20 kilometres apart. The airport was exactly midway between the two, but the area had more of the characteristics of the bustle and chaos associated with Rawalpindi than the relative calm of Islamabad.

Fortunately, the chap I was replacing, Selwyn Heaton, was there to meet us and whisk us away to the hotel in the more modern part of Islamabad. Selwyn was a New Zealand army officer who had been in my class at the Royal Military College, Duntroon back in 1974, and we had also been together at the army Staff College in 1987. He settled us into the Holiday Inn, which was the best hotel in town at that time. This hotel subsequently became the Marriott and it was later blown up by terrorists in a fiery inferno in September 2008.

Pakistan is a Muslim country and alcohol had been banned since the era of the former President, General Zia. However, the hotel served beer to non-Muslim foreigners in their room, provided that each guest filled in a declaration that basically stated he or she was an alcoholic and needed a drink to satisfy their addiction. We had a drink or two and then Selwyn announced that he and I would be off early the next morning to attend a graduation ceremony for newly trained Afghan land mine clearance staff. This was to be held at the training camp which had been established by the United Nations near Peshawar, about three hours' drive to the west of Islamabad.

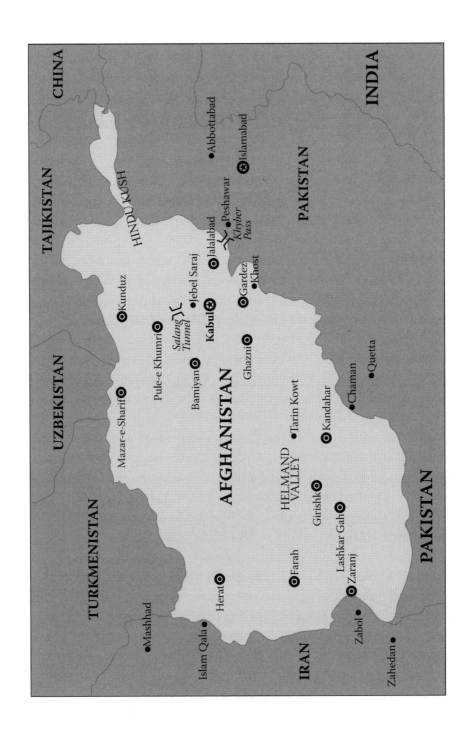

This news did not fill the family with joy, and when a few minutes later Zoe received a nasty shock from a faulty lamp switch in the hotel room and suffered a couple of bad burns, we were not off to the best of starts.

Selwyn collected me from the hotel at 05.00am the next morning in the obligatory white United Nations Toyota Landcruiser and the seemingly crazy Afghan driver. I was soon to learn that all drivers in the region were as crazy as I had been warned in the pre-deployment briefings. We set off from Islamabad towards Peshawar on the Grand Trunk road, which was more affectionately and appropriately known as the 'GT' road. In fact soon after our arrival in Pakistan I started to notice people, foreigners in particular, wearing T-shirts with the logo 'I survived the GT road' emblazoned on the front. Being relatively modern, the roads in and around Islamabad were in fairly good condition and there were restrictions on bringing animals like camels and donkeys into the city.

However, once we left the city outskirts the highway deteriorated and was full of potholes, but this did not seem to deter drivers from going as fast as they could. This would have been okay except for the fact that we were sharing the road with people, bicycles, donkey carts and camel trains. Every five minutes resulted in a near miss with another vehicle or some other unexpected event. The worst offenders were buses, aptly named 'Flying Coaches'. These were brightly painted with all manner of scenes shown on every panel and decorated with ribbons and chains that rattled on the ground, earning them the local nickname of 'jingly buses'. The buses were always crammed full of people inside, with more sitting on the roof and always a couple of young lads hanging onto the back.

'Are we going to get there alive?' I asked Mohammed the driver.

'*Inshallah,*' he replied. God willing.

I soon learnt that *Inshallah* was the standard response to all situations and I gradually became more and more fatalistic about unforeseen events in impoverished countries.

After about an hour of frantic driving we struck a traffic jam at the approach to a bridge. It was an old, narrow steel structure over a very steep gorge with a fast-flowing river down below. It had a faded sign posted on it stating 'only one vehicle at a time on the bridge'. The Pakistanis favoured large cargo trucks with wooden bodies, which were used to transport everything – from grain, dirt and animals to timber. The trucks were also brightly painted and decorated. When two trucks or jingly buses coming from opposite directions met on the bridge they could only pass each other with millimetres to spare. There was no thought of stopping and letting one truck pass through before the other crossed; they just met at the middle causing all sorts of arguments, shouting and delays.

Near the approach to the bridge a truck had mounted the concrete road divider and ripped out two wheels and an axle, which were perched forlornly on the concrete barrier. No attempt was made to move the vehicle, and it just lay on its side as half a dozen men were undertaking repairs in the middle of the road. When we were eventually able to proceed, we drove past the 'one-vehicle-at-a-time sign' and were quickly joined on the bridge by approximately 30 other vehicles!

Another hour down the road was the historic Attock Fort. This marked the border of the Punjab province and the appropriately named North West Frontier Province of Pakistan. Although only a provincial boundary, vehicles passing through the area were subject to a customs check. United Nations vehicles were exempt from paying any customs duty but commercial trucks and regular vehicles were pulled over and searched, usually with the result that the driver had to pay a 'fee'. I once asked my driver what was the best job in Pakistan and he replied without hesitation 'a customs official'.

The fort at Attock was built in British colonial times and was also the birthplace of the former British Prime Minister, Antony Eden. Now it was the barracks for a Pakistani Army commando unit. The fort overlooked a remarkable sight where the Indus and Kabul rivers met. The Indus was a bright, iridescent blue colour and flowed rapidly down its rocky course from the Hindu Kush Mountains, whereas the Kabul River was slow moving and a dark, muddy brown colour. When they met, the colours did not mix for some kilometres downstream, resulting in the amazing site of a two-coloured river disappearing off into the distance. Fortunately, a high, modern bridge had been built over the point where the two rivers met and down below were the remains of former bridges and areas where local families would stop and enjoy a picnic. Little did I know that some years later this picnic spot on the river bank would be the scene of much sadness for me.

We finally reached our destination at Risalpur Camp, which was about half an hour short of Peshawar. The tented demining training camp had been set up by the United Nations about two years earlier and it was situated at the end of a Pakistani Air Force base. The training camp had initially been established for what turned out to be a misguided attempt to address the landmine problem in Afghanistan.

The landmine problem in Afghanistan: a potted history

During the time of the Soviet occupation of Afghanistan it was estimated that six million Afghan refugees fled the country for Pakistan and another three million refugees crossed the border into Iran. The refugees in Pakistan were centred on the city of Peshawar in the north and Quetta in the central west, where they lived in huge tented camps and waited for the opportunity to return to Afghanistan. However, as the crisis dragged on their return was hampered by a number of factors.

The first was that a puppet Afghan communist regime, headed by Dr Muhammed Najibullah, still maintained control over Kabul and the major provincial cities. Najibullah had been in power some years before the final Soviet withdrawal in early 1989 and his government managed to remain in control for more than another two years. Secondly, it was known that the Afghanistan–Pakistan border areas and the villages that the Afghan refugees had come from were heavily infested with landmines. Finally, the tent cities had turned into sprawling, semi-permanent mud-walled villages in which the refugees had lived in poverty for almost 10 years. The refugees were reluctant to leave their 'new homes' in the camps, and it was obvious that should the refugees attempt to cross the border, an unprecedented human catastrophe would unfold with thousands of people wandering through unmarked minefields.

In 1988 the United Nations launched a general humanitarian relief program called Operation Salam, under the leadership of the late Prince Sadruddin Agha Khan. As a part of this program, the United Nations launched an appeal in October 1988 for funds to help train Afghans to clear the landmines. A 'village demining' concept was initially considered the best option. The United Nations would train Afghan refugees in basic mine clearance skills and when they returned home they would clear the landmines in their village and life would go on. The response to the appeal was very poor and only two countries responded with money. The vast majority of countries regarded landmines as a military problem, and not a humanitarian one.

Interestingly this latter group included Canada, which fortunately changed its opinions radically and later became the champions of the anti-landmine cause. A plan was devised whereby a number of predominately Western countries would provide military experts to train the Afghans. This group included Australia, Canada, New Zealand, Norway, Turkey, the UK and the USA. A two-week training course was developed and during the period 1989 to 1990 thousands of Afghans were trained in basic mine clearance skills.

However, the plan did not work for a number of reasons. The mine clearance training provided was of an extremely basic level and equipment such as sensitive military style mine detectors were not available. In one hurried but misguided attempt to solve the problem, 1000 commercial metal detectors were bought as a stopgap measure. These were orange coloured and of the type you often see people on the beach using as 'treasure hunters'. They were totally unsuitable for mine clearance operations or training, and they are still sitting unused in a storeroom to the best of my knowledge. Secondly, in an extremely difficult and volatile security situation, the idea of sending groups of Afghan ex-fighters, or mujahedeen as they were called, with a metal detector and a bag of explosives back into Afghanistan was not likely to stabilise the situation. Even if the 'deminers' had gone in, there would have been no method of enforcing safety standards or to properly record and regulate the work they were doing. In addition, had this scheme had worked, the ability to keep training such large numbers would have been curtailed because in February 1991 all the contributing nations, except Australia and New Zealand, withdrew their contingents from Operation Salam due to commitments in the First Gulf War.

By the time I arrived the United Nations had changed tack and was liaising with potential partner organisations to have them undertake mine clearance work on a more organised and controlled basis. There were well over 100 non-governmental organisations (NGOs) undertaking relief activities in Pakistan and Afghanistan at that time, but it was apparent that none specialised in mine clearance. The United Nations then undertook to create specialised organisations to fill this void. Fledgling Afghan organisations with names like Afghan Technical Consultants (ATC), Organisation for Mine Awareness (OMA) and the Mine Clearance Planning Agency (MCPA) were established from 1998 onwards. The training camp at Risalpur now trained fewer people but to a higher standard, and the graduates were employed by one of the new Afghan mine clearance NGOs, according to predetermined needs.

Although the small contingent of Australian and New Zealand army officers and sergeants delivered the mine clearance training, because the training camp was located on a Pakistani military base, it came under the overall control of their own camp commandant. In this case it was Colonel Sajaad, a charming Pakistani engineer officer, who was also a proud Pathan from the tribal areas of Pakistan bordering Afghanistan. On arrival at the camp Colonel Sajaad gave me a wonderfully formal salute, all the more remarkable given he was one rank higher than me! However, I was to find many Pakistanis, particularly in the military, were 'more British than the British' in their attitudes, manner and dress. Even though the mine clearance program was a civilian activity, and even though I was a lieutenant colonel, the Pakistanis, both military and civilian, called me by the generic title 'Colonel Mansfield'. Initially, I didn't want to use my military title in the job, but I soon came to see that in this environment, it was an asset – both at work and in day-to-day matters.

I was also reunited with the Australian contingent that I now commanded, having undergone the same pre-deployment training with most of them before leaving Australia. While I had previously commanded an engineer squadron in Australia, being responsible for a group of your own soldiers overseas in a hazardous environment was a particular challenge and honour. At this stage I had to admit that my thoughts were mainly focussed on succeeding at this, rather than any great commitment to the United Nations or providing humanitarian relief to the Afghans.

When nations provide troops to a formal United Nations peacekeeping operation they can only go into another country with the authority of a UN Security Council resolution. The resolutions authorise the soldiers to wear their national military uniform and the recognizable 'blue helmet' of the United Nations. It also allows them to carry weapons (depending on the type of mission) and to use their weapons in accordance with the so-called Rules of Engagement. The participating troops are also awarded the UN medal inscribed with the words 'In the Service of Peace' at the completion of their tour.

Operation Salam in Afghanistan was a humanitarian mission, so it did not have any Security Council backing. There had been no formal resolution authorising the deployment of foreign troops to Pakistan or Afghanistan, even though it was acknowledged that the only expertise in clearing landmines lay with the military. Because the project did not have Security Council clearance, the troops provided to Operation Salam enjoyed none of the recognised benefits and more importantly, none of the diplomatic protections normally accorded to peacekeeping missions.

A pragmatic solution had to be found and donor nations, in effect, provided their military mine clearance advisers on an individual basis and we were each afforded the United Nations contractual status of 'Experts on Mission'. This status was normally used for short-term civilian consultants, such as water engineers or agricultural specialists. We were unarmed and not allowed to wear national uniform or rank. A compromise had been reached and it was agreed that all nationalities could wear a dreadful looking, locally made khaki-coloured safari suit, with a United Nations badge and a national flag on the sleeve.

So, 24 hours after leaving Australia, here lined up in front of me at Risalpur Camp were 14 safari-suited Australians and three New Zealanders – the remainder of what had once been a contingent in excess of 100 military advisers from the original seven troop-contributing countries. I quickly came to realise that this was a blessing, because when the other countries had been involved there had been continuous debate and argument over the best equipment or procedures to use when teaching demining techniques. Everyone naturally thought their own way was the best, so now with only two countries involved, deciding a common approach was going to be much easier.

Twenty Afghan refugees had attended the four-week training course and now they were ready to graduate. These were the first Afghans I had ever met and they were all tough-looking bearded ex-mujahedeen fighters. They were dressed in the local attire called the *shalwar-kameez*, which consisted of loose-fitting pyjama-like trousers and a long over-shirt. I gave a stirring speech congratulating them on completing the training course and wishing them all the best for their dangerous work ahead. As soon as I finished, they punched the air and gave a rousing chant of 'Allah Akbhar, Allah Akbhar, Allah Akbhar!' – God is great. I rather naively thought to myself, 'This is going to be easy to motivate these Afghans'. This notion was quickly dispelled when the interpreter then started speaking and told them all that I had said!

After the parade I examined a display that featured most of the 40 types of mines that littered Afghanistan. There were large anti-tank mines, but most of the landmines that were on display were what the military blandly call 'anti-personnel' mines. Explosive devices designed to hinder the progress of an advancing army had been around for centuries. In the American Civil War wicker baskets filled with explosives were buried on roads likely to be used by the opposing force. When the attacking troops came near to the buried bomb, the fuse was lit by the defenders and it was timed to explode in the midst of the attackers.

MODERN LANDMINES AND HOW THEY WORK

Landmines in their current form were developed during World War I, initially by the Germans as a counter to the armoured tank, a British invention of the time. Anti-tank mines were large, bulky explosive devices that looked like a cake tin and were initiated by the weight of an enemy tank driving over the top of it. It was relatively easy for the opposition troops to sneak across no-man's land at night and dig up the anti-tank mines laid by the defenders, so a smaller anti-personnel version was often laid around the bigger mine to protect it. This smaller mine proved its worth and was soon used on its own to protect front lines and to break up enemy infantry attacks.

During World War II, anti-personnel and anti-tank landmines were used in enormous numbers by all sides, inflicting a large number of casualties and considerable damage to equipment and infrastructure. The mines were generally laid in patterns and the defensive minefields were fenced, signposted and accurately mapped. The situation changed during the Vietnam War period when, due to their low cost and ease of use, anti-personnel landmines were used effectively by the North Vietnamese as a harassing, guerrilla type weapon. They were used to disrupt ground troops and to inflict casualties on both civilian and military targets. In many other conflicts around the world anti-personnel landmines were used in this random manner, and then just left when the conflict was over.

The modern mines now on display at Risalpur Camp came in a range of shapes, sizes and colours and had been manufactured in a variety of countries, although the majority were of Soviet origin. The mines all had innocuous sounding military names, such as the PMN, POM-Z, bounding fragmentation mine and PFM-1.

One of the most commonly used landmines in Afghanistan was the Soviet designed PMN. As far as anti-personnel mines go, it is a particularly large one and belongs in a category called a blast mine. It is so called because it is the power of the explosive blast that causes the injuries to the victim. The PMN mine is circular in shape and about the size of a large coffee cup, with a brown bakelite body and a black rubber cap. Under the rubber cap is a pressure plate which when pressed fires a detonator, which in turn fires the main explosive charge. The mine is designed to be buried just below the surface of the ground and to explode when an unsuspecting foot steps on it. Due to the relatively large amount of explosive in the mine the blast wave causes severe damage to the victim's leg. Usually the whole foot of an adult will be blown away and most of the bone and muscle up to the knee will be ripped away. As the blast radiates in all directions, the victim's other leg will also be damaged. If a child steps on a PMN mine they are most likely to be killed.

One of the perverse aspects of anti-personnel landmines is that they are generally designed to maim, rather than kill. In a battlefield situation a soldier who steps on a mine will be screaming in agony, which will strike fear and caution in his comrades. It also requires a medic to treat the wounded person and then a number of stretcher-bearers are needed to evacuate the soldier back to an already over-burdened first aid post.

The next mine could best be described as a hand grenade on a stick. It is called a POM-Z and consists of a cast metal cylinder with knobbly indentations all around it. A high explosive charge is placed inside it and then it is placed on top of a short wooden stake, and thus the mine sits slightly above ground level. A fuse pokes out of the top and then trip wires are attached to it. A trip wire is a long, thin piece of wire, a bit like a fishing line. It is stretched out from the device for about 10 metres and then attached to a firm object at the other end, like a tree or a wooden stake. When someone walking through it stretches the trip wire, it pulls out a pin and the mine fires. The cast metal case is violently blown apart with jagged fragments flying out in all directions. People within a radius of 20 metres would certainly be killed and those further away may be wounded.

If an extensive minefield has been laid then a number of the trip wires may be interconnected, so when one mine is tripped, it sets off a chain reaction. You may well think that this type of mine would be easy to see or detect, but at night or in long grass, they are surprisingly difficult to spot. Also, after a number of years exposed to the elements, the wooden pole rots away and falls over, leaving the mine in a highly unstable and dangerous state.

A particularly nasty device is the bounding fragmentation mine. What this means is that the mine is buried, but when someone steps on it the initial charge shoots it up out of the ground to about waist height and then the main charge detonates, sending a burst of metal fragments in every direction. Again, the metal fragments have a lethal radius of at least 20 metres. The mine itself is about the size of a large tin can and the fuse on top can be set off by pressure, or it can be fitted with a trip wire. This mine is sometimes given the rather trivial nickname of 'bouncing Betty' and was once featured in a movie titled 'No Man's Land'. Unlike the movie where the hero steps on the mine and then doesn't move his foot, allegedly to stop it going off, in real life the moment you step on it, it fires.

Often press reports claimed that some landmines were designed to look like toys in order to attract children. This is not the case, as all landmines are military devices originally designed to kill or maim soldiers. However, the one that was the basis for these kinds of comments was another Soviet designed mine, with the military name of PFM-1, but more popularly known as the 'butterfly mine'. It is of plastic construction with two butterfly-shaped wings. One side is filled with liquid explosive; the other is a flat plastic stabilising fin and the whole thing measures about 10 centimetres across. A fusing mechanism runs down the centre. If someone steps on it or picks it up and squeezes it, pressure is applied to the liquid-filled side and the fuse mechanism explodes the mine. As it was somewhat smaller than the other mines on display, this mine usually blows off the fingers or toes of the victim.

The horrendous thing about the PFM butterfly mine is the sheer numbers in which it can be delivered. The mines are packed into various types of containers and each container can hold hundreds of individual mines. The mines are usually dispensed by aircraft or helicopter. Although many of the figures relating to the number of landmines in the world today have been exaggerated, when you consider that one helicopter pass can deliver thousands of these devices, large numbers are easy to come by. Again, you may think that because this mine flutters down and lands on the surface of the ground they would be easy to see, but their small size makes them difficult to spot and they come in either green or light brown colour in order to blend in with their surroundings. It is this shape and colour that often led to some reporters to describe them as landmines 'looking like toys'.

UNOCHA, NGO, HALO, MCPA and other useful acronyms

After the trip to Risalpur Camp I spent the next few weeks back in Islamabad getting to grips with the new organisation I was meant to be advising. The whole arrangement of providing humanitarian assistance in a post-conflict environment was still in its early days for the United Nations, and all rather ad hoc. The office I was attached to had the long title of the United Nations Office for the Coordination of Humanitarian Assistance to Afghanistan, or UNOCHA for short.

The role of UNOCHA was to coordinate the humanitarian response of the various United Nations agencies – mainly assisting Afghan refugees in Pakistan, but also including those refugees in Iran and the former Soviet Union. UNOCHA itself had the specific task of managing a number of aircraft that were leased to fly United Nations staff and supplies into Afghanistan. UNOCHA also ran an extensive and effective radio network. The base station in Islamabad was open 24 hours a day and through this we could communicate to United Nations regional offices in Afghanistan, to the aircraft and to vehicles fitted with high frequency (HF) radios. Both the aircraft and the radio network were the backbone and a most vital component of the United Nations relief efforts in Afghanistan.

There was also an associated political office dealing with Afghanistan located in Islamabad, which was headed by a veteran diplomat named Benon Sevan. His title was the Special Representative of the United Nations Secretary General and although I had served in overseas posts before, this was my first real exposure to high level international diplomacy in a conflict situation. Some years later Benon was named in the Iraq oil-for-food scandal, but at the time that I met him I was impressed with the flair he displayed and his skill with handling tricky situations. He was a career United Nations diplomat originally from Cyprus and I liked the way he always had time to talk to you and share a joke. The humanitarian side of the organisation was headed by Martin Barber, a tall British gentleman who had extensive experience in dealing with refugees in Cambodia during the Pol Pot period, both with the United Nations and the British Refugee Council. Martin and I were to develop a close working relationship and our paths were to cross many times in the following years.

STEPPING INTO A MINEFIELD

As a result of the Soviet invasion of Afghanistan, the United Nations agencies had withdrawn their headquarters from Kabul to Islamabad, both for political and security reasons. At that time in 1991, most United Nations agencies had kept a sub-office open in Kabul, but the majority of relief activities were focussed on the refugee camps in Peshawar and Quetta. The UNOCHA head office in Islamabad was housed in rented offices in the Pakistani Red Crescent compound, and this is where I reported to start my regular work.

The mine clearance effort at the time consisted of a series of separate projects, where each of the newly formed Afghan demining NGOs was given a specific task. Some were set up to do the actual mine clearance work, which we started to call 'humanitarian demining' or just 'demining' to differentiate it from the military combat term of minefield breaching. Another NGO undertook mine awareness or safety education campaigns in the refugee camps, and yet another was set up to conduct minefield surveys, produce minefield maps and to coordinate the work of the other NGOs. This latter task was doomed to fail, as traditionally NGOs dislike being coordinated by anyone, let alone another NGO.

UNOCHA had appointed a Norwegian national named Jan Haugland to oversee this loose arrangement of mine clearance projects. Haugland was an unusual man. He was very pleasant and an adventurer by nature, having previously been to the North Pole and now in his spare time, led camel safaris through the Pakistani desert. However, I found him to be quite erratic and he had a number of annoying habits. One was that he chewed tobacco and spat the juice into a spittoon under his desk while he was talking to you. The other was that he would sit in his office and shout out my name, 'Mansfield!' expecting me to come. As a colonel in the army I did not normally come when someone shouted my name. Fortunately for me a number of events happened to improve my lot. Due to some rather public criticism of the way the landmine problem was being dealt with in Afghanistan, UNOCHA had commissioned an independent evaluation to review the situation. At the same time Haugland decided to leave and Martin Barber asked me to manage the program until they could find a suitable United Nations replacement.

The independent review was quite critical of the whole mine clearance set-up and identified over 40 areas where improvements could be made. It recommended that in the absence of a recognised Government in Afghanistan, there should be more oversight exerted by the United Nations. At that time, there was not even one master database or map showing where all the known minefields were in Afghanistan. The main humanitarian concern was the potential return of refugees to their home villages, yet no agency could guarantee that the mines would be cleared before their return. Martin and I studied the evaluation report in detail and came up with a plan to introduce a more coordinated and centralised response to the problem.

As the whole operation depended on funding from foreign countries, we decided to hold a donor meeting to explain the reforms we were planning to introduce. Another United Nations colleague who was working on agricultural projects in the country at the time, Bob Eaton, said that he had heard about the meeting and came along as he expected us to be torn apart for all the past shortcomings. In his own words, he said I was 'brilliant' in accepting the deficiencies of the current arrangement, and then mapping out a strategy to deal with the landmine problem on a more organised and controlled basis. At that time exaggerated claims were being made of up to 10 million landmines being laid in Afghanistan and thousands of years being needed to clear them all. I broke the problem down into priorities, focused on expected population movements, and put a time scale of 10 years on solving the worst of the landmine problem.

The first thing I did was to move the organisation responsible for the survey and mapping of minefields from Peshawar up to our headquarters in Islamabad. A bright young Afghan named Sayed Aqa headed this organisation, called the Mine Clearance and Planning Agency, or MCPA. Afghans traditionally have a culture of respecting 'grey beards' or older people, yet Sayed was only in his late twenties and was ably managing an organisation that was starting to hire hundreds of staff and attracting an annual budget of millions of dollars per year. Sayed brought his minefield database and operations staff to Islamabad and he worked as my operations officer at a headquarters that was deliberately not military in character, but which had all the components of a responsive and centralised 'head office'.

The organisations involved with actual mine clearance were based in Peshawar and Quetta, and their teams undertook four- to six-week 'missions' into Eastern Afghanistan to clear minefields in areas that were under mujahedeen control. The reporting back of progress in terms of numbers of mines destroyed or square metres cleared was erratic, and there was little way of verifying what was actually happening on the ground. Rumours abounded of mines being dug up by various groups and subsequently being offered for sale in the bazaars in the tribal areas of Pakistan.

Another of the Peshawar-based Afghan NGOs, the mine awareness organisation OMA, delivered safety messages in the refugee camps in Peshawar or Quetta. Working in Peshawar had its own risks, a fact that was brought home to us when OMA's finance officer was shot and killed outside his home in January 1992. I didn't know what to make of this as I was still quite new, but as time went on there were many killings, kidnappings and accidental deaths of people working in Afghanistan.

Although the United Nations had decided on the policy of establishing Afghan organisations to undertake mine clearance work, two other international mine clearance organisations also had their beginnings around this time. The first was a British charity with the rather catchy name of the HALO Trust – standing for the Hazardous Areas Life-Support Organisation. HALO was registered as a charity in the United Kingdom in 1988 by Colin Mitchell, a somewhat eccentric former colonel in the British Army. Colin worked out of his home in London, their letterhead gave the rather quaint address of Drake House, Dolphin Square, London, SW1V 3NW and his wife, Susan, kept the books.

When I arrived in Afghanistan HALO were a small outfit, with only about 30 Afghan deminers and five British supervisors, working in and around Kabul. 'Mad Mitch' as he was known in the British press was famous for his exploits in saving the British garrison in Aden in 1967, and then successfully running for one term in the British parliament on the sole platform of saving his regiment, the Argyle and Sutherland Highlanders, from disbandment. The United Nations had funded some of HALOs early work, mainly to keep a balance between the vast majority of money going to Afghan NGOs working in the refugee camps in Pakistan and the mujahedeen-controlled areas of the Afghan countryside, compared with the small amount going to the Najibullah Government-controlled cities like Kabul.

The second international organisation with its roots in Afghanistan was again British, and it had the rather more focused title of the Mines Advisory Group, or MAG. The founder of MAG was an outspoken character named Rae McGrath. Rae was a former warrant officer in the British Army and had been employed by UNOCHA for a period. However, he had become disillusioned with what he perceived as the bureaucracy and slow progress of the United Nations, and so he wrote a very critical letter that was published in a United States newspaper. Not surprisingly, he left the UNOCHA shortly after. Although his NGO was not undertaking mine clearance activities at that time, Rae conducted the first survey of mined areas in some of the eastern provinces of Afghanistan and published a report under the name of MAG. He then left Pakistan to concentrate on starting MAG mine clearance activities in Cambodia.

As part of my effort to better coordinate and focus the work of the Afghan organisations, I instituted a series of monthly planning meetings. These were usually held in Islamabad, but we also held them in Peshawar, and later throughout all parts of Afghanistan. I chaired the meetings which consisted of United Nations staff, the attached military technical advisers and the directors of the Afghan NGOs. These were real cross-cultural events with all the differing languages, backgrounds and experiences coming into play. English was the official language of the program, but I discovered that there were many versions of 'English'.

At one meeting the Afghans kept going on about 'wehicles'. It took me some time to realise what they were on about. As a Norwegian, the previous manager Haugland had pronounced the letter 'v' like a 'w', so here was a whole room full of Afghans talking about 'wehicles'. The other source of confusion was my name. When Australians say the letter 'a' it often sounds to others like an 'i'. Many a time I spelt out my name with the result being written down as 'Mr Minefield', which proved to be a constant source of amusement to the Afghans that my name and my job were the same.

At one of the first monthly coordination meetings that I chaired, Colin Mitchell was out from England on a visit, so he attended the meeting. We discussed the draft annual mine clearance plan that we were working on, and then I put up an organisation chart outlining a more formal structure for the mine clearance program. The chart had my UNOCHA office at the top and then the various Afghan organisations shown below – allocated to various provinces or thematic responsibilities. I had placed HALO on the chart but with no connecting lines.

During the meeting we went around the table for comment and when it came to Colin, off he went. 'No-one has ever boxed in HALO Trust,' he exclaimed. For the next 10 minutes he made statements about the lack of competence in the United Nations and the inadequacy of the Afghan NGOs. This was all rather curious given that the United Nations had provided funds for HALO's work, and the room was full of the Afghan NGO Directors he was so roundly criticising. When he finished I thanked Colin for his comments, ignored them and just kept on with the meeting. That night we hosted drinks at our home where I had a lovely chat with Colin, and surprisingly I found him to be quite a charming person.

A brush with royalty – almost

Not long after we had arrived in Pakistan a major state event occurred with the visit of Diana, Princess of Wales. Her itinerary included a stay in Islamabad to meet with Pakistani Government officials and to attend a garden party on the lawns of the British High Commission. She was then due to travel to Peshawar to visit some Afghan refugee camps and also to travel up to the famous Khyber Pass.

Our office sent a message to the British High Commission, suggesting that a visit to the landmine clearance training school at Risalpur be included on her itinerary. I am sure that the message never got to her, but a reply came back saying that Diana just wanted to meet some refugees and that she was not interested in landmines. Fortunately, this situation was to change some years later, when for a short period Princess Diana became the very public face of the anti-landmine cause.

CHAPTER 3:

MEET AND GREET
IN AFGHANISTAN

Originally, the Australian Government had only provided the military experts to train Afghan refugees in basic mine clearance techniques at the Risalpur training camp in Pakistan. There had been no thought of the army instructors deploying into Afghanistan itself. However, as the United Nations program shifted from the ill-conceived mass training model to that of creating and supporting specialist Afghan mine action NGOs, the training requirement had reduced considerably. Also, as these recently formed Afghan organisations deployed demining teams to work in Afghanistan, it was very difficult to gauge the standard of work being performed and the accuracy of the reports being provided by them. Rumours circulated that the Afghan teams were not working properly, if at all, and that mines were being dug up and then sold in the bazaars in Peshawar.

In early 1991 UNOCHA sought approval from the Australian Government to allow members of the contingent to deploy into Afghanistan to monitor and report on the work of the Afghan teams. This was agreed, although initially it was on a case-by-case basis with the authority for each trip to be given by Canberra. The Australian servicemen were also allowed to enter minefields, which all the other troop-contributing nations had expressly forbidden. In time, this decision was to give us much credibility in our work.

The first Australian to 'go in' to Afghanistan under this arrangement was an officer named Major Graeme Membrey. Graeme had been assigned in January 1991 to work as a full-time technical adviser with the mine clearance organisation Afghan Technical Consultants, or ATC as it was better known. Unlike the rest of the training team who lived and worked together, Graeme was on his own working within

ATC. Mind you this did not bother Graeme because he was a tough character. In physical stature he was a short, muscly redhead and he had a determination to match. Graeme had previously applied to join the elite Special Air Service (SAS) regiment back in Australia, which was unusual for an engineer officer. Graeme undertook the gruelling SAS selection course and completed it, passing all the stages. As a result he was posted to the Commando Regiment, where he worked as the Senior Instructor – Water Operations and as an underwater demolitions supervisor.

By this time in late 1991, ATC was getting close to having 1000 staff and the Director was an ex-Afghan army officer named Kefayatullah Eblagh – or Kef as he was affectionately known by the foreigners. Kef was an excellent choice to be the Director due to his local status and manner, but he did not have experience in Western-style management. Graeme found that Kef was in charge of every single detail within ATC; he did not have a deputy and would not allow his subordinates to make any decisions. While many of the technical demining improvements made in the mine clearance program were agreed at our monthly meetings, Graeme realised that many organisational aspects needed to be improved within ATC to give the United Nations and the donors confidence in the organisation. He quickly became Kef's 'right hand man' by helping to develop updated operational techniques, writing proposals and reports for donors, suggesting improved office procedures and advising on training needs.

One time Graeme told Kef that he should trust his staff and not worry so much about minor details. He said, 'You are the boss, so you should be sitting back at your desk, smoking a cigarette and be thinking about the big picture.' Next day Graeme walks into Kef's office to see him smoking a cigarette.

'See, Membrey,' he said, 'I am thinking about the big picture.'

Another time Kef proudly showed me a huge new briefcase he had bought, like the ones airline pilots use. I told him that it was not appropriate. I said to him, 'Your staff should carry around all the detailed documents and background papers, but as the boss, you should only carry the final version of letters or contracts ready for signature – in a thin briefcase.' Next time we met Kef had the thin briefcase. We had some good-natured fun at Kef's expense in the early days, but he and I very quickly became lifelong friends.

Mind you, sometimes our Western ways did not always work. About a year later, one of the accountants from ATC ran away with a cash payroll of about US$100,000 that he was meant to be delivering to a camp in Afghanistan. Graeme and I were rather agitated and urged Kef to call the police. However, Kef calmly picked up the phone, called someone and said, 'You recommended that man to me, I want my money back.' The man was detained that night at Karachi airport trying to flee the country and all the money was returned. If we had gone to the Pakistani police, there is no way the man or the money would ever have been found.

Graeme undertook a number of trips in the eastern provinces of Afghanistan during 1991. He would check on the ATC demining teams at work and advise on improved mine clearance procedures, site layouts, casualty evacuation and camp management. Most importantly he would reconnoitre new sites for clearance teams to work. On one visit to a village the local mujahedeen commander challenged him and asked why the United Nations was wasting its time with manual demining and all these safety procedures – it was far too slow.

He said, 'When we were fighting the Soviets, we would just drive a tank back and forwards over the area and blow up all the mines.'

In response Graeme asked him to show him what he meant. The commander promptly reappeared with six of the PMN blast mines and had them buried randomly in a field. Then a Soviet T55 main battle tank also appeared and was driven back and forwards over the mined area. Four of the mines exploded, one was crushed (and thus became even more dangerous to handle) and the last one was never found! Graeme left well satisfied that the 'tank method' didn't work, and that the program should stick to more conventional and organised procedures.

Field trip to Khost

My first trip to Afghanistan came in February 1992 and it was to be an overland drive to Khost in the eastern part of the country. The plan was to accompany some of the NGO directors on a visit to inspect some manual demining teams and to observe two mechanical flail machines at work. The journey started with the now regular drive from Islamabad to Peshawar where our party assembled.

With me was Kefayatullah from ATC and Sayed Aqa, the Director of the survey organisation MCPA and a number of his staff. It was extremely difficult at that time for any foreigner to travel into Afghanistan, so the UN had been approached by two journalists who wanted to accompany us. As the demining work was donor funded, requests like these were usually approved as the publicity would help highlight the landmine problem. The two journalists were what are known as 'stringers' – they were basically freelance but had an arrangement to provide stories to regular media outlets. The first was Robert Adams, who did work for the BBC and the second was an Irishman named Gerry Burke, who wrote mainly for *The Guardian* newspaper. I quickly came to see that these stringers often took great risks in order to get a story, in the hope of one day getting a regular, salaried position with a news agency. This was also before satellite TV had become a reality, so getting video tape out of Afghanistan to be broadcast was also very difficult. In my later travels I would often carry video tapes for journalists back to Pakistan for broadcast.

We had planned an early start so we all assembled outside the demining office in Hayatabad, a relatively 'modern' suburb of Peshawar that backed onto the neighbouring tribal area. Despite assurances that all the vehicles would be ready, they were not. Most of them needed fuel. In the military, the golden rule is to always have vehicles fully fuelled so that they are ready to move at any time. Sayed Aqa explained to me that for the Afghan NGOs the opposite applied. They kept the vehicles as empty as possible, particularly overnight, to avoid petrol being siphoned out by petty thieves or to stop staff using the vehicles on unauthorised private trips. Time and again, I was to find it hard to fault the logic of a situation that was totally at odds with what I was used to. However, this Afghan logic caused about an hour's delay to the start of our trip.

The famous Khyber Pass is due west of Peshawar, but we headed south-west towards another pass through the mountains at Kohat. Our convoy of six white UN vehicles made its way past green irrigated fields and the smoky brick works where thousands of young children worked long hours making mud bricks. We then wound our way up through the mountains and into one of the Federally Administered Tribal Areas. Pakistan has four major provinces, but along the border with Afghanistan there are seven tribal areas and six frontier regions, which are loosely administered by Islamabad but largely independent.

The area is mainly inhabited by Pashtun tribes whose traditional influence spreads across the border into Afghanistan. In order to enter these areas foreigners need to have a permit, which we had duly obtained before setting off. However, when we arrived at the town of Kohat, we were stopped by tribal officials and great discussions ensued about our authority to proceed (and the need for an additional fee). After some time (and no extra fee) entry was granted and on we continued.

Our route took us along the banks of the Kurram River and then we turned off and headed west. At one stage we arrived at the top of a large, flat plateau to be greeted by the sight of a huge scrap metal yard. It seemed as if all the debris from the war in Afghanistan had been collected and brought to this site – there were all types of tanks, armoured personnel carriers, jeeps, aircraft, artillery pieces, bombs and other items of military equipment stacked in this huge expanse. I was keen to stay and explore, but we needed to push on to reach Khost before dark.

We took off again and soon the road disappeared and we were just bumping along rocky tracks and dry river beds. After a while I noticed that vehicles coming from the opposite direction were passing to the left of us. I commented on this to the driver and he replied, 'We are now in Afghanistan where we drive on the right side of the road, not the left like in Pakistan.' I must confess that this did not seem so important while bouncing along a river bed in four-wheel drive mode. I asked the driver when had we crossed the border between Pakistan and Afghanistan and he just shrugged – it didn't seem all that important. The whole area was desolate with very few signs of habitation or villages.

After a few more hours we came to a river crossing where all the vehicles screeched to a halt. There were quite a number of other 4WD vehicles parked around the area. All the Afghans seemed to know each other and then on some unseen signal, they all washed, lined up and commenced to pray. The Afghans conducted this ritual without any sort of self-consciousness and we foreigners just wandered around looking bemused, not quite sure what we should do. Given our time constraint only the 'short version' of the prayers was performed and soon we were off again.

Late in the afternoon we approached the city of Khost. We were driving parallel to a river and the town was about 300 metres away on the other side. All of a sudden the drivers abruptly pulled the vehicles off the road and took cover under some large trees. We got out and I asked Sayed what was happening. He pointed to the sky and moments later a lone MiG fighter jet with Afghan Government markings swooped down and dropped a bomb on the town. The ground shook and a huge black cloud of smoke arose from the centre of town. The jet circled around, made another pass and dropped another bomb. It then flew off to the north, presumably back toward Kabul. We waited a while to make sure that all was clear and then sped into town. We went to the sight of the bomb blasts and despite two large craters in the road, fortunately no-one appeared to have been injured.

Khost itself was a typical Afghan town, with mud-walled compounds and dusty streets leading out to irrigated fields, with goats, donkeys and dogs roaming at will. The town had been built in a broad river valley with huge brown mountains rising up on either side of the valley. Khost had been occupied for most of the war by the Soviets, but it had the rare honour to be the only city captured by the mujahedeen during the whole period of the occupation. This was partly due to geography, as the province jutted like a duck's beak into Pakistan, with the result it was able to be attacked from three sides. In reality, it appears that the Soviets withdrew and gave up the position, rather than due to any great military skill by the mujahedeen. After we checked around and confirmed that no locals had been hurt by the aerial bombing, we went to a compound on the outskirts of town where the demining teams had set up camp.

Due to the unstable security situation in Afghanistan all the demining teams were originally recruited from the refugee camps and trained in Pakistan. The teams deployed from Peshawar on six week missions into Afghanistan, and then they returned for one week's rest and to be paid. As there was a complete lack of infrastructure in Afghanistan, it was normal for two or three teams to deploy to an area, where a base camp would be set up to house all the deminers. This led to some criticisms of the program that it had a large administrative tail, providing tented accommodation, food, stores and medical support. But it had to be done, as these facilities did not exist in the countryside. We arrived at one of these base camps at dusk and enjoyed a traditional Afghan meal of rice, mutton and bread while seated cross-legged on the floor, and then retired for an early night.

The next morning I awoke early and went to the parapet of the mud-walled compound to take in the view. Strange as it may sound in a Muslim country, the whole scene reminded me of Christian Sunday school visions of biblical times. All I could see were brown mountains, other mud-walled compounds, fields, donkeys, camels – not a car, power line or modern building was to be seen. It looked so peaceful in the early morning light, and people were slowly starting to go about their daily routines. It was hard to reconcile this tranquil scene with the knowledge that just about anywhere landmines could have been buried, waiting silently for their victim.

After breakfast we headed off to see some of the manual demining teams at work. The site we arrived at was a former agricultural area on the outskirts of the town, and which the Soviets had mined heavily. The Soviets had controlled all the major towns in Afghanistan throughout their 13-year period of occupation. To protect themselves they had laid large defensive minefield belts around all of the towns, 15 to 20 kilometres out from the town centre. These were designed to keep the mujahedeen fighters, who controlled the countryside, far enough away so that they could not fire mortars or rockets into the towns. The minefields would consist mainly of anti-personnel mines, as the Soviets knew that the mujahedeen generally operated on foot. This minefield we were visiting was one of those forming the defensive perimeter around Khost. It was my first 'live' minefield and I was quite excited about the prospect of finally getting to grips with what I was advising about.

DEMINING IN ACTION THE MANUAL WAY

The training originally given to the Afghan deminers back in Peshawar by the foreign military contingents was based on a straight transfer of military skills. In the military, a platoon of about 30 engineer soldiers would be tasked to breach a number of lanes through a minefield, so that other troops or vehicles could then file through. In a battlefield situation, the military engineers accept that they may be fired upon by the enemy while conducting minefield breaching operations. Their task is only to clear a few lanes through the minefield and then move on. They would not necessarily be tasked to clear 100 per cent of all the mines and may be forced by time constraints to work in bad weather or at night. It was also accepted that in combat there may be casualties during a minefield breaching operation.

The initial Afghan teams had been arranged along military lines. They were grouped in teams of 30 men (the same as a military platoon – and only men worked as deminers in Afghanistan) and each breaching party consisted of three people. This gave a total of 10 breaching parties per team. The first member of the breaching party was equipped with a long stick or thin metal rod and he felt ahead for trip wires. The second was the detector man and he operated the metal detector. The third was the prodder man whose role was to gently prod into the ground to find the mine. In the military setting, the first person would also act as a lookout and would be armed with a rifle to provide protection.

Each breaching party was separated from the next one by about 25 metres, so that if there were an accident, only the person in immediate contact with the mine would be injured. The sequence was that the person with the trip wire feeler would start from a known safe area and lean forward, gently feeling with his long stick for trip wires. If no trip wires were found the metal detector operator would then take over and check the same area of the lane for buried metal objects.

As he advanced, the operator slowly swung the metal detector from side to side and he marked the edges of the lane with a red rock. The lane was one metre wide, as this was the distance covered by the sweep of the metal detector. If there was a buried metal object the detector made an audible sound. The operator then placed a marker cone 10 centimetres back from the point that caused the detector to sound off. He then backed off and the prodder man came forward to prod the ground, in order to discover what had caused the detector to sound off. Each member of the team was trained in each task, so they rotated through the different jobs every hour or so.

At that time the deminers had no protective equipment other than second-hand military uniforms and normal industrial goggles. To protect the prodder man, the drill was that he lay down just short of the suspect area and then he proceeded to poke in the ground in front of him with a prodding tool. This was usually a long sharp metal rod, but many of the Afghans favoured the shorter Soviet-style bayonet. The prodder man gently prodded the suspect area at a low angle – less than 30 degrees from the horizontal. This was done as a safety measure so that the prodding tool would only come in contact with the side of the mine and not the top of it (where the pressure of the tool would have set off the mine). If the deminer struck a hard object, he would gently excavate the area to uncover the object. More often than not it would just be a piece of scrap metal that caused the detector to sound off – a metal can, a bullet shell or a fragment from an exploded bomb or rocket.

If it was a mine that was uncovered, the prodder man would call for the team leader to come and confirm. The drill was then that all breaching parties would stop work and move back to a safe area. The team leader would then prepare to destroy the mine. The United Nations policy was that all mines were to be blown up in situ. This was by far the safest way to deal with a mine, as trying to lift it out of the ground and re-inserting the safety pin was dangerous and required a higher level of training. Also, if the mine was destroyed then there was no suggestion that it could be used again, or sold in the bazaars back in the tribal areas. Once the mine was blown up all the deminers would return to work.

The site we were visiting was well laid out, with a well-marked safe area where the vehicles were parked, an ambulance and medic were on site, and the teams and breaching parties were all working in lanes marked by red painted rocks. We sat on a small hill some way back and observed the whole process for an hour or so. My first reaction was that demining was horribly repetitive and boring. Every movement by the team members was slow and deliberate, and there was little to see as an observer. Each time the detector sounded all the prodder men ever seemed to find was a piece of scrap metal.

After a time, a number of questions started to go through my mind about the efficiency of the whole operation. Why did we need the trip wire feeler person when all the minefield completion reports indicated that intact trip wires were never found? Why did the third member of the breaching party have to observe the others – why not get whichever of the detector man or prodder were not actively working to observe the other? Why did the whole team stop work and leave the area when a mine was found – why not just mark the mine and blow them all up at the end of the working day? It also became clear that with all the pre-start checks, tea breaks, prayer breaks and early finishes, the teams were only actively demining for less than five hours a day. But the major question in my mind was why were they working here in the first place – was it really a minefield?

One of the main purposes of our trip was to see first-hand the work of two flail machines that UNOCHA had purchased in June 1990. In World War II tanks had been fitted with various attachments to the front of them to help them defeat landmines. These could be ploughs, rollers or flails – again with the military aim of just clearing lanes through minefields during combat, in order that other vehicles could follow safely along the cleared tracks. The ploughs simply turned the earth and pushed the mines aside, the rollers were heavy metal wheels that would explode mines due to their weight, and the flails were an arrangement of heavy chains rotating and beating the ground in front of the tank. The idea of using military tanks for our 'humanitarian demining' was not appropriate, but a British company had developed a civilian machine called the Aardvark flail. The United Nations program had purchased two of them in mid-1990 for about US$500,000 and they were given to ATC to operate in August.

On arrival at the site we were confronted with the sight of these strange-looking machines I was now responsible for. They looked like very long, white-painted tractors. At the front was the rotating drum with thick chains and hammers attached, the middle section was the motor and perched as far back as possible was the cabin where the driver sat. The rear wheels were normal rubber tyres but the front had a tracked wheel arrangement. The concept was that the machine would drive slowly over the mined area with the chains and hammers beating the ground and causing any mine to explode. Its purpose was to clear minefields containing the blast type anti-personnel mines, but it was designed to withstand an anti-tank explosion if it inadvertently hit one of those. The manufacturers had claimed that the machines could clear large areas of minefield every day at a rate of 2500 square metres per hour, but the machines were failing to achieve anywhere near that clearance rate.

There were the obvious logistical problems. Although the machine was powered by its own engine, having tracked wheels meant it was very slow and could only travel a limited distance. Therefore, to move it to a completely new work-site it had to be transported on a semi-trailer and there were not many of these available in Afghanistan. Obtaining clean fuel and spare parts was also an issue, and if a machine broke down it could take weeks for a part to arrive, so the machines often sat idle. Security was always a concern and the flail camp had already been bombed once from the air by Afghan government forces. Finally, selecting good sites for the machines to work was difficult. Despite the manufacturers' claims, they were not really intended for large scale area clearance of rocky terrain, and 100 per cent clearance could not be guaranteed.

Anyway, one of the machines was away in the distance and ready to go. The driver turned on the engine and started the chains flailing. A huge cloud of dust arose around the machine and it disappeared from view. This happened most of the time, so a system had evolved whereby a supervisor standing near us guided the driver via a hand held radio, as the driver could see nothing. We heard a couple of muffled explosions and saw black smoke mixed in with the cloud of yellow dust, as the machine hit some anti-personnel mines. With the demonstration over the machine returned to our viewing position. The journalist, Robert Adams, said that he wanted to get some action photos of the flail. He said he would lie on the road up ahead with his camera and could we get the operator to drive the machine towards him. We said it wasn't such a good idea but he insisted. What he didn't realise was that the chains were designed to rotate away from the machine so in case a mine was 'thrown out' it would go out to the front of the machine and not under it. When the operator started the machine Robert was showered with flying stones and rocks, and he hastily got out of the way.

I was not convinced by what I had seen. I thought that in principle it was good for the program to say that we used a variety of demining techniques – manual, machines and dogs. However, the limitations on their use, the high cost and poor clearance rate made me question their worth.

My first and worst landmine accident

Unfortunately, I did not get much time to discuss all this as we suddenly got an urgent radio message telling us about the demining accident involving the death of three men. As the deminers were from ATC, Kef was keen to go and find out what had happened.

It was quite a drive to the site of the accident and we arrived about an hour later. The team had been working around an abandoned village called Painder Khel, and the incident had occurred on a track beside a high mud wall. There was a large crater in the ground where the mine had exploded and bits of debris and red detonating cord were evident. The team leader explained that the deminer in the lane had found a suspicious object, so called his partner to have a look. They then must have called their section leader to come forward. At that moment the mine had exploded. From the size of the crater and the debris that had been found, they deduced that it had been two anti-tank mines stacked on top of each other and then rigged with some type of anti-handling device. There did not seem to be any reason to plant such a device in that area, as no vehicle could travel on the track. It must have been a cruel booby trap left behind by the retreating Soviet forces.

Finally, the team leader pointed out where the various parts of the deminers' bodies had been found. What was left of the bodies had already been taken back to the demining camp and buried straightaway, as was the local custom. That night back at the camp the mood among the other deminers was sombre but calm. They were sitting around and those who could read were reading their Korans, while others just sat quietly. I know that religion provides comfort to many people, but I was particularly struck by how it provided a sense of peace to these men and how easily they accepted the will of Allah.

I was both saddened and shocked by what I had seen. I knew about the power of explosives but this had only been in the context of training and blowing up inanimate objects. To see the effects of a blast on the human body was shocking – particularly a blast this big. At least the end would have come quickly for them, unlike some later accident victims I saw who suffered limbs blown off and horrific injuries. I did not know the three deminers personally so while I was deeply saddened by their loss, I was not emotionally devastated. Still being relatively new to mine clearance and Afghanistan, I did not have a context in which to place the accident – did this happen all the time, were the accidents always this destructive? However, I knew that I was responsible for the overall mine clearance program and this accident made me determined to make sure that the deminers got the best training, equipment and supervision that we could arrange.

The next morning the deminers were back at work and our party went off to attend the first of many *shuras* that I would take part in during my time in Afghanistan. A *shura* is a meeting of village elders or leaders to discuss matters of concern to their village or tribe. We joined about 30 bearded men sitting cross-legged in a circle and through our interpreter explained the purpose of our visit. While Kef or Sayed Aqa could have spoken on our behalf in Pashtu, it was better that I do it. The Pashtuns have a code of honour that they must offer hospitality to guests, and as the United Nations official I could avoid getting too embroiled in local issues. I thanked them for their cooperation and said that as the area was relatively peaceful and refugees were starting to return, we wanted to send more mine clearance teams to the area. We also had plans to set up a training camp in the town so that we could conduct refresher training on site, rather than sending teams back to Peshawar. They agreed with this proposal and offered us some sites for our camps. Then some of them became quite forceful and demanded a range of other assistance like food, medical support and assistance with agriculture and so on.

Through the interpreter I said 'I am only responsible for the mine clearance program, and I guarantee I will deliver what we have just agreed about the mine clearance teams. I am an honest man and I will not promise you other things that I have no control over. However, I will take your message back to my head office and see what I can do'.

My open approach seemed to appease them, and although I was only responsible for the mine action program, it dawned on me then that to these people I represented the whole 'United Nations' system, and the distinction between the different agencies meant nothing to them. I thought my honest statement to the shura would have been 'quotable', but when I looked the two journalists had already packed up their notebooks and were walking away.

So, after about five days on the road, my first trip to Afghanistan was coming to an end and we headed back towards Peshawar. It had been fascinating to meet the people, see the countryside and better understand the conditions under which mine clearance was conducted. The accident had etched in my mind how serious and dangerous mine clearance was, and that it was not just some sort of amateur endeavour. It was clear to me that a huge task laid ahead, and that we had to get more efficient in the way demining was undertaken. There was also a need to improve the type of equipment available to the deminers and the way it was used.

The family settles in to Pakistan

Meanwhile back in Islamabad, Margaret and the children were settling into life in Pakistan. Most people in Islamabad lived inside high-walled compounds, which may contain as many as two or three houses. Large extended families lived together – usually with a new bride coming to live with her in-laws. We rented a large villa in the compound of a senator serving in the Pakistani parliament. There were frequent power cuts in Islamabad but they didn't seem to affect the senator's house. We got used to the muezzins' call to prayer every morning and learned about the Muslim celebrations like Eid. The smaller of the Eid festivals involves the sacrificial slaughter of an animal, and at that time there were flocks of fat-tailed sheep and goats being herded around the city streets and offered for sale.

We explained to our children, Zoe and Charles, what the festival was about, but told them that they wouldn't need to see anything. 'That's okay,' they replied, 'we were just up on the balcony and watched our neighbour slaughter a goat!' That evening we were duly presented with a fresh leg of goat from the neighbour, as was the custom.

The downside was that all the offal from the slaughtered animals was dumped in the communal rubbish bins at the end of each street. Despite the authorities liberally sprinkling lime powder all around the bins, the stench was unbearable for a few days.

Water was interesting. It flowed to the compound for only an hour or two per day through semi-open pipes and went into a concrete tank buried at the side of the house. You then had to pump the water up to a smaller concrete tank on the roof, where gravity would deliver water to the taps inside the house. No-one told us about this, so we had a few dry days to start with. The trick was of course was to fill up the top tank just before the water flowed into the bottom tank. With two full tanks we could last about a week if anything went wrong. Which it soon did.

One hot, dry summer and without any warning, the local Monday newspaper proclaimed that Islamabad would run out of water by that Friday. Mild chaos and angst ensued until the city started to deliver water by tanker trucks. However, this quickly broke down as people hijacked the trucks or bribed the drivers to fill up their home water tanks. In the end, each water truck had two armed soldiers assigned to it to ensure a fairer distribution of water. We came to discover that the Pakistan army was the only organised and trusted institution in the country.

I was provided a vehicle for my work and the kids caught the bus to the American school, but Margaret needed a car to get around town. Most of the taxis in Islamabad were old Morris Minor cars that had been patched together and kept going. They were solid and reliable and the Pakistanis had a great affection for them. Often you would see 'for sale' ads where the owner would proudly proclaim that the vehicle had been driven overland from the United Kingdom to Pakistan in the 1950s and 1960s. As Margaret had learned to drive in a Morris Minor in England, I secretly bought one, had it renovated and surprised her with it. It was properly registered in Pakistan but I wanted to get the United Nations number plates, as these were regarded as diplomatic and the driver could not be stopped by the police. We were eligible for the United Nations plates, but the bureaucracy just ground on and on and the plates never came. In frustration I went to the bazaar, got some United Nations number plates made and attached them to the car. She was never stopped after that and the car provided faithful service during our time there.

Zoe and Charles settled in quickly at school as they were used to moving around. It was called the International School of Islamabad (better known by its initials as ISI) but it followed a US curriculum and had links with the US Embassy. Unlike the Australian school system which follows the calendar year, this one had the long (Northern Hemisphere) summer break over June to August and the school year started in September. As a result Zoe and Charles 'lost' six months, but it helped them adjust to the new subjects they had to study. There were over 800 kids at the school from year 1 through to year 12 and there were over 40 nationalities represented – a real mini-United Nations in itself. One slightly humorous aspect of the school's name was that the Directorate of Inter-Services Intelligence was the premier intelligence gathering organisation for the Pakistan military, and it had been responsible for supporting the mujahedeen in their fight against the Soviets. It also went by the acronym ISI. The shared acronym did not really cause any confusion, but some years later the school did change its name.

Acknowledgement from home

The Australian Army team of 15 officers and senior non-commissioned officers was based in two houses in the suburb of Hayatabad in Peshawar. The teams rotated through every six months, so by now about 50 individuals had done a tour. While I was the overall commanding officer of the team and the other technical advisers, a major looked after the day-to-day activities of the training team in Peshawar. The army policy at that time was if you were posted for more than 12 months your family could accompany you. If it was less than 12 months, it was unaccompanied. This meant that people like Graeme Membrey and I had our families with us, but those on the shorter tour did not.

At the end of 1991 Australia was heavily committed to the UNTAC peacekeeping mission in Cambodia. This was dominating the headline news back in Australia, particularly as one of my outstanding former army bosses, General John Sanderson, had been appointed the military commander of UNTAC. At its peak the Australian commitment reached nearly 600 troops in Cambodia. This made our little team of 15 stuck away in Peshawar feel a little forgotten and neglected. Morale was high because the men were all experienced non-commissioned officers and the work was highly rewarding, but a few days before Christmas 1991 we had only received one greeting message from Australia.

I was annoyed, so I took the rather bold step of directly telephoning the Chief of the Australian Army, General John Coates.

I said to General Coates, 'Sir, we are seeing on the news all sorts of messages and gifts going to the Australian troops in Cambodia, but my men, who are separated from their families, have received nothing. The only parcel that had arrived for the team was from a returned servicemen's club in New South Wales. While the men are all experienced officers and senior NCOs and there is no problem, they do feel a bit like the lost tribe.'

General Coates was genuinely concerned and asked, 'Didn't you receive my personal message?' to which I replied, 'No, we have not received messages from anyone.'

General Coates assured me that he had sent a greeting to the team and that he would look into the situation. Good to his word, the next day we were flooded with messages and greetings from various army and government officials.

This must have stirred the nest because in February 1992 I was told that we would be visited by the Australian Minister for Defence Science and Personnel, Gordon Bilney and General Coates. They flew directly into Peshawar (from Cambodia) and only stayed a few hours. When they first landed the Australian Defence attaché came running up with a message for General Coates. He said that a report had just come in that Lieutenant Colonel Russell Stuart had been shot in Cambodia.

General Coates asked, 'Is he dead?' to which the attaché replied, 'No.'

'Good,' said Coates, 'let's get on with the visit.' I smiled to myself. Russell had also been a classmate of mine at Duntroon and he had just become the first member of our class to be wounded. He had been flying in a helicopter over Khmer Rouge territory in Cambodia when he was shot through the arm from some ground fire.

The visit by Bilney and Coates to Peshawar went well and they left with a very favourable impression of the dedication and hard work of the team. On behalf of all the teams, past and present, I accepted a Chief of the Army Commendation presented by General Coates for our 'exemplary performance of duty'.

CHAPTER 4:

TRIP TO KABUL

A few weeks after the field trip to Khost, I made my first visit to Kabul in March 1992. Although the Afghan national airline, Ariana, still operated some flights out of Kabul, it only flew to New Delhi and to some airports in the former Soviet Union. There were no direct flights to Pakistan and driving to Kabul was tricky, due to insecurity on the roads and the need to 'cross lines'. However, the United Nations leased a number of aircraft which were vital to the relief effort and allowed relatively safe travel throughout Afghanistan.

The United Nations political office still operated a large DC9 jet aircraft – a hangover from the days of Prince Sadruddin – and it was fitted out with a VIP configuration, albeit with some space for cargo. This plane was used extensively by the United Nations political envoy, Benon Sevan, to ferry him to negotiations with neighbouring countries to try to end the stalemate between the Najibullah Government and the mujahedeen factions. On other occasions the plane was used for 'milk runs' to ferry staff and supplies between Islamabad and Kabul, and it was on one of these flights I found myself heading to Kabul.

The United Nations always obtained clearance from all parties and factions before a flight took off. Although the 'neutrality' of the UN was recognised by most groups, the big fear for aircraft was an attack from the ground by a rebel group using Stinger missiles. These missiles had been supplied to mujahedeen groups by the USA during the war. The weapon had been a critical factor in breaking the Soviets' air superiority and one of the factors leading to their eventual withdrawal from Afghanistan. The Stinger missiles had an effective slant range of about 4500 metres, which made aircraft particularly vulnerable when taking off or landing. Many of the missiles provided to the mujahedeen were now unaccounted for.

The DC9 had been designated as 'Salam 01' and it was crewed by contracted Swiss pilots, all reportedly former jet fighter pilots. Their strategy to avoid the Stinger threat was to come in low and fast. After we left Pakistani airspace and approached Kabul the pilot descended to a few hundred metres in altitude – well below the top of the brown mountains that surround Kabul and out of sight from most of the city. Then at a designated point he banked the plane sharply, slipped through a gap in the mountains, dropped the plane on the runway and brought it to a screeching halt. I love flying and had complete faith in the pilots, so I was never scared or apprehensive taking the trip. It was always an exciting way to arrive in Kabul.

The airport at that time was relatively unscathed and there were plenty of old Soviet-era aircraft parked around the airfield. As we stood on the tarmac and handed our passports over to Afghan officials, I noticed a fully bombed up government MiG fighter jet take off and head to the south. I thought to myself, 'You're probably the same bastard who tried to bomb us in Khost a few weeks back!'

Being involved with both sides of a conflict was a bit surreal at times. Moscow was still delivering some aid to Afghanistan by air, but the Russian air force had a different tactic to counter the missile threat. The large four-engine Antonov transport aircraft would fly over Kabul at about 10,000 feet and then suddenly spiral down. Every few seconds they would pop out anti-missile flares which were designed to confuse heat-seeking anti-aircraft missiles. It was quite a spectacular sight to see these huge aircraft hurtling down to earth with their spiral trajectory clearly marked by the white smoke of the flares.

The Afghan demining NGOs were not working in Kabul at this time as they were based on the mujahedeen side. However, the UNOCHA Mine Clearance Program had a liaison officer based in Kabul. His name was Fred Estall and he had been a warrant officer with one of the early New Zealand army training teams. However, Fred had taken leave and stayed working on a UNOCHA contract. Although a New Zealand national, he was originally from one of the Pacific Islands and he had their typical strong, muscular build.

Fred was a very outgoing personality and he was famous for organizing memorable parties. Although there was a curfew in Kabul at the time, alcohol was still freely available. Fred's answer to the curfew was that no-one should go home, and his most famous all-night party had a caveman theme, where everyone came dressed in nothing but animal skins. His job involved liaising with the government to inform them what the United Nations mine clearance program was doing, keeping in touch with the HALO Trust office, establishing a mine awareness project with the Afghan Red Crescent Society and overseeing part of the so called 'Soviet pledge'.

Although the Soviets did not clear any mines before they left, they had pledged some mine clearing tanks, metal detectors and other demining equipment through the United Nations. Fred had been criticised in the evaluation report for only focussing on the Soviet equipment pledge and the report recommended replacing him with a more senior person, who could deal with the liaison aspects of the job. Fred had offered to resign but it was not accepted.

I found Kabul to be a fascinating city. Most buildings in the downtown area and suburbs were relatively undamaged at this time and there were only a few mined areas within the city itself. Shops were open, government ministries were sort of functioning and a number of foreign countries maintained their embassies in Kabul. Most vehicles on the roads were old and of Soviet origin, like Volga taxis and Kamaz trucks. The standouts were the ubiquitous white land cruisers used by the United Nations and aid agencies. UNOCHA had a compound on the edge of the upmarket suburb of Wazir Akbhar Khan, which is where Fred had his office.

After the inevitable cups of chai we met the local United Nations officials. The United Nations employs two types of staff – international staff from outside the country and locally engaged national staff. The national staff are employed for their local knowledge and contacts, language skills and other specialist's skills like health, agriculture and so on. They do not hold senior positions in United Nations country offices, are paid less and, most significantly, are not evacuated in times of crisis – because they are already home. Many of the local Afghan staff were to endure great hardship in the years to come, and I always admired their dedication and commitment. It was also great to meet the local Kabul-based radio operators with whom I had spoken to many times on the radio but had not met before.

We undertook a series of visits, with the main meeting intended to be with an office the Government had set up called the Department of Mine Clearance. I was quite shocked and dismayed with what we found. The 'department' consisted of only two men who were sitting at empty desks. They had no documents, maps, minefield records – nothing. Through the interpreter we tried to understand what their role was and what they did, which turned out to be very little. They complained that they were given no resources from the Government, had no access to minefield records and had no control over any demining work done by the Afghan Army.

The HALO team kept them informed of what they were doing, but the Department had no control over HALO's tasking. It was clear that the UNOCHA Mine Clearance Program had a much better idea of the landmine problem throughout all of Afghanistan, and had significantly more resources to deal with it. It also became clear from other meetings that most of the Afghan government ministries were just 'hollow shells' and the government itself only controlled Kabul city and little else.

I was also keen to visit the HALO Trust office and operations, particularly given Colin Mitchell's earlier criticism of the Afghan demining NGOs. While dealing with the HALO head office in London was always a bit tiresome, invariably their staff on the ground were easy to get along with. The expatriate staff were generally ex-captains from the British Army, although usually not engineer officers or bomb disposal experts. One famous case was David Hewitson, who had been a submarine officer in the Royal Navy! David actually turned out to be one of their best operators – despite the lack of sea mines in Kabul.

I met with the current head of the HALO office in Kabul, Julian Gregson and two of the operations officers, Tim Goggs and Tim Porter, along with their local manager Dr Farid. They explained that they had five expatriate supervisors and had employed about 60 deminers by that time. Most of their operations were centred on a base at Pol-i-Khumri, in Baghlan province in the north of the country, and from that base they demined in three neighbouring provinces. They were also starting work based around the village of Jebal Seraj, about 75 kilometres north of Kabul. We then went to visit a demining site at the ancient fortress of Bala Hissar in Kabul, and I was very pleased to see that the HALO mine clearance procedures, techniques and equipment were much the same as the United Nations program. The only exception was the vehicles – being British, they had imported four-wheel-drive Land Rovers.

While in Kabul we stayed in the UN Guest House. This was a lovely old building set inside a large walled compound, only a few blocks from the city centre. It was probably built in the 1930s and had the feel and charm of an old country club or officers' mess. There was an oak lined bar (as drinking alcohol was still allowed at this time in Kabul), a dining room, library and billiard room. It also had a large entry foyer and lounge room with a huge fireplace. About 15 bedrooms were split between upstairs and down. Only UN international staff were eligible to stay in the guest house. As satellite TV had not reached Kabul in early 1992, there was usually a convivial atmosphere in the Guest House in the evenings. This provided a good opportunity to meet colleagues working on different projects and to discuss the latest developments in Afghanistan.

Surviving the Salang Tunnel

As we were in Kabul over the weekend, Fred Estall suggested that we take a drive to see the famous Salang Tunnel. The tunnel had been built by the Soviets and was completed in 1964. It's situated on the major north-south connection road in Afghanistan and provides the only year-round crossing of the Hindu Kush Mountains. At the time it was built it was the highest road tunnel in the world. A deadly fire in the tunnel in 1982 had killed 64 Soviet soldiers and 112 Afghans. Also, as the main supply route for the Soviet forces during their occupation, the road leading to the tunnel had been subject to numerous attacks and ambushes by the mujahedeen.

I was keen to go even though it meant a 'cross line' journey from the Government controlled area around Kabul, to the mujahedeen controlled areas north of the city. Fred also invited along Alan Craven who ran the United Nations radio network and a diplomat from the

Hungarian Embassy in Kabul. We set off early Saturday morning in Fred's white king-cab pick-up truck, complete with the standard blue 'UN' markings on the doors. Although the distance to the tunnel is only about 120 kilometres, we anticipated the journey would take three to four hours each way.

We left Kabul and decided not to take the road through the village of Charikar due to security concerns, even though it was slightly shorter. Rather we took the newer road via the former Soviet airbase at Bagram. The road ran through a sparsely vegetated, rocky valley and you could see a series of inter-connecting observation posts on the top of hills overlooking the road. These had obviously been used by the Soviets to guard convoys running between Bagram and the city. We passed by the huge airfield and town of Bagram and started the climb towards the mouth of the Pansheer Valley, stronghold of the famous mujahedeen commander, Ahmed Shah Masood.

At some point we had 'crossed the line' out of the government-controlled area but it was not obvious where this was. We passed by a number of villages and agricultural fields, but there were very few other vehicles around. At one point along the road we passed the site of what had been a major mujahedeen ambush of a Soviet fuel convoy. The burnt-out remains of about 20 fuel tankers lined either side of the road. Each one had a large hole in the side of the tank caused by rocket-propelled grenades (RPGs). One could only imagine the horrible, fiery death that the tanker drivers must have suffered.

We started to climb into the Hindu Kush Mountains and the road became quite narrow and windy. Patches of snow started to appear on the roadside and soon we were passing under long shelters that had been built over the road. These were intended to keep the road open and safe even during an avalanche or rock falls. Finally, we reached the entrance to the tunnel. We stopped to take in the surroundings and being at 3400 metres altitude the air was quite thin. The tunnel itself looked foreboding. It was carved out of the rock and was not lined with concrete. Water was dripping down profusely from the roof of the tunnel. The entire tarmac had gone from the surface of the road and it was a basically series of water filled potholes.

Fred started to drive through and of course there were no lights working in the tunnel. The vehicle headlights tried to cut a beam through the thick, blue diesel smoke haze that lingered inside. The tunnel is 2.6 kilometres long but it took us nearly 20 minutes to get through. Coming out the other end was like entering a new world. There was crisp, clean white snow, a beautiful blue sky and fabulous views of the mountains. We were stopped by three uniformed and armed guards from the 'army' of General Dostum, who controlled most of northern Afghanistan. We offered them some cigarettes and motioned about going further. They said no, which was fine, as it was time for us to turn around and get back to Kabul before dark.

The trip back through the tunnel was no less spooky and once out of it we were pleased to be on our way back down the mountains. After about half an hour a man and a young boy aged about 15 years old appeared on the road and indicated for us to stop. Both were armed with Kalashnikov rifles. The man went to Fred's side of the car and boy came towards mine. Thinking we were going to stop and have a chat with the locals like on the trip to Khost, I opened the car door and already had one foot out of the vehicle. Just then the boy raised his rifle and put the barrel through the gap between the car body and the open door – pointed directly at my head. Instinctively I drew my leg back into the vehicle and pulled on the car door. The rifle barrel rode up the inside edge of the door and I just kept pulling the door handle until the door finally closed.

Meanwhile, Fred was talking and gesturing to the man. None of us spoke any Dari but it was clear he wanted food and medicine. Fred was gesturing that we had none and kept repeating the only two words in Dari that he knew: 'Melal-e-Mutahed, Melal-e-Mutahed' meaning 'United Nations'. Eventually they let us pass after it became clear that we had nothing to give to them.

A few kilometres on we pulled over at a small lay-by on the edge of a sharp bend in the road. We were still high in the mountains and quite exposed, but we got out to stretch our legs and reflect on the road block incident. After a couple of minutes two shots rang out. There was a lot of echo due to the mountains all around, so we could not tell where the shots were coming from. We all looked at each other, jumped back in the vehicle and kept on going. Things went smoothly again for a while and when we got down to the valley we decided to go via Charikar as it was shorter, even if there were more villages to pass through. Then things got worse. Every couple of kilometres groups of armed men would come onto the road and stop us, demanding money, medicine or food. Every time Fred would stop and repeat his mantra of 'Melal-e-Mutahed'. After being stopped about 10 times I was getting a bit agitated and thought to myself, 'Why doesn't Fred just drive through them?' But he wisely stopped each time and talked our way through.

One of the last 'checkpoints' consisted of only one man and his Kalashnikov. He stopped us and then jumped into the back of the pick-up, indicating he wanted a lift. The United Nations has strict rules that weapons are not allowed in UN vehicles, so Fred jumped out and shouted at the bloke, 'Get the fuck out of my truck!' The bearded, mujahedeen warrior with the Kalashnikov meekly got out of the vehicle and skulked away. To this day I still cannot decide if it was the silliest or the bravest act I have ever seen. We were all somewhat relieved when we finally pulled into the United Nations guesthouse back in Kabul as darkness was falling.

Changing of the guard: Mujahedeen forces take over Kabul

Although I was not involved with the political side of the United Nations work, April 1992 was a momentous month that brought sweeping changes to the political landscape, and which affected everyone working in or around Afghanistan. The Geneva Accords had been signed on 14 April 1988 between Afghanistan and Pakistan, with the United States and the Soviet Union acting as guarantors. The accords consisted of several instruments, one of which related to the voluntary return of Afghan refugees from Pakistan and another set a timetable for the Soviet withdrawal. The withdrawal officially began in May 1988 and ended on 15 February 1989, thus closing the chapter on the nine-year Soviet War in Afghanistan. The various mujahedeen parties based in Pakistan had not been invited to the negotiations, nor signed the Geneva Accords. Consequently, they refused to accept the terms of the agreement.

Since 1987 Dr Najibullah had been the President of Afghanistan. He was heavily dependent on Soviet support to stay in power, and even then his forces only controlled Kabul and the major provincial towns. Immediately after the Soviet withdrawal he still received economic and military aid, but with the collapse of the Soviet Union in December 1991 he was left without any foreign assistance. This led to an economic crisis and instability within his government. During this time, the UN Secretary-General's envoy, Benon Sevan, was working feverishly to get a political agreement for President Najibullah to step down and hand over power to a coalition of the major Mujahedeen groups.

The *Los Angeles Times* on 21 April 1992 ran the following story: Appealing to all Afghans to 'refrain from revenge' the UN envoy trying to broker an urgent peace in the country said Monday that regime leaders and Muslim guerrillas massed outside the capital are moving closer to compromise. But he stressed that the safe departure of ousted dictator Najibullah is 'part and parcel' of any interim agreement to fill Afghanistan's power vacuum.

It was then reported that Benon Sevan had guaranteed safe passage to India for President Najibullah. However, in a dramatic turn of events when attempting to fly Najibullah out of the country, their convoy was turned back at Kabul airport by dissident troops. Benon had no option other than to take Najibullah back to the compound that housed the United Nations political office. The *Los Angeles Times* went on to say that 'it was clear Monday that the process of Afghan reconciliation is snowballing down a route totally apart from the UN brokering process. Coalitions continued to form throughout the country between the Afghan army commanders and the leaders of the mujahedeen guerrillas, who have battled them for the past 13 years. One by one, in every key city except Kabul, heavily armed rebel groups pulled out of their bunkered siege positions. The army's defence lines came down and opposing commanders sat down together for the first time to form interim coalition councils.' However, the situation in Kabul didn't last long and by 25 April 1992 the various mujahedeen forces had occupied Kabul.

STEPPING INTO A MINEFIELD

I was back in Islamabad at this time but was receiving first hand reports. Fred Estall had left back in March and we had replaced him in Kabul with Graeme Membrey. Graeme had finished his attachment to ATC and he had decided to take leave from the Australian Army and stay in Afghanistan to work on a United Nations contract. I was in regular touch with Graeme on the radio throughout this period. He said that on the night the mujahedeen took control of the city he stood on the roof of the UNOCHA building and watched a spectacular 'fireworks' show light up the night sky over Kabul. It went on for hours. However, they were not fireworks but rather tracer rounds, rockets, flares and any other explosive device that the mujahedeen fighters could get their hands on.

Graeme said he was enjoying the roof-top show until rounds started to fall all around him, so he took the precaution of getting under cover. A number of locals were killed that evening due to falling bullets.

Although I was now filling a United Nations post, I was still the Commanding Officer of the Australian Army Mine Clearance Training Team and responsible for the team members travel and security. A few days before all this turmoil, and when the situation had still looked stable, I had deployed two sergeants, Dean Beaumont and Danny Shaw, to Kabul. They were meant to then drive to Pol-i-Khumri to run refresher training courses for HALO Trust deminers. However, they got stuck in Kabul due to the start of fighting on the road to the north, so I ordered them to return to Peshawar.

As the dramatic events in Kabul quickly unfolded all the United Nations flights were cancelled, because one of the Afghan warlords, Gulbuddin Heckmatyar, had threatened to shoot down any aircraft he thought may be taking Najibullah out of the country. In the end both Dean and Danny managed to get themselves on an Ariana flight to New Delhi at 30 minutes' notice. As the passenger jet was taxiing out at Kabul airport, its front tyre had a blow-out due to some shrapnel on the runway. Dean said it was quite bizarre standing on the runway as they jacked up the plane and changed the tyre – with all the locals milling around smoking cigarettes near the aircraft. I was most relieved when they both eventually they made it safely back to Pakistan, via New Delhi.

Naturally the Australian government was getting concerned about the confusing political and military situation in Afghanistan, and they were questioning whether the Mine Clearance Training Team should be withdrawn. All the members of the team were keen to stay and continue their mission. Most of them had developed a good rapport with their Afghan counterparts and the work was challenging and meaningful.

I argued with my counterpart in Army Headquarters in Canberra by saying, 'I reckon that with a flood of refugees from Pakistan and Iran now expected to return to Afghanistan, the need for demining work will increase dramatically. I believe that many areas of the country are safe to work in and that the risks are acceptable.'

Also, the Australian Army's knowledge of mine warfare, which had been dormant since the Vietnam War, was now second-to-none. The Australian Ambassador in Islamabad, Ted Pocock and the Defence Attaché, Colonel Brian Cloughley, both supported my view in their official cables back to Canberra. The Australian Government decided that although their foreign policy interests in Afghanistan at that time were negligible, the ongoing provision of the team was consistent with its 'good international citizen' objectives and that we could stay. However, the Defence Minister at the time, Senator Robert Ray, directed that no Australian members of the training team could enter Afghanistan without his permission.

Analysing another serious demining accident

Unfortunately I had to go back to Kabul much sooner than I expected. On 8 July 1992 reports started coming in over the radio that there had been a serious demining accident involving some of the HALO Trust staff near Kabul. It was believed that some people were dead and others seriously injured. Differing stories about the cause of the accident were starting to be reported on the local news. Graeme Membrey was in Kabul and was able to provide regular updates to us.

Graeme explained that Tim Goggs and Julian Gregson had started to use one of the Soviet mine clearing tanks to clear an unsealed road near the village of Kare Samir, north of Kabul. They used the heavy rollers fitted to the front of the tank to detonate an anti-tank mine, which unknown to them had been booby-trapped. As a result of the subsequent explosion the Afghan tank driver, Shah Mohammed, was killed, Julian Gregson died later that evening and Tim Goggs a few days after. This was a tragic and horrible event which shocked the whole demining community.

As the United Nations had provided HALO Trust with the mine clearing tank through the Soviet pledge of equipment, and as the task had loosely been coordinated with Graeme Membrey, my UNOCHA boss Martin Barber asked me to go to Kabul and report on the accident. The Australian government agreed with the request, so I flew back to Kabul on the next flight.

The UNOCHA mine clearance program had decided not to use the Soviet tanks for a number of reasons. In the Soviet inventory they were officially called BMR-2 mine clearance tanks, which was a T55 tank fitted with KMT-7 rollers. The rollers were heavy steel wheels that were mounted on arms out in front of the tank, and the rollers were slightly wider than the tracked wheels of the tank. The idea was that as the tank went forward into a suspect area the roller would hit any mine first and detonate it, without causing damage to the tank itself. In a combat situation, in order to cross a minefield, other main battle tanks would then follow exactly in the tracks of the mine clearing tank.

Because the BMR-2 was used in combat it was painted in camouflage colours and often still fitted with its huge gun barrel, and could also be equipped with a heavy calibre machine gun. This was an unacceptable situation because of the United Nations principles of 'neutrality' and unarmed status, and led to the decision not to use the tanks in any United Nations funded projects. In addition, during the time of the Najibullah Government it would have been impossible to transport the tanks into mujahedeen territory, and UNOCHA had already purchased the two white, civilian Aardvark flail machines for road clearance tasks. However, as a non-governmental organisation, HALO was not bound by the restrictions on the use of military equipment and had decided to try using the BMR 2 tanks. Tim Goggs in particular had shown an interest in using the tanks and he had already operated them with some success up in Baghlan province.

When I arrived in Kabul some days after the accident, the local head of the HALO office, Dr Farid, took me out to the site of the accident which was about 15 kilometres out of the city. It was a sobering scene indeed. The main highway north out of Kabul was a sealed road and it had been the main supply route for the Soviets – and it was the same road we had driven back along when returning from our trip to the Salang tunnel. The Soviet forces had placed huge minefield belts on either side of the main highway to try and prevent ambushes on their convoys by the mujahedeen forces. An unsealed road branched off the highway through one of the minefields towards the village of Kare Samir. At this time, the villagers could not use the road for fear of being blown up and they were forced to take a long detour to get anywhere.

When we arrived at the site Dr Farid parked on the sealed road and then we walked the 200 metres to the disabled tank, following the tank track marks visible on the dirt track. Dr Farid assured me that the area around the tank had been checked for other mines, but I was still cautious.

The task HALO had started to undertake was to clear the road so that the villagers could use it and dramatically reduce their travel time to Kabul city. The mine clearing tank had been brought to the site and Tim assumed the role as the commander of the tank, Julian was the crew member and Shah Mohammed was the driver. The tank had only gone 200 metres when they saw an anti-tank mine laying on the surface of the road in front of them, so they stopped the vehicle just short of the mine. They then walked back along their tracks to get a demolitions kit from their vehicle.

One technique to destroy mines like this is to place another large charge of TNT next to the mine, back the mine clearing tank off a considerable distance and then remotely detonate the TNT, which in turn would set off the mine. For some reason when they returned to the tank with the demolitions kit, they chose not to do this. Rather they decided to close up the hatches on the tank and hit the mine with the rollers to make it explode. The tank had been designed to withstand this type of blast and Tim had had used this method previously. Also, there had been no prior evidence of booby trapped mines in this area.

STEPPING INTO A MINEFIELD

When they hit the mine it exploded, but it also set off another large explosive charge (possibly an aircraft bomb, an artillery shell or another anti-tank mines) which had been buried back from the mine, a distance that placed it right under the belly of the tank. This was an improvised technique designed specifically to 'defeat' tanks with rollers. The second explosion blew a hole in the floor of the tank and ignited the fuel tanks. Tim and the driver emerged from their hatches, but Julian did not. Tim went back into the tank to pull Julian out, despite it burning fiercely. By now the clothes of all three men were on fire and these were extinguished by the Afghan medical team that was supporting them.

They were taken to hospital in Kabul where Shah Mohammed was pronounced dead on arrival, and Julian died later that evening from burns and smoke inhalation. Tim had burns to 20 per cent of his body and arrangements were made to fly him out the next day on a United Nations plane to Karachi, where he would be collected by one of the worldwide aero-medical companies. Unfortunately, when he was being transferred by ambulance to Kabul airport the next day the vehicle was turned back by mujahedeen fighters, who suspected it was a United Nations plot to smuggle the former President Najibullah out of the country. Tim was eventually flown out the following day on a Red Cross flight and evacuated to the UK. A few days later Colin Mitchell sent us a telegram saying that sadly Tim had died. The cause was severe lung damage, caused by smoke inhalation, almost certainly due to his re-entering the tank.

I had only met Julian Gregson once, but had known Tim Goggs reasonably well. Tim had come to one of our monthly meetings to brief everyone on his work with the tanks. I had seen him a few weeks before the accident walking along a road in Islamabad. I offered him a lift and invited him home for lunch, but he said he had some errands to do and then had to head back to Kabul. He was a fine, dedicated young man who had died doing what he believed in. I finished up my accident investigation report and we sent a copy to Colin Mitchell in London. Colin later advised us that my report had been submitted to the UK Coroner's Court inquest into the deaths and was accepted as the most complete and accurate version of the events. The following year in July 1993 Tim Goggs was posthumously awarded the George Medal for bravery.

A complicated power-sharing arrangement

Despite the initial euphoria of the country being 'liberated' by the mujahedeen, things quickly started to go bad in Kabul. The power-sharing arrangement, which had been worked out with seven of the major mujahedeen parties, was meant to rotate people through different positions like President and Prime Minister, and also share ministries.

The first President, Sibghatullah Mojadeddi, was appointed on 28 April 1992. I had met him once at a reception and he seemed a pleasant if innocuous chap. His main claim to fame while President is that the Ariana plane on which he was a passenger was hit by a rocket-propelled grenade (RPG) while landing at Kabul airport. Fortunately the aircraft landed safely with no casualties. The forlorn-looking jetliner, with no nose cone, was a familiar sight at the airport for years to come.

Mojadeddi only lasted as President for three months when he was outmanoeuvred by Burhanuddin Rabbani, who was allied at the time with General Dostum from the north and Ahmed Shah Massoud, both of whom had been responsible for capturing Kabul. Unfortunately, the leader of another party, Gulbuddin Heckmatyar, did not accept these arrangements and a stalemate ensued. Kabul started to be divided up among the various factions and the downhill spiral for control of the city and its residents had begun.

Around this time it was announced that the recently appointed United Nations Secretary-General Boutros Boutros-Ghali would be visiting Islamabad. All the senior United Nations staff from the various agencies were invited to meet him. As I was filling a United Nations post I was included and was quite excited about the chance to see a leading world figure up close.

We all stood around in the searing afternoon heat in our jackets and ties waiting for Boutros-Ghali to come out of meetings with Benon Sevan and other leaders. With all the protocol and arrangements surrounding the event, to me his presence seemed more like a royal visit than a working mission.

When he finally appeared, Boutros-Ghali walked up and down a line that had formed, shook everyone's hand and then left. No rousing speech about a grand plan for the United Nations to help Afghanistan. Not even a 'keep up the good work' or 'thanks for your efforts'. Nothing! It was quite disappointing and we all left wondering why we had bothered to stand there for so long.

Cricket pride in Pakistan ...

Margaret, on the other had had a much more interesting visitor. Pakistanis are fanatical about cricket and it was one common topic that Australians could easily share with the locals. The passion for cricket reached fever pitch on 25 March 1992 when Pakistan won the World Cup cricket competition for the first time ever by defeating England.

The match was played in Melbourne so this automatically increased Australians standing in the eyes of Pakistanis. We were actually in Lahore for the weekend at the time the match was being played and in every bazaar, alley way or tea shop the Pakistanis were huddled around TV sets watching the game. The city had virtually come to a standstill. When we said we were from Australia, we were always invited in to share a cup of tea and join in the excitement. However, the excitement got a bit out of hand when we were travelling home in a motor bike taxi after Pakistan had won the match, and many of the locals were out in the street firing their weapons into the air.

Being in Lahore at the time was doubly thrilling because it was the home town of the captain of the Pakistan cricket team, the charismatic Imran Khan. This was still in the period of Imran Khan being cast as a playboy, and when he came home he was feted as a national hero who could do no wrong.

One day Margaret was at home in Islamabad when she received a call from a Japanese friend, who was also a representative for the children's fund UNICEF. The friend said to Margaret, 'Would you like to come around for afternoon tea? Bring the kids; I have Imran Khan coming to discuss some UNICEF matters.' Margaret did not need a second invitation and was around to the house in a flash.

When I got home that evening Margaret was still in a besotted state. She said that it was just the four of them – the Japanese lady, Margaret, Zoe and Charles sitting around for two hours chatting with Imran about cricket, the World Cup and Australia. Imran signed cricket bats for Zoe and Charles and even gave them a few tips on batting and bowling. The photo Margaret had taken sitting next to Imran took pride of place in our house in Islamabad, and it certainly raised our standing among our Pakistani friends.

CHAPTER 5:

DEMONSTRATING DEMINING TO DONORS ALL IN A DAYS WORK

Despite all the political turmoil and insecurity in Afghanistan throughout 1992, the UNOCHA mine clearance program was going from strength to strength. Parts of the country were relatively peaceful and following the fall of the communist government, refugees had started to return to their homes in provincial areas. One such area in this category was the eastern part of the country, centred on the town of Jalalabad. It is the first major town you arrive at after entering Afghanistan by road from Pakistan, through the famous Khyber Pass.

The area had been heavily populated before the war and it had been a large agricultural area. Politically, a governor named Haji Abdul Qadeer had emerged and he was able to cobble together a stable coalition in all of the eastern provinces that lasted for a number of years. Many of the refugees in the camps around Peshawar had come from these eastern provinces, but even if they were ready to return to their villages it was believed that the presence of landmines would deter many of them.

Around this time the head of UNOCHA, Martin Barber, had the idea to start taking some donor country representatives on visits to demining sites. It was very difficult for Westerners, in particular, to get into Afghanistan now. There were no longer commercial flights to Kabul or other provincial cities, and driving alone anywhere in the country was unsafe. Also, this whole concept of 'humanitarian demining' as it was now being called was new and not a topic diplomats or development donors had ever had to deal with before. Quite understandably, many donors wanted to see that their money was being well spent. As a result it was decided that I would lead a donor visit to Jalalabad.

I briefed the NGO directors and it was agreed that Kefayatullah would set up a display of manual demining with one of his ATC teams, Fazel

Karim from the Organisation for Mine Awareness (OMA) would arrange a mine awareness briefing and Shohab Hakimi, the head of the Mine Dog Centre, would show some mine dogs working. I asked them to coordinate among themselves and I set about making all the other arrangements. We did not want to overnight in Afghanistan, so we arranged to meet the donor representatives at the Pearl Continental Hotel in Peshawar the night before the visit. That evening after dinner I showed our eight guests some inert landmines, explained the landmine situation throughout the country and briefed them on our trip the next day.

Next morning a convoy of six white UN vehicles left Peshawar early and drove through the magnificent Khyber Pass towards the border with Afghanistan. We stopped at the top of the pass to admire the view and take in the history of the area, as well as submit our paperwork for passing through the tribal area. Down at the bottom of the pass the scene at the border crossing point at Torkham was one of absolute chaos. The border was in a narrow gorge and there were two huge metal gates that marked the border, and they were closed.

About 50 jingly trucks were parked along the road blocking access to the gates and harried Pakistani customs officials were shouting at everyone. Off to one side in a large hollow was a scene reminiscent from an Indiana Jones movie. There was obviously a good deal of smuggling going on and there were shipping containers, crates, sacks and barrels of every description being loaded on to trucks, camels and donkeys. After much pushing and shoving we submitted our papers to the Pakistani officials and we manoeuvred our vehicles forward and passed through the border gate. There were no checks on the Afghan side, so we just drove on.

The road was in varying condition on the 50-kilometre run to Jalalabad. As we passed through villages, scruffy young boys stood on the side of the road with shovels. As you approached they would half-heartedly shovel some dust into a pothole and then put out their hand for a tip. Just short of Jalalabad we turned off and went to the ATC demining site. Kef had done well and set up chairs around a map and provided refreshments. His team leader gave a good briefing on what they were doing and then the donors were taken to see the deminers at work. The visitors were shown the Schiebel mine detectors which the teams were using.

GUARDING AGAINST SCRAP METAL COMPLACENCY

We called them 'mine detectors' but in fact they were metal detectors. They were green in colour and were exactly the same device that militaries use. The detectors send out an electronic signal and if the resulting magnetic flux is broken by a metal object, the detector sounds an alarm. They were rated to be able to detect a small piece of metal to a depth of about 14 centimetres under the ground. This was adequate as most mines were only buried to a shallow depth – normally a couple of centimetres. The detectors have to be checked against a tiny metal test piece each day before they are operated to make sure that they are calibrated properly. They also used up a lot of batteries.

One big problem working in a war torn country is the huge amount of scrap metal littered around, particularly, it always seemed, near minefields. There could be tin cans, bullets and all types of metallic objects on or below the surface. If an artillery shell, rocket or mortar had exploded in the vicinity, there would be metal shards and fragments scattered for hundreds of metres in every direction.

When working the deminers had to investigate every time the detector alarmed. Invariably, it was a piece of scrap metal. At times the 'failure rate' could be a thousand to one, that is for every mine that had been found the operator may have investigated hundreds and hundreds of false readings. It wasn't really a 'failure' as the detector was doing what it was designed to do (i.e. detect metal), but it meant that the job became very boring and repetitive for the deminers. As a result of this situation, every demining site had a huge pile of scrap metal off to one side and we had to guard against complacency among the deminers.

One of the deminers was introduced to the visitors and he spoke very good English. He was dressed in the standard deminer's uniform of green trousers and shirt. He explained that he was actually a member of a small team of minefield surveyors working in the area. Their job was to go ahead of the demining teams to try to determine the boundaries of a mined area, map it and then mark the area with red rocks. This was done both to warn local people and to show the demining teams where to start when eventually the area was scheduled to be cleared.

The man then explained that some time ago when working, he had accidently stepped on a mine and lost his leg. To prove the point, he rolled up his trouser leg and showed us his prosthetic leg. The visitors were impressed and said what a brave man he was. With a twinkle in his eye and feigned modesty he replied, 'No, no, no. My colleagues here go out to the minefields and every day they are risking two legs. Me, I am only risking one leg.'

This response was greeted with laughter and applause. On subsequent visits, I noticed that no matter where we went this chap magically turned up and told the same story. I did not mind as he was a great ambassador for his country and he so eloquently portrayed the positive spirit that we had in the mine clearance program.

These days you wouldn't dream of taking a visitor into a minefield without wearing protective clothing and equipment, but at that time not even the deminers had any to wear. I had stressed to the NGO directors that they were not to plant any mines, but if they had found some that day, or the day before, to leave them in the ground and not blow them up until after the visit. Fortunately, the team we were visiting had found a few of the POM-Z and PMN anti-personnel blast mines that morning.

One by one the donor representatives were taken forward in the demining lane and shown the half-uncovered mine that the deminer had detected with his metal detector and then gently revealed. It never failed to have an impact on visitors. Around you is a normal looking field or track, and yet here in front of your eyes, buried a few centimetres under the ground and unseen until a few moments ago, is a cruel and indiscriminate device that would have blown your leg off had you stepped on it. This was always a sobering sight for anyone who witnessed it.

Once they had all seen the mine we backed off, a deminer placed a charge of TNT beside the mine and when it was wired up, one of the donors was invited to press the button on the detonator machine and explode the mine. People who have no experience with explosives are always amazed at how noisy and powerful a small amount of high explosive can be. The Afghans would also joke with the visitors and reassure them that these were 'peaceful' explosions.

We were getting a bit behind schedule at this stage so we quickly headed off to the next display, which was to be a mine awareness 'class' in a village. This was about 30 kilometres away on the other side of town and it took an hour to get there. Inside a mud hut were a group of 30 young boys of all ages who had been assembled for a lesson.

MINE AWARENESS CLASSES FOR THE LOCALS

In these 'classes' instructors explained what mines looked like and what to do if you found one – do not touch and report it to someone.

You may wonder why bother warning people, as many of the mines are buried, but there are often some tell-tale signs that mines have been planted in an area. Sometimes you can see small craters in the ground caused by earlier mine explosions, or the carcasses of dead animals which have stepped on a mine, evidence of military positions or trenches and so on. Often the locals knew what fighting took place and it was not uncommon to see an overgrown field next to two ploughed ones – the overgrown area obviously being mined. Finally, some of the mines like the POM Z (the fragmentation mine on a stick) or the butterfly mines were found on the surface of the ground, so could potentially be seen by local villagers.

As women and girls are as equally vulnerable to landmines as men, OMA had set up a separate women's program. This area of Afghanistan was deeply conservative and they followed the code of Pashtunwali – a concept of living or philosophy for the Pashtun people and which is regarded as an honour code and a non-written law for the people. Part of this code or culture involved women staying separate and not going outside the family home unless fully covered and escorted by a male relative. People blame the Taliban for introducing the all-covering 'burkha' that women had to wear, but it was in widespread use in rural areas of Afghanistan even at this time.

Setting up the mine awareness training and getting acceptance for it had been difficult, but it was working well. The female instructors were usually the wives of the male instructors and they could travel with them. Curiously, they did not object to us foreign men going into the room to see the women's class underway. The instructors covered their faces with their shawls and the girls giggled like any kids. At least they were getting the same information as the boys.

The 'horse and dog show' – detector dogs and disappointment

By now we were way behind schedule so we quickly set off to see the dogs. After another hour's drive we came to their work site, and I realised that we were back near the place we had been in the morning. The dog program had been set up by the Americans and they were currently in the process of negotiating the transfer of it to become a non-governmental organisation under the UNOCHA mine clearance program.

The dogs being used were German Shepherds and Belgian Malinois – both big strong breeds of dogs. The director of the dog centre, Shohab Hakimi, briefed the visitors and then the dogs went through their paces.

Dogs do not 'clear' mines; they are just another form of detector. They are trained to sniff out explosives using their amazing sense of smell. The technique being used was to have the dog on a long lead and it was trained to sniff out along an imaginary straight line to about 20 metres from the handler, and then turn around and sniff its way back. If it smelt a mine they were trained to sit and 'point' at the spot. The handler then called it back and rewarded it with a rubber ball to play with. At this stage, a regular deminer would need to come forward with a metal detector or prodder in order to pinpoint the mines exact location and uncover it.

There was a fair degree of scepticism among the visitors. Would you walk on a piece of land that a dog has sniffed and not indicated anything? Shohab had one trick up his sleeve. We went to a safe area where he gave one of the visitors an inert mine and said go and bury it where you like. The person did so and dug a few more fake holes to stop the dog using the sight of disturbed ground as the cue. Sure enough, when the dog arrived on the scene it quickly found the mine and the visitors were slightly more convinced.

I explained to the assembled donors, 'The dogs have great potential in areas where there are high levels of metal fragmentation in the ground, because they will ignore the fragments as they are only trained to react to the smell of explosives. The dogs are also useful in detecting some of the mines that only contained a minimum amount of metal.'

However, at this time UNOCHA did not control the dog project and privately I felt more work was needed to be done to fully utilise the potential of the dogs and to gain greater confidence in declaring areas safe after dogs had been used.

By now it was getting late in the day. We were meant to call by the Governor's office in Jalalabad, but as we were on the wrong side of town I made the decision to finish up. We had to get back to the Torkham border crossing before dark when the border gate would be closed for the evening. We returned through the border with much less difficulty, as the crowds of trucks and people had subsided somewhat. As we drove back up the Khyber Pass the sun was starting to set, camel trains were passing by and lights from various encampments were flickering all over the mountains. It was a glorious end to a great day.

A few days later my boss, Martin Barber, called me into his office and said that some of the donors had contacted him. They said that they had enjoyed the visit immensely but were disappointed they had not met the Governor. I took the point and quickly realised that although my world revolved around demining, it did not for others. For the diplomats and donors the political dimension was equally important. It made them look good if they reported back to their capitals that they had been to Afghanistan and met with certain political leaders. I didn't make the same mistake twice.

At the next monthly meeting I thanked the NGO directors for arranging the visit, but then gave them a stern dressing down for not coordinating better over the timing and the sequence of the visits. I said to them 'In the army the commander gives an intention or order and then the subordinates carry it out, and that was what I had expected them to do'. Another lesson I had just learned was that I may have to have a more hands-on approach to certain activities. I also warned them that we had to be careful not to be seen to be putting on a 'dog and pony show' – a good army expression for a display that is all show and no substance. When preparing for a later visit Kef said to me, 'I know; you don't want the horse and dog show.' I had to laugh.

Overall, the visit had been a huge success and was soon showing signs of generating more financial contributions for the program.

A medical emergency

Martin decided to continue with the visits and the next one a few months later followed the same format. This time in my vehicle was my Afghan driver and I in the front, with the two diplomats in the back. One was a small, fat little middle-aged man with round glasses and a clipped moustache. He was very 'old fashioned' looking and from one of the European embassies in Islamabad. When we were crossing the border into Afghanistan at Torkham he looked a bit pale and I saw him take a pill. I asked if he was okay and he said yes, so I assumed it was car sickness caused by the winding roads through the Khyber Pass. I thought no more of it.

This time we had to drive through the centre of Jalalabad to get to a demining site. There were large crowds of people in the busy town centre and the bustling bazaar area, along with the usual confusion of trucks, donkeys and camels. Our vehicle was just crawling along through the crowd when I heard a noise from the back of the car. I looked around and saw that the little man's arms were flailing wildly and beating at his chest, and then he slumped down in his seat. I jumped out of the car and ran around to his side and opened the door. The man was motionless, did not appear to be breathing, had blood-specked foam all around his mouth and had wet himself.

We had all done advanced first aid training before we left Australia and were authorised to carry certain drugs like morphine in our personal medical kits. However, our training had focussed on treating traumatic mine blast injuries and not so much this type of situation. My mind was racing. I was sure that he had suffered a heart attack and was dead.

STEPPING INTO A MINEFIELD

By now a large crowd of local Afghans had gathered around and we had become separated from our other vehicles. My plan was to pull him out of the vehicle, lay him on the road and try to resuscitate him. I remember thinking, somewhat selfishly, that I did not look forward to giving him mouth-to-mouth resuscitation in this condition. For some reason I decided to first check for a pulse. I put my fingers on the side of his neck and could feel a faint pulse. I was confused – I was sure he was dead so why was there a pulse? As I tried to detect if he was breathing he made a slight groan and moved. Thank goodness he wasn't dead. I then decided the best idea was to head to the Red Cross hospital, which I knew was only a few blocks away.

I got on the radio and called my colleagues in the other vehicles. The golden rule is never to swear on the radio (because everyone is listening) but I said. 'We have a medical emergency. I'm heading to the Red Cross hospital. This is serious shit!'

When we arrived at the hospital the chap was in luck. A Canadian doctor had flown into Jalalabad that morning in the small Red Cross plane to conduct a clinic. The man still could not walk or talk, but I described what had happened and the doctor looked at his pills. The doctor (correctly, as it turned out) diagnosed that the man had suffered an epileptic fit. The doctor said that they would look after him and take him to Peshawar when they flew back that afternoon. We then joined up with the rest of our group and continued on with the visit.

The only other excitement on the trip, and I know it sounds like a stereotype, involved the Japanese ambassador who ran out of film for his camera in the middle of the minefield. He just suddenly turned around and started to walk out of the safe lane to get back to the car. He was quickly stopped. I didn't want to lose two diplomats in one day.

When I was back in Islamabad a few days later I went to visit the European diplomat to see how he was. He confirmed that he was an epileptic and said that after the pre-visit briefing in Peshawar he had suffered a nightmare, where he imagined he had gone into a minefield and stepped on a mine. When we had arrived in Jalalabad the next day it all got too much for him and this had triggered the seizure. I rebuked him slightly and said, 'You should have told me about your medical condition before you agreed to come on the visit, or at least wear a medical bracelet so that people will know what they are dealing with.' He apologised profusely.

Making a friend – Gunter Mulack

It was also during one of the donor visits that I met Dr Gunter Mulack, who was to become a great friend and colleague. Gunter was an experienced diplomat who had been the German ambassador to Kuwait during the first Gulf War. He spoke fluent Arabic and was something of an Islamic scholar. On one visit to a minefield it was just Gunter and I, so we let him set some explosive charges and then moved back to detonate them.

He said to me, 'You're very safety conscious.'

I replied, 'This is just normal procedure, mate.'

He then told me when he was in Kuwait he and some colleagues had found a box of hand grenades on a beach. They stood there and pulled out the safety pins, threw the grenades into the sea and watched them explode underwater!

Gunter came to love Afghanistan and during our spare time he enjoyed going into bazaars looking for interesting artefacts. He was based in Berlin, but our paths crossed many times and he was to help me out more than once in the years that followed.

My caution with explosives had been based on a bad experience with safety distances that always stuck in my mind. In 1977 I had been seconded to the Papua New Guinea (PNG) Defence Force and served with them in Wewak, on the north coast of PNG. A raging flood had washed away a large 40-metre long concrete causeway at a major river crossing point near some villages. The overturned causeway was now acting like a dam wall and the water rushing around it was causing severe erosion at either end.

I was tasked to blow it up into smaller segments that could be bulldozed away, to allow a new bridge to be built. I worked with my PNG team for about a week setting the explosive cutting charges all over the causeway. The big day came and we posted sentries up and down the river, as well as along the road and a couple of tracks.

Warnings were shouted out through a megaphone. The sentries gave the all clear so I lit the fuse and moved back about 500 metres to a sandbag bunker.

Then wouldn't you know it – two local tribesmen just popped out of the jungle about 100 metres from the bridge and started to walk towards it, right where hundreds of kilograms of high explosive were about to go off. We had time so I sent a vehicle down to collect them. The look of shock on their faces when the bridge was blown to pieces was priceless, but I had learned the truth of the saying 'if it can go wrong, it will'.

CHAPTER 6:

MANAGING THE DEMINING PROGRAM

Every month we would hold a coordination meeting for all those involved with the UNOCHA mine clearance program. I would chair the meeting and all the Afghan NGO Directors would attend, along with the various technical advisers and other support staff. The meetings were usually held in Islamabad or Peshawar, but as time went on we held them in Quetta (in central-west Pakistan) or in Jalalabad, Kabul, Kandahar and Herat in Afghanistan. They were useful, focussed meetings and throughout 1992 we were working hard to implement many of the recommendations made the previous year in the independent evaluation report.

The first issue to address was the organisation of the mine clearance program. The evaluation had called for greater centralised control directed by the program manager – which was now me. I had already moved Sayed Aqa and the staff of his organisation, the Mine Clearance Planning Agency into the 'headquarters' in Islamabad. They worked as the operations and planning staff for the program, particularly focussing on survey. It was unusual to have United Nations and NGO staff working together like this, but we had the United Nations staff on the top floor of our building and the NGO staff on the ground floor.

The entire donor funding for the program came through UNOCHA so we were able to exercise tight control over the Afghan NGO's financial activities. UNOCHA had a number of excellent Pakistani finance staff who oversaw this. The logistic officer, medical adviser and some other administrative staff of the program were also Pakistani.

STEPPING INTO A MINEFIELD

Each of the NGOs had their own emblems and of course the United Nations had its official logo, which could only be worn or displayed by United Nations personnel or equipment. Although seemingly not a big issue, I decided we should have an additional logo for the Mine Clearance Program, which every organisation could display to show that we were all part of the national demining effort. The monthly meeting reviewed some suggested designs and in the end we agreed on a green circle (the colour of Islam) with the words 'Demining' in English and 'Mine Paki' (meaning mine clearance) in Dari. The use of the demining logo became widespread among the program and was well recognised throughout Afghanistan. It certainly helped promote the impression of a unified program and one in which everyone felt they were an equal partner.

We were always making contingency plans to move the program headquarters to Kabul if the security situation allowed. With the fall of the Najibullah Government in April 1992 this looked like it may be soon. I was keen to replace some of the Pakistani headquarters staff with Afghans to facilitate such a move. We advertised for a program officer and received plenty of applications. Because the term 'demining' was still fairly new, we always received mistaken applications from people in the 'mining' or minerals extraction industry. We would write back and say that we were in the business of digging up landmines, not gold, but they were free to have their application considered if they wished. They never did.

In the United Nations system a program officer is usually a young graduate whose job is to research topics, draft project proposals, compile reports, arrange meetings and so on. One applicant for our vacancy stood out and he said in the application that he worked for an NGO coordinating body in Peshawar. I had to go to a meeting of that group, so I arranged to interview him afterwards. At the start of the meeting a young looking Afghan man came out to welcome everyone and got the meeting going. I was impressed by his manner, confidence and knowledge of his subject. I whispered to my colleague that I hoped this was the man we had come to see. He sure was and I offered Mohammed Shakir the job on the spot. He came to Islamabad and easily fitted in to the office environment and quickly earned the respect of the rest of the program.

The next issue to address was the lack of information about the landmine problem throughout the country, and the subsequent setting of priorities of where to clear next. Before my time, the NGOs obtained information from the refugee camps and would subsequently demine in the areas where the refugees said they came from. However, often the refugees did not go back. The evaluation report recommended that we focus on those areas where people had already started to return and 'reward' them for doing so with demining work. To do this we still needed better data.

A survey reveals the ugly landmine truth

Sayed Aqa had long proposed that we undertake a national level survey and plans were drawn up for the National Survey of the Mines Situation in Afghanistan. The aim of the survey was to better quantify the landmine problem in Afghanistan, to help establish priority areas for clearance and to assist with effective long term planning of mine clearance operations in Afghanistan. It took some time to arrange funding for the survey from the European Commission and for MCPA to train over 75 data collectors.

The survey was to be conducted by interviewing people all over the country by trained interviewers, including both men and women. The survey did not get underway until early 1993 but the results were staggering when they came in. It was found that throughout Afghanistan up to 20 civilians were being killed or injured by landmines every day. Over 900 villages in 162 districts were reported to have a mine problem, and 2,300 minefields were identified covering an area of 380 square kilometres.

This survey, along with refugee tracking figures provided by the United Nations High Commissioner for Refugees (UNHCR) provided the basis for our planning for many years to come. Because the total area affected by landmines was so large, we had to classify each minefield as high or low priority and a set of criteria were agreed upon before an area would be scheduled for clearance. They were:

- The area must be secure and free from fighting
- The population must be able to draw immediate socio-economic benefit
- All local groups must be united in requesting assistance
- Some support is to be provided by the local population
- Refugees must already be returning to the area
- Other funded rehabilitation or development projects are being delayed due to mines
- The area is free from opium poppy cultivation

At the more technical level we needed to speed up the manual demining process. Manual demining was the main method of clearance we used, and despite being slow it was still the most reliable method for achieving complete clearance. It also had the added advantage of providing employment in war torn Afghanistan. At this time we had well over 2,000 Afghans employed and they were receiving a good salary, were insured and received training. In the following years the NGOs continued to grow and eventually employed more than 7,000 people and they were believed to be the biggest employer group in the country. Most importantly, these Afghan deminers did not have a gun in their hands.

Looking at the organisational level we found it most efficient if the demining teams deployed from their bases in Peshawar or Quetta into Afghanistan for up to six weeks. They would then return for one week's rest, resupply and administration. To reduce daily travel time to the worksite we continued to establish field base-camps near the mined areas inside Afghanistan which could support up to four demining teams at any one time. At the micro-level we reduced the minefield breaching parties to two people – just the detector man and the prodder man. We did away with the trip wire feeler and observer as we were not finding any trip wires, and a section leader could easily observe his four breaching parties.

Refining demining techniques and equipment

Raging debates were held over certain demining equipment and techniques, particularly prodding for the mine. Most demining accidents occurred during prodding, as this is when contact is made (hopefully) with the side of the mine. The reason the deminer was currently required to lie down to prod was because if a buried blast mine went off, the blast wave went upwards in the shape of a 'V'. If the deminer was down low and back from the mine as far possible, he could avoid serious injury. A number of deminers survived a mine blast with just the loss of a few fingers and a massive headache, all because they were lying down when the mine went off.

The official prodder was a long thin fibreglass rod with a handle – a bit like a double length chopstick. However, due to the hard ground in Afghanistan most deminers preferred to use the bayonet from a Kalashnikov rifle. This was better for digging away the earth from the mine, but as it was much shorter brought the deminer in closer to the mine. It was tiring prodding with your arm outstretched and it was just human nature that the deminers would raise themselves up a bit to try to see what they were uncovering. A number of people, including HALO Trust, started to argue that it was more natural and comfortable to prod while squatting or kneeling. The argument went that if the deminer was more comfortable, could see better what he was doing and had more control over the prodder, he was likely to have less accidents.

While I could see the merits of the argument and knew that some deminers were squatting in spite of the rules, the problem was that a squatting person was directly over the mine. If the mine exploded the deminer would take the full force of the blast on his chest and face. A number of deminers had been blinded as a result of blast accidents. Previously the program had issued industrial plastic goggles to deminers to try and protect their eyes, but these were useless as they were just blown straight off by the mine blast. Until we had some better face protection I was not prepared to officially alter the prodding technique.

Our logistic officer, Tariq Zuberi, was a former colonel in the Pakistani army. I tasked him to come up with a range of options for helmets and visors that may suit our needs. Most of this type of equipment resided with the military and the problem we faced was that even innocuous items like metal detectors and helmets were deemed to be 'dual use' – that is they were civilian in nature or were intended to be used in a civilian context, but could be misused by other people for aggressive purposes.

As a result, a lot of military items were subject to a sales embargo and we could not buy them for use in Afghanistan. Tariq finally sourced a helmet with a visor that looked promising. It looked much like a motorbike helmet but was made of Kevlar and came with two thicknesses of clear perspex visors. He also obtained some other items like a visor with just a headband, a bit like a clear welding shield. We decided to conduct some tests to see what would best suit our need.

Tariq managed to obtain some PMN blast mines and POM Z fragmentation mines from the local bazaar. I did not ask too many questions about this. We then went to a range area and set up the helmets and visors on dummy deminers made of sandbags, set them back the same distance from the mines as the squatting deminer would be and then exploded the mines. Even though it had been well fitted, the visor on the headband just blew off. With the helmets and visors, the heavy metal fragments from the POM Z had penetrated the thinner visor easily and some parts of the thicker visor. However, the results from the helmet and visors in front of the blast type mine were more encouraging. The visor was sandblasted with dust and dirt from the explosion, but the inside of the visor was clean, meaning it had stopped the blast and would protect the deminers face and eyes. During other trials, the main problem with the helmets was that they were found to be hot and heavy to wear for long periods of time.

This was all totally unscientific but we were satisfied we had the answer. The thicker visor was too heavy, but as most of the accidents were occurring with the buried blast mines we felt the helmet with the thinner visor would protect against blast injuries. The problem now was money. The helmets were about $500 each, so it would cost over half a million dollars to equip the whole program. We did not have the money at the time. The monthly meeting also felt that in the interests of fairness, all deminers should be issued the protective helmets at the same time.

During my visits around the program I would try to get to the local hospital to visit injured deminers. Shortly after these helmet trials were held I went to Quetta and visited the local Red Cross hospital. I was shown a deminer who had accidently knelt on a mine. He had lost both

My parents, Fred and Annie Mansfield on their wedding day on 17 August 1940. They were married in Christ Church cathedral in St Arnaud in Victoria. It was a modest ceremony due to war-time restrictions. My father worked for the Shell oil company and my mother was a nurse. (Photo: Ian Mansfield)

My father, VX102775 Captain Fred Mansfield, (back row, centre with glasses and pipe) served with an infantry battalion battalion in Papua New Guinea for four years during World War 2. He only got home once during that time. (Photo: AWM 075918)

The Mansfield kids. My oldest brother Alan (standing) was born before Dad went to the war, the rest of us – Brian, Peter, me and Helen were born in quick succession after the war. This photo was taken in late 1953 and is the earliest photo I have of me. (Photo: Ian Mansfield)

I grew up in country Victoria and attended Ararat West primary school. This is me trying to look tough in Grade 3 in 1961. (Photo: Ian Mansfield)

This photo appeared in the Ararat Advertiser newspaper on 4 November 1962, the day before bonfire night. The caption read 'It was a cracker night last night and here two boys prepare for the big occasion. They are Glen Rundell and Ian Mansfield (right). The boys say they were well aware of the danger of crackers and said they would use every care'. Maybe my interest in explosives started here? (Photo: Ararat Advertiser)

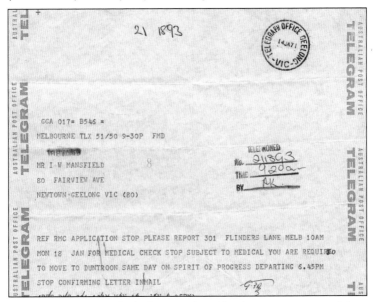

The army moved fast. I got my high school exam results on Thursday, 13 January 1971 and then received this telegram from the army on Friday, telling me to report to the recruiting office in Melbourne on Monday. From there I would be 'sworn in' and then travel by overnight train to start as a cadet at the Royal Military College, Duntroon the next day. (Photo: Ian Mansfield)

The Sydney Daily Telegraph newspaper ran a feature on life at Duntroon on 20 October 1972. I was in the same section as the Crown Prince of Thailand, Maha Varjiralongkorn, who was better known as 'Mr Mahidol' while at the college. In the photo I am sitting with the Prince at dinner. (Photo: Ian Mansfield)

Left: Armed with a degree in civil engineering and commissioned as a lieutenant, I graduated from Duntroon on 10 December 1974 – to serve as an officer in the Royal Australian Engineers for the next 20 years. (Photo: Ian Mansfield).

Right: Taking a break during training to walk the famous Kokoda Trail while living in Papua New Guinea in 1978. A group of eight of us walked the trail from Kokoda village to Owers Corner in five days, carrying all our own equipment. Standing at the back are Captain Dave Gratwick (left) and Flight Sergeant Kim Palfryman (right). (Photo: Ian Mansfield)

Gunsmoke seen near May Downs

ENOGGERA: Sappers from the 20th Divisional Engineer Support Squadron recently deployed 2000km north-west of their home base for Exercise Gunsmoke.

After a four-day road move, the Sappers deployed into the sparse rocky area around the May Downs Camp, near Mt Isa, Qld, for five days of revising engineer skills.

During this phase the Squadron practised demolitions, live firing of mines, booby trap training and camouflage.

The second phase of the exercise, also held over five days, required the unit to deploy eight times in a tactical setting over 180km.

The final deployment was carried out on a blustery, rainy and moonless night in NBC gear – TOPP – along narrow boggy tracks.

An almost inevitable NBC strike forced the unit to adopt TOPP 3 until the end of the exercise.

OC, Maj Ian Mansfield, said the Sappers benefited from the training, particularly the different location and long convoy journey.

★ **ABOVE:** Maj Ian Mansfield displays an M14 anti-personnel mine and its effect on a GP boot.

While commanding an engineer squadron in 1986 I ran a mine laying exercise near Mount Isa. This photo in the local paper shows me proudly holding a boot damaged by a landmine. This is now rather ironic given my later involvement with humanitarian mine clearance programs around the world and my support for a ban on landmines. (Photo: Ian Mansfield)

PMN anti-personnel blast mine (Photo: GICHD)

A box of PMN anti-personnel blast mines (Photo: GICHD)

Left: POM-Z anti-personnel fragmentation mines (Photo: GICHD)
Right: Valmara anti-personnel bounding mine (Photo: GICHD)

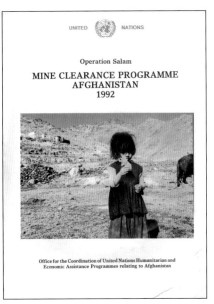

Left: PFM anti-personnel mine, better known as a butterfly mine due to its shape.

Right: The cover of the first national mine clearance plan for Afghanistan, which I prepared in 1992 and which outlined our priorities, funding needs and mine clearance goals for the year. The young Afghan girl in the photo is holding a PFM butterfly mine (I did not take the photo of her). (Photo: Ian Mansfield)

The Directors of the first Afghan mine clearance organizations – (from the left) Kefayatullah Eblagh (ATC), Fazel Karim (OMA), Sayed Aqa (MCPA) and Engineer Pushtoon (SWAAD). I kept this photo on my desk at work to show that we were all part of the landmine clearance 'family'. (Photo: Ian Mansfield)

During combat operations, the military only aim to clear lanes through a minefield and then continue with their mission. While similar equipment and techniques may be used, civilian, or humanitarian demining, focusses on clearing all landmines and returning land to productive use. (Photo: GICHD)

An Afghan instructor teaches a new demining recruit how to use a metal detector to find buried landmines. Of course any metal object would make the detector sound the alarm, and in operations there are often hundreds, if not thousands of pieces of scrap metal uncovered for every landmine found. (Photo: MCPA)

After the metal detector gave a signal, the 'prodder man' would gently prod at a low angle in the ground to see if the suspicious object was a buried landmine. The deminers had to be careful not to hit the top of the mine, as this would set it off. Most accidents occurred during prodding (Photo: Ian Mansfield)

During my first trip to Afghanistan I saw the Aardvark flail machines working near Khost. The armoured machine had rotating chains and hammers at the front that were designed to detonate any landmines that they may strike. (Photo: Ian Mansfield)

Each morning before starting work the Afghan deminers would test their equipment and then pray for a safe days work. (Photo: ATC)

The Australian Army provided teams of officers and non-commissioned officers to train and advise the Afghan demining organizations. This is Team 7 in late 1991. (Rear row from left) Captain Mick Lavers, Sergeant John Kirkham, Lieutenant Guy Dugdale, Captain Mark Willetts (Centre row) Staff Sergeant Des O'Hanlon (with beard), Major Graeme Membrey, Major Warren Young, Major Rex Wright, Staff Sergeant Mal Quigg, me – in my role as Commanding Officer of the Mine Clearance Training Team (Front row kneeling) Sergeant Dean Beaumont, Sergeant Steve Charlesworth, Staff Sergeant Wayne Schoer. We were allowed to grow beards in order to show sensitivity with the local Afghan culture. (Photo: Ian Mansfield)

In February 1992 the Australian Minister for Defence Science and Personnel, Gordon Bilney, visited the team in Peshawar. Briefing him during the visit are (from the left) Kefayatullah Eblagh (Director ATC), Gordon Bilney, Colonel Sajaad (Pakistan army and commandant of the mine clearance training centre) and me. (Photo: Ian Mansfield)

A Soviet T55 tank fitted with mine clearance rollers. The rollers were designed to blow up landmines in front of the tank tracks during combat operations. A number of these tanks were provided to the United Nations through a 'Soviet pledge of equipment' but they were unsuitable for humanitarian demining. (Photo: Ian Mansfield)

Margaret meeting Imran Khan in Islamabad in mid-1992. Imran was the captain of the Pakistani cricket team when they won the World Cup Cricket series in Melbourne in March 1992; with a result he had super-star status in cricket mad Pakistan. (Photo: Ian Mansfield)

At the top of the famous Khyber Pass in October 1992. Most visits to eastern Afghanistan involved driving over the Pass and it was always a spectacular sight. The Australian army teams would travel to Afghanistan to inspect Afghan demining teams, conduct on-the-job training or undertake accident investigations. (From left) Lieutenant Bruce Vivers, Afghan deminer, Major Lee Unbergang, me, Sergeant Michael Durnin. (Photo: Ian Mansfield)

Inspecting a POM-Z fragmentation mine close up. In the early days of the Afghan mine clearance program we had no protective equipment available – either for deminers or visitors. If this mine exploded it would kill or injure people within a 20 metre radius. (Photo: Ian Mansfield)

Small teams of Afghan instructors would travel to the refugee camps and Afghan villages giving landmine safety briefings to the population. Due to cultural reasons, this involved women giving separate lessons to women and girls. (Photo: Ian Mansfield)

Dogs were trained to use their amazing sense of smell to sniff out buried landmines. They had the advantage of ignoring the millions of metal fragments that littered Afghanistan, but needed regular training and good back-up veterinary support. (Photo: Ian Mansfield)

The Australian connection. Dave Edwards, Bill van Ree, me and Ian Bullpitt at a large team leaders meeting held in Jalalabad in 1994. At these meetings we would discuss a wide range of operational and safety issues with the Afghan NGO staff. (Photo: Ian Mansfield)

The demining logo we designed and which was used by most of the demining organisations in Afghanistan in the early 1990's. This badge was worn on uniforms and placed on vehicles to show that everyone was working as part of the one national program – regardless of what organization they were employed by. (Photo: Ian Mansfield)

An Afghan civilian only a few minutes after he stepped on a landmine. He is being treated by medics from a demining team which happened to be in the area (who also took the photo). (Photo: ATC)

A deminer preparing to blow up a PMN mine. When they were found, the mines were left in-situ and some TNT explosive would be placed close to the mine. When the TNT was set off the explosion would also destroy the mine. (Photo: ATC)

My family and I at the top of the Khyber Pass. From left; Margaret, Zoe, Charles and me. Margaret and Zoe would usually wear a headscarf when travelling outside of Islamabad. (Photo: Ian Mansfield)

legs, one arm, his face had been sandblasted and he was blinded. He was not in a good way, and although I'd never thought I would see the day when I felt that someone would be better off dead, that thought now crossed my mind.

I was deeply moved by this man's plight and that night I telephoned Tariq Zuberi and told him to order 300 helmets and visors. I told him that I would find the money when I got back. I also said that we had no choice but to have a phased introduction of the helmets throughout the program, but hopefully, we could issue helmets to all deminers over the period of a couple of months. Fortunately we were able to get more money fairly quickly and we eventually issued helmets and visors to all the deminers. Mercifully, the deminer in Quetta passed away a few days after my visit.

We did not have any answer to the question of chest protection. The military style full body bomb disposal suits were entirely unsuitable. Deminers could not move in them, they were too hot and they were prohibitively expensive. The more common army style 'flak jackets' were also too hot and heavy and they did not extend down to cover the deminer's groin area. In any case, we could not buy these items as they were prohibited for sale being 'dual use' pieces of equipment.

The evaluation report recommended that we standardise on one type of metal detector. The detectors provided under the Soviet pledge of equipment were heavy, cumbersome devices. Informal tests undertaken by the different military advisers in the past found them to be unreliable and they felt that the Soviet detectors basically didn't work. We were also using four brands of other commercially available detectors that were common at the time. Some were having reliability problems and the requirement to provide training, maintenance and spare parts for four types of detectors was a big logistic problem.

It was interesting to note that in many Western armies at that time most of their mine detectors would only be used for training a couple of weeks of the year. The rest of the time they would sit on the storeroom shelf. In Afghanistan the deminers were using the detectors six hours a day, six days a week, 48 weeks a year, and our detectors were physically wearing out.

An Austrian company called Scheibel made a good general purpose detector called the AN 19/2 and the demining organisations were happy with it. As Scheibel had never raised their price, provided spare parts within 24 hours and had trained some Afghan repair men, we decided to standardise on their detector. The US Army had also just placed an order for 40,000 Scheibel detectors, so we were confident that they would have conducted extensive testing on the detector, and their large volume purchase helped keep the price down for our much smaller orders.

The final logistic challenge was to ensure the safe supply of explosives to the demining teams in the field. The United Nations policy remained unchanged – all mines that were found had to be destroyed in-situ. The normal method of destroying a mine was to place a stick of TNT next to the mine, insert a detonator and then light the fuse or fire it electronically. The power of the TNT exploding would cause the mine to detonate.

Fortunately we were able to buy TNT and detonators from the Pakistan Ordnance Factory at Wah Cantonment near Islamabad and they would transport the explosives from the factory to Peshawar or Quetta. The demining teams would collect it from there and take it into Afghanistan. Temporary storage facilities were then established at the site camps. Moving explosives around Afghanistan could be fraught with danger, but luckily we suffered no major incidents.

Navigating the wildlands of Peshawar

With the focus of much of our work being in eastern Afghanistan, I was spending a lot of time in Peshawar. Peshawar was a real frontier town and if incidents associated with living in Islamabad were often amusing, in Peshawar they could be deadly. The law and order situation was often confused because drugs and weapons were openly available and official corruption widespread. Many people were armed and rival Afghan mujahedeen factions and other 'foreign interests' often sorted out their differences on the street. The main hotel in town was the four-star Pearl Continental and it had a sign at the front door saying 'Check your guns here'.

Graeme Membrey had been replaced as the technical adviser at the demining organisation ATC by another Australian major, Paddy Johnston. Paddy had his wife Cheryl and two children living with him in Peshawar, but he was getting concerned about the poor security in town, which included house break-ins, robberies and kidnappings. When out shopping one day Cheryl had to hide in the back of a stall in Sadar Bazaar because automatic rifle fire erupted. The fact that it turned out to be 'happy fire' because the Pakistan cricket team had arrived in town didn't really help matters.

A more serious shooting incident occurred in June when Paddy was at work in his office at ATC and he heard some gunshots. He went outside and saw that a Japanese man had been shot in a car in the driveway next door. Paddy opened the car door and checked for vital signs and started to try to resuscitate the man. He then saw that the back of the man's head was missing and Paddy could do nothing to stop the bleeding and the man died in his arms. The Afghan staff of ATC then started getting concerned in case 'any foreigner' may have been the target and also they did not want Paddy to get taken in by the Pakistani police. The rumour was that the Japanese man had been seeing Afghan women and this was some kind of payback or warning to foreigners.

Immediately after the shooting incident Paddy decided to send Cheryl and their children to stay with us in Islamabad, even though they were due to go on holidays in a few days' time. Margaret and our driver picked them up at Islamabad airport, but on the way home they got caught up in an anti-Benazir Bhutto protest. The police were firing tear gas all over the place so Margaret put the kids on the floor of the vehicle and our driver took off cross country through a park and some fields.

After the Johnston family returned from their holiday in Europe it was decided that his family should return to Australia and Paddy finished out the year in Peshawar on his own.

Just out of Peshawar there is a town called Dara Azem Kehl – which is famous for two things – hashish and homemade weapons. It is in one of the tribal areas so foreigners needed a permit to go there. During a relatively calm period I arranged a trip for a couple of families to go and visit the town. The town itself looked like it was straight out of a cowboy movie. There was one dusty street down the middle, with drug shops on one side and gun shops on the other. It was a truly amazing scene. Tribal men operating primitive metal-working lathes could turn steel bars into most kinds of weapons – pistols, shotguns, rifles, semi-automatic weapons and so on. For a few rupees you could buy a couple of magazines of ammunition and go out the back of a shop and fire off the rounds. We couldn't resist, so Margaret and the kids fired a Kalashnikov and a pistol. You could even fire an RPG but it cost the equivalent of US$200, so we thought that was too expensive. We didn't go to the other side of the street and after about an hour in the town we decided that it would be prudent to leave.

Kefayatullah's organisation, ATC, was based in a suburb of Peshawar in a series of houses which had been turned into offices. One day he had a lucky escape when a Mirage fighter jet from the Pakistan Air Force crashed into the house next door and exploded in a fiery inferno. The wing of the jet flew off and smashed into the balcony outside Kef's office. Fortunately he wasn't injured, even though he was sitting at his desk at the time. The speculation around town was that a young air force officer had been showing off to his girlfriend by undertaking low level manoeuvres over the city, when things went horribly wrong for him.

A Peshawar story with a happier ending was Kef's second marriage. Kef had been married for some time but had no children. In an Afghan's mind the problem was clearly with the woman, because it could not possibly the man's fault. Kef decided to take a second wife, which was permitted under their law. Margaret and I were invited to attend the ceremony which was to be held in Peshawar. Initially we declined because we did not agree with the concept, but Kef insisted and out of friendship and curiosity we decided to attend.

This was our first Afghan wedding and it was an eye opener. For a start it was segregated – hundreds of men were in one compound and the women were all in another. Margaret and I went our separate ways. I just stood around talking to the few people I knew and later we were served a sumptuous Afghan meal.

Later when I caught up with Margaret she had a much more interesting story to tell. In the ladies' house there was a stage and on it sat wife number one and wife number two, along with Kefayatullah himself. As I was Kef's friend and Margaret was the only foreign woman in the room, she was invited to join the bridal party on the stage. The actual marriage had taken place earlier and everything was harmonious, because wife number one had had a say in choosing wife number two.

The women had not eaten by the time we left, because the women do not get to eat until after the men had finished. Margaret got talking to one of the few Afghan women who could speak English. When asked what she did, the lady said she was a gynaecologist and her job was to examine brides-to-be to make sure they were 'intact'. When Margaret asked what happened if they were not, the lady whispered that she repaired the damage. The happy end of the story is that both of Kef's wives became pregnant and bore him a number of sons, so in the eyes of an Afghan man all was good. We naturally didn't agree with a lot of this, but who were we to judge?

CHAPTER 7:

HEADING OUT WEST TO HERAT

The one geographic area of Afghanistan that we had not paid much attention to was the western part of the country, and in particular the historic city of Herat. Strategically located, Herat lies on the ancient trade routes of the Middle East, Central and South Asia. The roads from Herat to Iran, Turkmenistan and other parts of Afghanistan are still as important today as they ever were. More recently, Herat was one of the popular stops on the 'hippie trail' of the 1970s and it was visited by hundreds of young adventurers on overland journeys from London to Sydney. Herat was occupied by the Soviets throughout the period of their invasion, but following the fall of the Najibullah Government it had quickly come under mujahedeen control. Unconfirmed reports suggested that the city and surrounding areas were heavily mined.

The United Nations had sent a small fact finding mission to Herat shortly after the change of government in April 1992. They found that the city was calm and under the control of a governor, Ismail Khan. Most of the basic services like electricity, water and sanitation and health care were not working. The area around Herat had previously been famous for its grapes and other fruit, but the mission found the city and surrounding areas devoid of trade and agriculture, mainly due to landmines. It was agreed to send a follow-up mission and I was asked to go and assess the extent of the landmine problem.

As I was still in the Australian Army I needed to get permission from army headquarters in Canberra to go on the trip, which was duly granted with no conditions. On 20 May 1992, a small group of experts from different United Nations agencies flew in Salam 01 from Islamabad to Herat, along with a large quantity of medical supplies. We flew over Kabul and then due west over the rugged and uninhabited brown mountains in the central parts of Afghanistan.

The airport in Herat had been built by the Americans in the 1960s and was used by the Soviets during their occupation, so the large runway was still in good condition. We were met by a delegation of local officials and taken to meet the governor. The road from the airport to the city was in terrible shape with huge craters and potholes everywhere. Some of the craters were so large vehicles in front would disappear from view and then reappear on the other side.

The journey of a couple of kilometres to the governor's office took nearly 30 minutes. The governor, Ismail Khan, was quite slight and short, had a long grey beard and wore a checked turban. He did not have an imposing physical presence and his manner was quiet, but his cold grey eyes left no doubt that he was the man in charge. He had been in the Afghan Army but led a mutiny against the Soviet occupation in 1979. When he was subsequently driven out of the city he had become the leading mujahedeen commander in the west of the country. On the departure of the Soviets he had become the self-appointed governor.

Ismail Khan welcomed our group, offered us chai and outlined the needs of Herat. His presentation, delivered through an interpreter, was all logical, well thought out and he showed a real concern for his people. He pledged to work with the United Nations to allow aid and assistance to be delivered. Someone jokingly said that the road from the airport should be the first priority. Ismail Khan replied that it would be the last road to be fixed, as it should serve as a reminder to all visitors as to how bad the conditions that they had endured had been. He also did not drink any tea, which was unusual for an Afghan. I was later told that he did not eat or drink during daylight hours, in honour of his men who had been killed fighting against the Soviets.

Herat had suffered badly during the occupation. To the west of the city, the Soviets had levelled a belt of houses over five kilometres long and one kilometre wide to lay minefields for their defensive perimeter, and to allow a clear view to fire their weapons if attacked. We were cautious driving around and it was clear from piles of rubble that some mines would be deeply buried, and that the levels of metal fragmentation would be very high. Other parts of the city and surrounding areas were also mined, as well as along the road to the Iranian border, which was 70 kilometres away.

As we were only on a one day visit it was agreed with the governor that I would return with some of the Afghan NGO directors and we would develop a plan to demine Herat. It was going to be a large undertaking. There was also a sense of urgency about the situation as there were reportedly two million Afghan refugees from this area living in Iran. There were regular rumours that the Iranian Government would soon force these refugees to repatriate home.

Late in the afternoon we boarded Salam 01 and flew back to Islamabad. We were all very pleased with the results of the visit and as this was the VIP plane we relaxed in the leather seats and drank a few champagnes. I arrived back home fairly late, had some dinner with my family and went to bed. Around 11 pm the telephone rang and it was the duty officer from army headquarters in Canberra wanting to know if I was back safely from this 'dangerous' mission.

I said, 'Yeah, I'm back. I was going to call in the morning.'

He got a bit irate and said, 'Don't you realise that this mission was personally authorised by the Minister for Defence and that there are a chain of people waiting to hear that you are back safely?'

I apologised and told him I was not aware that the trip had been cleared at that level. As I hung up the phone I smiled to myself, as it had been one of the safest and most comfortable journeys I ever undertook in Afghanistan.

I made a number of trips back to Herat soon after that initial visit. On the next trip I took Sayed Aqa from the survey organisation with me, with the aim of getting a better understanding of where the minefields were located and recording them. We met with the former Afghan army garrison commander who handed over some minefield maps. However, as was often the case, when maps were handed over they were usually incomplete or lacking in detail.

On one or two occasions alleged minefield maps were offered to the United Nations for sale, but we had a policy of not paying for them. The occupation had lasted over nine years so minefields had been fought over, additional mines could have been laid and other mines may have been lifted. The maps could guide you to a general area, but they were nowhere near reliable enough to give to a demining team to start clearance work. Additionally, the mujahedeen had often randomly laid mines and these were not recorded.

Now that we had a better idea of the problem we set about planning the solution. It was agreed that instead of setting up a new 'western Afghanistan based' demining NGO, we would draw on our existing organisations. As the most experienced demining NGO, Kef's organisation would send instructors over and conduct the initial training for new recruits.

In a bit of a twist we decided that Fazel Karim's mine awareness organisation, OMA, would expand its scope and would take over responsibility for the demining in Herat. In the previous year's evaluation of the UNOCHA mine clearance program, it had recommended that OMA should close down as most refugees had received some form of mine awareness training. Fazel had lobbied hard to stay afloat, to the point of getting down on one knee in my office one day pleading for OMA to continue. It made some sense to have him oversee the demining and if refugees did return from Iran there would also be a need for mine awareness training in Herat. Fazel's organisation was now well established with logistic and finance systems, so he could 'hit the ground running'. With the addition of a few new technical staff he could easily adapt to mine clearance work.

Then there was the question of money. I did not have any. I had some promising interest and potential pledges from some donor countries, but no cash in the bank. The World Food Program (WFP) was very active in Afghanistan and Pakistan, particularly in the refugee camps. They had one scheme called 'Food for Work', which involved paying people with food rather than money. This was particularly useful for labour intensive tasks, like digging irrigation canals or undertaking road repair, when no money was available for salaries. The workers received bags of flour, cans of cooking oil or vegetables like dried beans or lentils in return for their labour. I knew the local head of the World Food Program quite well so went to see him. I managed to persuade him to agree to provide food in Herat to pay the new deminers when undergoing their training, plus cover their initial work until I could get the cash. I was very pleased with myself.

I flew to Herat and briefed Governor Khan on my plan. He said 'no'. I was quite stunned and disappointed.

I asked him 'why?'

The Governor said, 'I have heard that all the demining teams in the east are paid in cash, and I want the deminers in Herat to be paid in cash as well.'

I replied, 'I have some pledges from donors but I will not have the money available for a few months.' I then pulled a cheap shot and said, 'Governor, there are civilian mine accidents happening every day in Herat. Every extra month's delay will mean that more of your people will suffer.'

He looked me squarely in the eye and said, 'Our people have suffered for nine years. Another month or two will not make any difference.' I didn't know what to say. I was annoyed that he rejected the food plan after all the trouble I had gone through to arrange it, and our instructors were ready to start. On the other hand, I should have consulted him earlier and part of me was impressed that he was willing to hang on to get the best deal for his people.

Once the funding had been secured we had to recruit the deminers. An experienced UN colleague suggested that a good way to go about it was to make sure that the local partners were involved with the recruitment process. He said if you need 20 staff, give the local governor/official/warlord the job criteria and ask them to recommend 30 people. This way they would appear to be in control, could put up their relatives or people to whom they had an obligation, but would not lose face if someone was not selected. On our side, the 'patronage' applicants would be easily identified and rejected, or if they met the criteria then they were suitable anyway. This made a lot of sense so we decided to try this method in Herat.

We wanted about 100 deminers but only 54 names were produced. One of the Australians sent over to supervise the training asked around and a woman said to him, 'My son has survived nine years of Soviet occupation … and now you want him to die in a minefield?' However, once the training started and people saw how well organised and supervised the demining process was, and that they were paid in cash, new applicants flooded in.

Just as the situation looked settled there was a completely unforeseen incident in October 1992. Some rebel groups opposed to Ismail Khan launched unprovoked attacks on the city. From the Australian Army side, we had sent Staff Sergeant David Mitchell and Sergeant Craig Egan over to Herat to organise and supervise the training of the second intake of new deminers. They were staying in the United Nations guesthouse when it came under sustained rocket and artillery fire.

The United Nations quickly evacuated its 10 international staff, including Mitchell and Egan, by road to Mashhad in Eastern Iran, which was the nearest town to the border. I became very concerned about this situation because I had lost contact with the two. They were serving soldiers travelling on official Australian passports into Iran with no visa or proper United Nations status. There was huge potential for a diplomatic incident. Fortunately, the United Nations offices and the Australian Embassy in Tehran were able to look after them and arrange their safe exit from Iran. I was most relieved when Mitchell and Egan called me to say that they were safe and well, and on their way back to Islamabad.

On another visit I was told that a mass grave had been found on the outskirts of the city. As the highest ranking United Nations official in town at the time, I was asked to go and have a look at it. The people showing me the site were vague about when it may have happened and who was involved. Even before the Soviet invasion in 1979 there was a substantial presence of Soviet advisers and their families in the city, and I got the impression the grave had something to do with the immediate pre-invasion period. A hole only about a metre deep had been dug in the rocky brown soil. At the bottom of it I could see at least 10 human skulls, each with a single bullet hole in the head. Some remnants of dark-coloured clothing could also be seen. The whole scene was very disturbing and confusing, and later I heard that more remains had been discovered. I reported what I had seen when I returned to Islamabad.

Success and progress

Despite these few setbacks, Herat quickly became my favourite place in Afghanistan. Because of its isolation from the rest of the country, it rapidly became peaceful again and on every trip you could see progress and improvements in the lives of the people. It was far from perfect and there was still a huge amount of work to be done, but at least it was going in the right direction. I developed a good working relationship with the governor and the demining work soon got underway. He re-opened schools, including those for girls – even if the 'school' was just kids sitting under a tree or in a mud-walled room with no roof.

The security situation became so good it soon reached the stage where we started to bring donors on overnight visits to Herat. We would include visits to the *Jama Masjid* or Great Mosque of Herat and the famous minarets. Another favourite attraction was a tiny factory that made ceramic tiles for the mosque and also hand-blown blue glass. A small hunch-backed man slaved in front of a burning furnace using the same technique that had been used for centuries. It was a fascinating time warp. The glass was very brittle and every piece was misshapen, but this added to the appeal of it and all the visitors tried to carry some home.

The mine clearance work, particularly in the huge minefield belt in the west of the city, was making good progress despite numerous difficulties. The houses had been constructed from a mixture of concrete or mud brick, and all the buildings were inside compounds surrounded by high mud walls. Over the years these walls had been knocked down or fallen over from lack of maintenance. This meant that many mines were now deeply buried. Often the deminers had to work vertically along a face to detect mines that were buried two or three metres deep. We often joked that we should be measuring our progress in Herat in cubic metres, rather than square metres.

The work was intensely satisfying because as soon as a compound was cleared the owner would move in the next day and starting rebuilding the mud walls. Often local kids would be hanging over a new wall watching the deminers work next door. The deminers would chase them away for safety reasons, but the kids soon came back.

Life goes on despite the dangers

On one donor visit we saw a civilian man sitting on a low wall just near a plot of land that had recently been cleared. He had lost one leg and looking at the bandages his accident had obviously only happened recently. I thought to myself this is not going to go well – he will complain about the slowness of our work or the lack of help being provided. Instead I was pleasantly relieved. He said that he had attended mine awareness training and he had been told not to go onto his land because it was mined, but he went anyway. Winter was approaching and he wanted to rebuild the family home before the snow fell. Tragically this story was often repeated in mine-affected countries around the world. Local people are aware of the presence of landmines, but through economic necessity they are forced to take risks.

On another visit the assembled donors were shown a large area marked with red rocks and we told them that this was a very dangerous minefield. As if on cue, a local man with his donkey and wife appeared in the distance and walked along a narrow track right through the middle of the minefield. They knew it was dangerous – they just had to get on with their lives.

Dealing with cash – the Afghan way

The main problem for us with Herat was providing logistic support, due to its remoteness. Travel by air from Pakistan or by road from Iran was the only options for the United Nations. There were no banks operating in Afghanistan at that time and the local currency, the Afghani, was worthless. The United Nations paid its local staff and NGO projects in US dollars. Getting cash to Herat was always difficult. Soon after the United Nations reopened its offices and started projects in Herat, the UNOCHA finance officer asked me quietly if I would be prepared to carry cash when I visited. I said yes of course and often I would fly into Afghanistan with over US$50,000 cash in my bag. I never told anyone except my wife that I was doing this, for obvious reasons.

On one occasion the organization OMA had prepared a large cash payroll in Peshawar to fly to Herat. The driver of the vehicle and guard were severely bashed and robbed on their way to Peshawar airport, and the money was never recovered. I had never heard of it before but there was an illegal money transfer system operating around the Middle East called *hawala*. It worked like this. You went to a man in a dingy office in say, Peshawar and gave him US$100,000 cash. He would deduct a fee of around 3 per cent and then telephone his 'agent' in Herat. Our demining person in Herat would then go to the 'agent' the next day and collect US$97,000 in cash. After the robbery of the payroll we turned a blind eye to OMA using this system, as it worked and the fee was worth all the hassle that it removed.

Further west to Iran

The landmine problem in Herat also led to my undertaking a number of visits to the Islamic Republic of Iran. The first was an overland journey from Herat. The drive to the border was only about 70 kilometres along a reasonably good road. As we left Herat there was ample evidence of the previously healthy livestock and agriculture sectors, with large abandoned farming complexes and sheds on either side of the road. Herat had been famous for grapes and even wine in the past, and the method of growing the vines was interesting. There were no wire fences to trail the vines in ancient times. Instead long earth bunds about 2 metres high had been formed and the grapevine was planted at the top of the mound. As the plants grew the vines draped down the sloping side of the bund from where the grapes could be easily picked when ripe.

The houses here were also different. In the east of Afghanistan most of the mud houses had flat roofs and used timber poles as roof beams. Here in the west, there was very little timber and the mud houses all had attractive domed roofs, made of mud bricks and mud render. Halfway to the border our party stopped and they showed me an area where oil was oozing out of the ground. I had never seen this before and there was a strong, acrid smell of tar in the area. Apparently it was not commercially viable, but the locals all came and collected the gooey black oil to burn for heating and cooking.

The border with Iran is marked on the map at a town called Islam Qala. Calling it a town is a bit generous. There were a couple of dusty buildings on the Afghan side, a checkpoint across the road and then some more buildings on the Iranian side. The only difference was that the Iranian buildings all had large portraits of Ayatollah Khomeini painted on the side. Our visas were in order so we passed through easily and drove on to Mashhad. The purpose of the visit was to meet with Iranian officials and the staff from the United Nations refugee agency, UNHCR, to discuss the refugee return situation and assess the need to provide refugees with some form of mine awareness information.

We toured some of the suburbs where the Afghan refugees lived in Mashhad and conditions were certainly different and better than those on the Pakistani side. The refugees were living in suburbs with paved roads, mains electricity, street lighting and even telephone boxes. Many of them were employed. Traditionally many Afghans had worked in the construction industry in Tehran, so the influx of people into Iran may not have been as dramatic as it first sounded, but it was still a big problem. The other striking thing is that other than UNHCR, there appeared to be very little United Nations presence or activity in the area. In our spare time we visited the famous Imam Reza shrine, which is one of the largest mosques in the world. In Pakistan and eastern Afghanistan most people are Sunni Muslims, so it was interesting to see and learn about the Shia Muslim religion, which was dominant in Iran.

My next trip was at a much higher level. The Iranian government regularly complained that although they were hosting two million refugees, unlike Pakistan they were receiving very little support from the United Nations or the international community. It was a valid point. UNOCHA considered a range of proposals and it was agreed that we would provide US$500,000 to the Iranian government to fund mine awareness activities. The plan was to set up a station at the border at Islam Qala, where returning refugees would have to attend a mine awareness safety class before they would be issued some food and cash to help them repatriate.

The government nominated an organisation called the Refugee Relief Group of Ansar to implement this project. 'Ansar' is a Persian word that means helper, but no-one had heard of these helpers before. It turned out that they came under the control of the notorious Revolutionary

Guard, which left us rather uncomfortable. The government claimed that they had experience in community-based training, but the reality was that the authorities would not have allowed any other group to operate near the border regions.

I applied to get my visa at the Iranian Embassy in Islamabad. I got shunted around and was repeatedly told to go away, come back, go away and so on. In the end I shouted at the visa official, 'I am going to Tehran to give your government half a million dollars!' It didn't make any difference at the time, but I felt better and I eventually got the visa.

By now the United Nations special envoy had changed. Benon Sevan had left and he was replaced by Sotirius Mousouris. A Greek national, Mousouris was a career UN diplomat who had spent most of his time in New York. He said his mandate was only to keep a watching eye on the situation in Afghanistan and not to try to influence events. I never felt he was overly interested or committed to Afghanistan, and yet now I found myself sitting next to him on the United Nations plane bound for Tehran.

On arrival at Mehrabad airport in Tehran we were whisked away to the VIP lounge and greeted by a Foreign Affairs functionary. We then got into a convoy of black Mercedes vehicles, complete with police motor cycle escorts and took off. And I mean took off. We were travelling at well over 120 kilometres an hour through the streets of Tehran with police lights and sirens blaring. There was no need for any of it as we were just going to the Government guest house to stay for the evening. Later we were given a tour around parts of Tehran, including driving past the former United States Embassy compound where the US staff had been held hostage by Iranian 'revolutionary' students for one year and two months in the late 1970s.

The next day we met with the foreign minister and government officials to discuss the refugee situation. At a small signing ceremony, Mousouris signed the half a million dollar project with his Iranian counterpart. Mousouris hadn't even read the document. To him the important element was the political aspect that the United Nations was seen to be doing something with Iran. We also negotiated with the central government that if any Afghan deminers were severely injured in Herat, they could be brought to the medical facilities in Mashhad in Iran. We needed this assurance as previous local arrangements had broken down and there had been cases of injured deminers on their way to Mashhad being turned back at the border.

The project got underway and I had a few more trips to Iran in the following years. On one occasion I flew from Tehran to Mashhad with my new-found Revolutionary Guard colleagues. They were actually very pleasant and efficient in what they did. One chap always carried a black briefcase and never went through the airport metal detector or security. He obviously had a weapon, but I wasn't sure if he was meant to be protecting me or checking that I wasn't going to do something that I shouldn't. It was probably a bit of both.

The Revolutionary Guard had established their mine awareness tent at the border at Islam Qala. We had provided the content and training materials to the Revolutionary Guard and they had faithfully translated them into the Persian language and were using what we gave them. The border post was full of open-bodied trucks containing people and loaded high with all their worldly possessions. They duly sat through a 30-minute 'landmine safety lesson' which covered what to look out for on their return home, were issued some food and money, and then got back onto the open trucks for their journey to Herat.

As a fascinating end to this trip, I was taken further south to the border town of Zahedan. Forty-five kilometres out of town it is extremely desolate and the landscape and dusty sky merge into one as a sandy-coloured blur. But it is the point where the three borders of Iran, Afghanistan and Pakistan meet. The Iranian side was heavily mined in an effort to stop drug smugglers, people smugglers and normal smugglers from moving into Iran. It looked like an impossible task because when we pulled up at a river near the border town of Zabol, there was a flourishing movement of goods going on. As occurred on the Pakistani side, appliances like TVs, air-conditioners, other electrical items and even vehicles were flown from a variety of countries into Afghanistan where there was no duty to pay. They were then smuggled over the border into the neighbouring countries of Pakistan or Iran, where they were sold at much lower prices than legally available goods.

Establishing Mine Dog Groups

Despite all this travel and high politicking, there was still work to be done to improve the efficiency and effectiveness of the mine clearance program. One area that still bothered me was the dogs. A United States company called RONCO had run a mule program during the war, providing mules to the mujahedeen to ferry supplies through the mountains into Afghanistan. This had more recently been converted to a mine detecting dog program. RONCO had done an excellent job of establishing the kennels, veterinarian services and training facilities at a place called Pabbi on the outskirts of Peshawar.

The training regime for the dogs appeared sound, but their employment and tasking in Afghanistan had been haphazard. The United States wanted to move on from this commitment, so we agreed to reorganise the project to become an Afghan NGO called the Mine Dog Centre, working under my direction. An elaborate handover ceremony was held and Shohab Hakimi was appointed the first director.

Fortunately, my good friend Dr Gunter Mulack from Germany had a shown an interest in the mine dogs and took up the funding gap caused by the departure of the USA. Germany continued to fund the dog centre and provide technical experts for years to come. I negotiated the visa and contract for the first German technical adviser and he wanted the provision of four cartons of beer every month to be included in his contract. He knew Pakistan was a Muslim country and he wanted his beer. Unfortunately, we were not able to comply with his demand.

Recruitment of locals on the other hand was no problem. It was a common story that Afghans do not like dogs. However, Shohab once explained to me that Afghans do not dislike dogs and every village always has dogs running around. They just do not keep them in the house as pets, like we do in the West. Soon after the handover of the dog centre Shohab advertised for 20 new dog handlers. Pabbi is 24 kilometres away from Peshawar but over 2000 men turned up applying for these jobs. Chaos ensued and Shohab had to shut the centre down for the day until calm was restored. There was certainly no evidence of Afghans not wanting to work with dogs.

Up until now the method of employment of the dogs was to assign a couple of dogs and their handlers to a manual demining team. The theory was that they were just another type of detector available to the team leader to use as he saw fit. The reality was that most of the team leaders did not trust the dogs. We often found that the demining team leader would run the dogs over an area, and even if they found nothing, would still go over the same area with his manual deminers. This was because the team leader had to sign a paper at the end of a job stating that the area was clear of landmines. The result was that it actually took more time, not less, to clear an area when this happened.

We discussed this for a long while and then I had an idea to turn the whole thing on its head. Why not make the dog team leader the person who had to sign the certificate declaring the area was clear? We set up some trials of these new 'Mine Dog Groups' as we called them, to test this idea. The new groups had four dogs and handlers, along with a section of manual deminers. The dog team leader was in charge.

The results were brilliant. The speed at which these groups could work was amazing. By using the dogs to their full capability, they were very quickly able to eliminate areas as not being mined and these were declared clear. To reduce the risk of a missed mine as much as possible, we would put two or even three dogs over the same area to make sure nothing was missed. The manual deminers who investigated the spots where the dogs had indicated could not keep up with the dogs, so we added more manual deminers to the teams.

We were on a winner and the introduction of the mine dog groups over time sped up our clearance rate significantly. Some people then wanted to qualify on our records that an area was 'cleared by dogs' or 'cleared by manual deminers'. I refused, because to me if an area was clear, it was clear. It didn't matter what method you used, it was the result that counted.

Some years later the United Nations headquarters in New York came out with a standard saying that a 99.7 per cent clearance rate should be achieved. This caused much angst and confusion in the demining world. It was a silly concept that had been hijacked by lawyers, who claimed that you could never achieve absolute certainty. This might be fine in some industrial process, but when you are standing on the edge of a piece of land next to an illiterate farmer, you have only have two choices – you can tell the farmer that it is safe to use the land, or that it is not safe.

Jumping through bureaucratic hoops

Another feature I discovered about working in a donor-funded environment was the requirement to undergo external evaluations or assessments. While UNOCHA had itself arranged the big evaluation back in 1991, the requirement to undergo an evaluation was usually imposed by the donor country itself. This was understandable, as it was their money, but as the program grew and we had more donors, the obligation for evaluations could become quite time consuming.

One of the first external assessments I recall was conducted by Alistair Craib and Phil Bean, on behalf of the United Kingdom. Alistair and Phil were both ex-British army bomb disposal officers and they had operational experience in Northern Ireland and Kuwait.

During the evaluation they would look into technical matters and make recommendations, but given their experience, it was also useful to get an outside opinion on what we were doing in a broader sense. They would also ask seemingly simple questions like 'What is the rate of mine clearance' and 'How much does it cost to clear landmines'? Good questions indeed, but very difficult ones to answer. The daily rate of clearance by a manual deminer varied greatly, depending on the conditions. If there was a lot of metal fragments in the ground then progress would be slow, and if lots of mines were being found it took time to organise to blow them up.

A rough average figure we came up with was that a manual deminer could clear in the range of 10 to 100 square metres per day. Not very precise, but it was the best we could do and it highlighted how slow manual demining was. The clearance rate for dog teams was much higher and while the advertised clearance rate for the flail machines was also much higher, we rarely achieved it. After a review done by our senior technical adviser, Bill van Ree, we decided to park the flails in a shed and not use them anymore, because of their high operating cost and low clearance rate.

The cost of mine clearance was also not easy to determine. We were all ex-military people or Afghan NGO directors, not economists. We could easily tally the amount of contributions we received from donors, but other support like seconded technical advisers and grants of equipment were more difficult to monetise. Did we include the equipment provided under the Soviet pledge, even though we didn't use it? As rough measure we would total up all our different types of 'income' for the year and divide it by the total number of square metres of land all the NGOs had cleared. This consistently would work out about US$1 per square metre and this was a figure we would often publish. In much later years, more detailed studies by the Geneva International Centre for Humanitarian Demining (GICHD) could only come up with a worldwide average in the range of US$1 to US$10 per square metre.

The cost of clearing an individual landmine was even more problematic. Again, by dividing our total annual income by the number of mines found we came up with a figure of US$300 per mine. This figure was widely used in the international press, particularly to highlight the fact that a weapon that cost only a few dollars to buy and place in the ground, was now costing hundreds of dollars to clear. The problem was that this figure had to be qualified. If teams were working in large, defensive minefield belts they would find lots of mines quite easily and the cost per mine would go down. However, a road or an agricultural field would only need a couple of mines planted in them to stop people using the area completely. Although we would try and reduce the area that needed to be cleared down to the minimum using the survey teams, often large areas may be cleared with only a few mines being found. In these cases the cost could rise as high as US$1,000 per mine.

The next question was always about the impact and effectiveness of the work, and this was virtually impossible for us to quantify at that time. We may be doing 'the job right' but were we doing 'the right job'? We would try to estimate how many refugees had returned to their homes in any given area, or how many kilometres of road had been opened, or how much agricultural land was returned to productive use, but these were rough estimates. In the mine clearance program we did not have the time or the expertise to address these issues properly. Also, there was a complete lack of baseline data in Afghanistan for any sector like agriculture or transport, so even the experts could not come up with meaningful figures.

We were fortunate that clearing landmines seemed such an obvious precursor to any relief or development activity, coupled with the fact that the program was well organised and could produce reliable clearance statistics, that we were usually able to attract sufficient funds.

Too soon to leave Afghanistan

By the end of 1992 my Australian Army posting was coming to an end and I received a posting order back to Australia. I had just completed the most amazing year. I had held down three jobs – acting as the Program Manager of the UN Mine Clearance Program, I was still officially the senior technical adviser to the program (my original posting) and I was the Commanding Officer of the Australian Army Training Team. I was responsible for overseeing the work of eight NGOs in three countries – Afghanistan, Pakistan and Iran.

In conjunction with Martin Barber, I had helped to raise the US$15 million a year we needed to function. Decisions I was making affected people's lives and welfare, and we were clearing increasingly large areas of land in Afghanistan where refugees were returning. The icing on the cake for me was that in the Australia Day honours list of 26 January 1993 I was awarded a military decoration called the Conspicuous Service Cross, for my services as commanding officer of the training team. I didn't want to leave what I was doing.

There was no possibility of an extension of my army posting, as my successor had already been named. I discussed it with my family and they were all more than happy to stay. I approached Martin Barber and he said he would be delighted if I would continue on, and said that he could arrange for me to go onto a temporary United Nations contract. I wrote to my army supervisor and said that I wanted to take my long service leave and then leave without pay, in order to stay and work in Afghanistan with the United Nations for another year. I received a rather strange reply in return.

The commander wrote sternly that I had been offered a good posting in a sought after location, that my decision would cause a snowball effect on other people's postings, and that my future career chances may suffer as a result. However, he reluctantly approved my request. He then wrote in hand at the bottom of the letter: 'PS. I would have done exactly the same if I were you!' So, on 1 January 1993, I started on a one-year temporary contract and was issued my first light blue United Nations 'Laissez Passer' passport.

My army successor was Lieutenant Colonel Greg McDowall. I knew Greg from a number of army courses we had done together back in Australia. He was a solid and reliable operator and we got on well together. Because we were the same seniority our army bosses seemed concerned that there may be some conflict between us, because I would effectively be Greg's supervisor. However, the way I saw it, I had taken leave from the army and had my United Nations job as the overall program manager to do, and Greg had his army responsibilities. We never had any issues between us.

In any case, Greg had a strong feeling that due to the worsening security situation in Kabul in particular, the Australian Army was highly likely to end its commitment to UNOCHA and withdraw the training team before the end of the year. With my new United Nations hat on this would cause some problems, as the Australian Army teams had all done an outstanding job. The team provided 15 reliable, responsible and well trained individuals who were providing technical advice, refresher training, accident investigations, quality control checks and good old common sense throughout the program. We were pushing the boundaries on the security side, but no-one wanted to leave.

In August of 1993 Greg had first-hand experience of the ever present dangers of landmines when he and another of the Australian military advisers, Captain Harry Jarvie, were on a mission in eastern Afghanistan. Greg wrote the following account of an incident they witnessed.

Captain Harry Jarvie and I were visiting a minefield survey task near Gardez in the Paktia Province of Afghanistan. During the morning we heard a mine explosion approximately 1 kilometre away and a local guide went to investigate. The guide returned through an unsurveyed lane in the minefield to advise us that an Afghan boy had been blown up by a landmine and was severely injured.

We decided we had to do something to help. The boy's injuries were horrific. His face and right side had been sandblasted to a pulp by the soil which had covered the mine, and his right forearm hung by a few sinews from his elbow. While Harry gave the boy a morphine auto-injector I prepared a methoxyflurane inhaler to ease his pain until the morphine took effect. Harry did his best to bandage the arm and, with the help of the locals, loaded him on to a stretcher for the one-hour drive to the nearest doctor.

As we headed back to our worksites we passed a tent and noticed a smaller boy huddled sobbing inside. On closer inspection we discovered he was bound hand and foot with a length of heavy white cord. There were a few turns around his neck for good measure. Muhammed Gul had been with his older brother in the minefield trying to lift mines. Tying him up had been his father's way of teaching him a lesson. Deciding he had learned enough for one day, we untied him and helped him clean his brother's blood off his hands. We tried to comfort him for a while and instructed another relative on how to treat him for shock.

We headed back to the minefield shaking our heads at how tough life was in Afghanistan. We later learned that the injured boy had mercifully died soon after he reached the doctor. At least we had made his last hour or so a little less painful.

CHAPTER 8:

KANDAHAR: CLEARING, KIDNAPPING AND KILLING

If Herat was my favourite place in Afghanistan, then Kandahar was my least favourite. Everything was difficult in Kandahar. When the Soviets withdrew in February 1989, four different Afghan warlords continuously fought each other for control of the city and different parts of the surrounding countryside. Killings, kidnappings, vehicle hijackings and general lawlessness always seemed to prevail. Tribal affiliations and obligations outweighed any other consideration.

Like all the other regional cities, Kandahar had been heavily mined during the war and the inevitable huge minefield belts surrounded the city. As happened throughout the country, but very noticeably here, landmines had been used as part of the Soviet strategy to depopulate villages to prevent effective local support for the mujahedeen. Mines were therefore laid in houses, irrigation systems, agricultural land and grazing areas.

Within the UNOCHA mine clearance program, an Afghan NGO had been established called the South West Afghan Agency for Demining, or SWAAD. It was based in Quetta in central-west Pakistan and like its sister agencies in Peshawar, sent teams across the border on six week rotations to conduct mine clearance in and around Kandahar. The director was a local from the area named Engineer Pushtoon. Afghans used the title 'engineer' to signify their profession as an engineer, in much the same way as we use 'doctor'. Pushtoon spoke very good English and had been educated at the American University in Beirut. He was a qualified town planner – a profession that wasn't in much demand in Afghanistan at that time!

During the early days of the initial, ill-conceived scheme involving the mass training of thousands of Afghan refugees on the short training course, a training centre had been operating at Baleli Camp near Quetta airport. However, this camp was closed soon after I arrived. There were also two New Zealand army officers and one Norwegian civilian remaining on secondment as technical advisers to SWAAD, but they all departed at the end of 1991. The only foreigner now left working for the mine clearance program was Mr Tahsin Disbudak. Tahsin had been a Turkish army engineer officer with one of the original military teams. He then came back when the program hired him to be the regional manager for the program in Quetta. His English wasn't so good, but he was as straight as they come and he was always reliable and totally loyal to me.

My first trip to Quetta, and then into Kandahar, was remarkably uneventful and may have lulled me into a false sense of security. Engineer Pushtoon and I drove from Quetta to the border post at Chaman on the Pakistan side (and Spin Boldak on the Afghan side) and then the 115 kilometres on to Kandahar. We were stopped once or twice on the road at checkpoints, or 'chains' as they were called, because heavy metal chains were stretched across the road to force you to stop. However, Pushtoon seemed well known so we were waved through. We visited demining sites around the city and then one of the site offices near the border between Kandahar province and Uruzgan province.

We didn't go into Uruzgan province because our records indicated that there had been very few mines laid, and only eight minefields had been identified near Tarin Kowt. Little did I realise that 10 years later Uruzgan province would feature heavily with the Australian Army, as this was the province assigned to Australian troops in late 2001, following the US invasion of Afghanistan. There was to be a future connection for me at a more personal level too, but more about that later.

As I continued on with the visit to Kandahar province with Engineer Pushtoon, I found the demining work we visited was much the same as that being undertaken by the NGOs working out of Peshawar, except that I assessed the standard of work and discipline to be slightly lower down here. When we returned to Quetta the next day, Pushtoon invited us to his house for dinner. Given his education and travel I expected that that we would meet his family, but no. Because he had invited other local Afghan dignitaries the men were all in one room and the women, unseen, in another.

While clearly quite intelligent, Pushtoon's manner was a bit odd. At the monthly meetings he would often make outlandish and unsubstantiated statements, or climb on the conference table to demonstrate a proposed demining technique. Incidents started to be reported back from Kandahar about his behaviour. He was engaging in local political activities and as a result, a number of SWAAD vehicles had been hijacked. On one occasion, he was kidnapped and held for a few days.

When they were established, each NGO had a steering committee comprising respected Afghans. The SWAAD steering committee was heavily influenced by the Gailani family who were prominent in Afghan life. The Gailanis contacted Martin Barber and I saying that Pushtoon had to go. As I had my doubts about Pushtoon as well, it was decided that we would replace him. I wrote to Pushtoon telling him that we had lost confidence in him and that he was going to be replaced.

Pushtoon did not take this news well. The Gailanis went mysteriously quiet and I was left to carry the can, but as UNOCHA controlled the flow of money to SWAAD we were able to exert our will. However, for months Pushtoon fought the case and despite our offers to compensate him, he kept at it. He was good friends with the then governor of Kandahar, Gul Aga, and we received a message that the governor wished to meet me. I flew to Quetta and Tahsin arranged for us to meet in the SWAAD offices. Gul Aga stormed into the room. He was very young by Afghan standards to be a governor, only in his mid-30s, but he had forged a reputation as a fearless fighter during the Soviet occupation. He was a big, burly man with a huge black beard and wore the long black turban that was fashionable in this area. He had two equally fearsome looking bodyguards with him, both toting Kalashnikov automatic rifles.

I said to him, 'You know it's against United Nations regulations to have weapons in the building?'

He responded with, 'It's an NGO building and I can do what I like.'

I stated the reasons why the United Nations had made its decision, but I soon discovered that all the clever arguments in the world do not count for much when you have two men holding rifles on the other side of the table. The discussion went around in circles. I was not going to back down and he kept insisting that we reinstate Pushtoon. The meeting ended in a stalemate.

As it was getting late, we went home to Tahsin's house, where I was staying the night. In a cruel twist of fate, Tahsin lived next door to the house where Gul Aga stayed when he was in Quetta. We got a stiff drink and went to sit in some chairs near a big bay window that overlooked Tahsin's front garden. Both of us simultaneously picked up our chairs and moved them to the back of the room.

I said to Tahsin, 'I wouldn't be surprised if a grenade comes over the wall tonight.'

He responded, 'I was thinking exactly the same thing!' Thankfully nothing happened.

We appointed the SWAAD deputy, Haji Ali, as acting director while we looked for another person. Haji Ali was a lovely, older man and I admired him for standing by his post under very trying conditions. It was a very difficult selection process to get a new director for SWAAD. Different groups were pushing their own people to get the job, while a number of suitable people we approached did not want to touch it. People were threatened and allegations were made against potential candidates.

After about six months we found a suitable person in Engineer Abdul Sattar. Although originally from Kandahar, Sattar had worked for a number of years as a local staff member for the United Nations in the north of the country. No-one seemed to know him or object to him – he was the ultimate grey man. In fairness, Sattar settled in well and steered a moderate course. One of his first decisions was to rename SWAAD as DAFA – the Demining Agency for Afghanistan.

Everything took a long time to achieve in the south of Afghanistan and there were always complications. At one stage DAFA had five vehicles that had been hijacked and stolen – three by one particular warlord. On a visit to Kandahar with Sayed Aqa, I was determined to get the vehicles back. We opened negotiations through intermediaries and the commander said that if we came to his village he would give them back.

The warlord was a particularly nasty person and had a reputation for kidnapping people and locking them in a wooden box for days on end. I like a bit of adventure and have parachuted, done scuba diving and ridden motorbikes, but I'm claustrophobic. I remember during my army engineer training we had to practise clearing tunnels in a mock Vietcong village. It took me every ounce of my willpower to lower myself into those narrow, dark tunnels with my shoulders squeezing against the side walls, so I did not fancy being locked up in a wooden box for the sake of a couple of vehicles. Sayed wasn't too keen either, so we negotiated with the commander to meet at a neutral location. After a sleepless night worrying about being kidnapped and locked in a box, Sayed and I went to the designated location – but the warlord never turned up.

On that same visit we went to see some teams working on the outskirts of Kandahar city. As I had observed previously, the teams seemed less disciplined down here. Some teams had even gone 'on strike' in the past over alleged grievances. When they heard that the 'big boss' was visiting, a number of deminers came up to me and slipped me notes outlining various grievances. I just passed these on to Engineer Sattar to sort out. Then a beautiful thing happened. An old man came up to us holding a bunch of flowers. He asked to speak to me and through the interpreter he said the he was extremely grateful that we had cleared his farming land. He said he could now die in peace, knowing that his family had a future. He gave me the bunch of flowers which he had grown on his land and then got down on his knees and kissed my hand. Wow! I did not have to draw my pay that month in order to feel job satisfaction.

As time went by we posted Tahsin to Kabul, and he was replaced by Dave Edwards as regional manager for the mine clearance program in the south. Dave was yet another Australian Army warrant officer who had been with one of the training teams, and then left the army to come back and work with the program. Dave was bright, energetic and a good all-round operator.

The one-man demining drill

At our monthly meetings we were always looking for new ways to improve efficiency. The latest proposal was for a one-man demining drill. In the current system, the detector man swept along the lane first. When the metal detector sounded he would place a marker just short of the spot, and then walk back 20 metres to the safety point and hand over to the prodder man. He would go forward, lie down and start prodding just short of the marker and work his way forward. When he found something he would report it to the team leader.

The idea of the one-man drill was that when the detector man heard the sound of the detector, he would gently place the detector on the ground behind him and then lie down and investigate the reading himself. This would have to be quicker as it cut out the walking back and forward. Also, as he had seen the spot where the detector sounded the detector man should also have a better idea in his mind of where to prod. Hopefully, this new procedure would help to reduce accidents as most of them occurred during prodding. As such a change would have equipment and training consequences, we decided to conduct a trial. Dave was selected to set up the trial down in Kandahar and oversee it.

Two teams were chosen and Dave found an area where they could both work under similar ground conditions. Training on the new one-man drill was conducted and then the teams were briefed on the recording process. Each team leader was to maintain a daily log of square metres cleared by the deminers. One team worked under the old method and the other used the new one-man drill. After a week of demining the results came in and the new team were clearing less square metres than the old team. We could not believe it, as it did not make sense.

Dave continued on with the trial for a few more days, and even with regularly visiting the site the outcome was the same. He then did a bit of checking around with various people, including his chief trainer Mohammad Sharif, and discovered that a rumour had gone around DAFA that if the one-man drill was adopted every 'second man' would get the sack.

The new team had deliberately been working slowly to stop the one-man drill being adopted. Armed with this knowledge, Dave reassured the deminers that this was not true and that DAFA would be buying more detectors so every man would keep his job. The trial resumed and within a few days the new team was working around 30 per cent faster than the team using the old method. A similar trial was conducted in the north under another technical adviser, Noel Spencer, and when the results were confirmed the drill was implemented program wide.

However, one of the problems with the new procedure was that the Scheibel mine detector came in two parts – the handle fitted with the detector head and a separate control box which the operator slung over his shoulder. This was cumbersome and wasted time when placing the detector on the ground. Enquiries to Scheibel identified that an attachment was available that allowed the control box to be fitted on the long handle. At the same time Dave had spoken to the technician of DAFA about the problem. The technician devised a simple tin bracket that could do the same thing and could be produced locally. It transpired that the cost of the Scheibel purpose-made bracket was around US$6 per item while the locally produced tin bracket cost 50 cents from the local metalsmith. As the program had over 1000 Scheibel detectors this was a 'no brainer' and the local design was passed to all NGOs to commence local production. Afghan ingenuity and a simple solution had saved the program some money.

But money raised its ugly head again in a different way. The teams would work in Afghanistan for six weeks and then return to Quetta to be paid and go on leave. The average monthly wage for a deminer was US$100, so you can realise that six weeks' pay multiplied by almost 400 deminers added up to a decent-sized payroll. Dave had set up the system where the team breaks were staggered, so only a few teams were in Quetta at any one time. The only exception was around the main Eid religious holiday, when DAFA closed down completely.

In preparation for Eid in March 1995, Dave had staggered the teams' return by a couple of days, but a number of them were delayed at the Chaman border crossing. The size of the payroll in the DAFA safe grew to about US$100,000 and on the night of 1 March 1995 armed men entered the office, bashed the guards and stole the safe. The two Pakistani policemen who were meant to be on guard outside the office had mysteriously disappeared. No-one was ever arrested for the robbery, but it was rumoured that some new group called the Taliban may have been involved.

What happened next lessened my faith in the United Nations somewhat. The robbery was reported to the UN headquarters in New York and Geneva. UNOCHA immediately despatched two senior staff from Geneva to come and investigate. To me, the money technically did not belong to the United Nations anymore, as it had been granted and transferred to DAFA. There had been other robberies that were not investigated at that level and in a program that was now running at around US$20 million a year, it was a significant loss, but not the end of the world. On the other hand, no-one had ever bothered to question our safety record, or our mine clearance rate, or any other operational matter. In 1993 six Afghan deminers had been killed and 31 injured in workplace accidents, yet no high level delegations had rushed out from Geneva to investigate these incidents. It seemed to me that at headquarters the loss of money was more important than the loss of Afghan deminers' lives.

Investigating demining accidents

The number of demining accidents had always been a major area of concern within the program. It was the one area where we had not made as much progress as we had in other aspects of our work. While everyone knew that clearing landmines was inherently dangerous, with proper training, appropriate equipment and good on-site discipline, we should have been able to reduce the number of accidents and the severity of them.

Despite numerous studies and investigations that we undertook, we could not pinpoint a single cause of the accidents. The Afghans were brave and fearless people, but they were not foolhardy. I remember visiting one deminer who had lost his leg in an accident just hours before. He said, 'My friends asked why I wasn't crying. I told them there was nothing to cry about, I was just doing my job.'

Illegal drug use among deminers was once rumoured, but we never found any evidence of that. One survey found that accidents tended to occur the longer the time deminers spent in the field away from their last long break. Each accident was investigated and documented to determine its cause. The results from these investigations were analysed to look for trends or identify areas of weakness.

Because the demining teams worked throughout Afghanistan where there were few functioning medical facilities, each team had its own ambulance, medic and driver. The medic was trained to provide immediate first aid and then assist with transporting the injured person by road back to hospital in Peshawar or Quetta, if they were working in the east of Afghanistan. In Kabul they would be taken to the Red Cross hospital in the city, and in Herat we had negotiated the arrangement to take severely injured people to Mashhad in Iran for treatment. The evacuation would often involve a long difficult drive taking over a day, so in those areas where we had established site offices that hosted up to four demining teams, we established Field Medical Units. These were staffed by a doctor, held a better range of drugs and could provide a higher level of care.

As UNOCHA was now operating two 10-seater Beechcraft King Air aircraft, I obtained agreement from Martin Barber that I was authorised to divert the planes to pick up an injured deminer in serious, life-threatening cases. This may happen three or four times a year, often at great inconvenience to other passengers, but most people understood.

One time when I was in Islamabad the phone rang at home on a Saturday morning. My wife, Margaret, answered the phone and the radio operator said that a deminer had been seriously injured and that the flight crew urgently needed my permission before they could divert the plane to collect him. I was actually with the kids at school soccer about half an hour away, and we didn't have mobile phones in those days. Margaret told the radio operator to wait a moment. She paused for a short time and then said, 'Colonel Mansfield cannot come to the phone at the moment, but he says it is okay to divert the plane.' There is one Afghan deminer who is alive today thanks to the quick thinking of my wife.

UNOCHA had also arranged insurance for the deminers through a Pakistani insurance company. The NGO staff were all covered, but the United Nations owned the policy and paid the premium – which at its peak was nearly half a million dollars a year. The cover provided US$20,000 for death and then had a reducing scale for loss of limbs, blindness and so on. The cover was expensive, but the benefits were quite generous by Afghan standards and insurance was not common in their society anyway. Normally the United Nations would not provide insurance cover for NGO staff, but everyone felt it was necessary in this case. Some of the NGOs argued that a self-insurance scheme where each organisation contributed into a common pot of money we would control would be better, but I was not confident. The temptation to delve into the pot when money was short would be too great.

Normally the insurance company would require a death certificate before making a payment, but such procedures did not exist in war-torn Afghanistan. Each accident that occurred was formally investigated, at first by the Australian Army team members and later by Afghan supervisors. Initially, we found that witnesses to an accident would not be truthful or forthcoming about the cause of the accident, as they did not want to harm the chances of the injured person receiving compensation. We deleted any reference to insurance from the accident reports and assured everyone that they would get the insurance payment no matter what the outcome of the investigation.

Fortunately, we had hired a retired Pakistani doctor, Dr Aleem, as the medical adviser to the program. Dr Aleem was a charming man and an old-fashioned gentleman. He had been the medical officer on a number of major mountain climbing expeditions in the past, and although now he was well into his 70s he was still very fit and active. Most importantly for us and unlike many Pakistanis, he was honest and well respected. The insurance company agreed that if Dr Aleem certified the death or injury then they would pay the benefit to the deminer's family.

Meanwhile, back in Islamabad ...

On the home front back in Islamabad things were never dull. Margaret had been talking to the senior United Nations official in Pakistan at a reception one evening and outlined how back in Australia, she had been involved with an organisation that helped defence families settle in when transferred to a new city. He asked her to come up with a proposal and next day Margaret got a part-time job as the first United Nations Community Liaison Officer in Pakistan, and only the second in the world.

Her role was to help newly arrived United Nations families settle in, find housing, get kids into school and be a friendly face. The United Nations had also established a social club and she became President of the Management Board. The club was located in a large house that had been converted to include a bar, restaurant, recreation room and a pool was installed in the back yard. Overseeing this club was not as easy as it sounded, because alcohol was involved and men and women would be swimming together in the pool. A cautious path had to be followed.

United Nations staff and diplomats had access to alcohol through a United Nations post exchange and a diplomatic store respectively. The monthly quota for United Nations staff was generous – four bottles of spirits, a dozen bottles of wine and four cartons of beer. An agreement was reached that any unused quota could be transferred to the United Nations social club, where it could be sold to members and guests. Pakistanis were not allowed into the club and only foreigners holding a passport from a non-Muslim country were admitted. The club did a roaring trade and even though it had an excellent local manager, Margaret had to be vigilant against corruption and illegal alcohol sales.

One evening at around midnight the club manager, Mr Ishtiak, called us at home and said that there had been an incident at the club. Apparently a Danish man working for an oil company had slipped on the stairs and fallen through a large glass window. The injured man had been taken to hospital and Ishtiak said he had boarded up the broken window. Margaret decided she should go and check, so we got up and drove to the club. Ishtiak showed us the window, which was now securely boarded up, so we went back home to bed. At 1am the phone rang again. It was Ishtiak and he sounded very anxious. He was now at the Islamabad General Hospital with the Danish man who was in a bad way, because they could not stop the bleeding – could we come and help?

When we arrived at the hospital we were greeted with a scene of absolute chaos. A jingly bus carrying a full load of people from a Pakistani wedding party had crashed causing numerous casualties. Eight dead bodies were laid out in the foyer and injured people were lying all about screaming and crying. We searched around and found the Danish man lying unconscious on a blood-soaked gurney, with Ishtiak holding a compress to his chest. A Pakistani doctor came in and shouted at us to get out of his operating theatre. We shouted at him to stop this man's bleeding.

When we all calmed down he said that we would have to go and buy the blood for his transfusion. Margaret went to the blood store and pushed her way in and bought the blood, boldly marked 'Tested for HIV/AIDS'. When she asked if they could guarantee the blood was clean, the orderly replied 'no'. However, there was no choice, so the man was operated on and given a transfusion. When we visited him next day he said he was so drunk that he couldn't remember a thing, which was perhaps for the best!

With Benazir Bhutto now back as Prime Minister of Pakistan, political agitation on the streets increased and we became more cautious about our daily movements. When Margaret pulled up at the traffic lights one day, some bearded mullah types in the next car called out something to her. She wound down her window and said, 'Pardon?'

'You American whore!' they shouted back.

In her best English/Australian accent she replied, 'I will have you know I am not American, thank you,' and drove off. Another time she got caught in the middle of a riot and the police hit her beloved Morris Minor with their long batons and shouted at her to get away.

In the holiday periods our family managed to undertake quite a bit of travel in the region. Some visits did not seem so significant at the time, but we were often reminded of them later. Once we flew to Skardu high in the Karakoram Mountains. On the flight we had a stunning view out of the plane window of K2, the second highest mountain in the world standing majestically at 8600 metres above sea level. Another time we drove to Gilgit and then up the Hunza Valley towards the border with China. This area was extremely remote and reportedly the people in this region live the longest of anywhere on earth. One theory is that they eat lots of apricots that grow in the region, and many of the people had orange-coloured skin (as if to support the theory).

Crossing by road from Pakistan to India was often difficult as there is only one border crossing point, and it was regularly closed. During one period of reduced tension, we flew to Lahore in Pakistan and then drove in a taxi to the border point at Wagah. The border was manned on both the Indian and Pakistani side by the most magnificent looking soldiers. They wore splendid ceremonial costumes and undertook exaggerated marching and drill movements – each side exactly mimicking the other.

We walked past the soldiers into India and then caught a taxi the 32 kilometres to Amritsar, which is the site of the Golden Temple, one of the holiest sites in the Sikh religion. The temple had been closed to outsiders following a massacre in 1984 and it had only recently been re-opened to the public. The temple and surrounding ponds were beautiful and there was an entrance gate on each of the four surrounding walls – signifying that people from any direction or any religion were welcome. A memorable feature was a huge communal kitchen, which offered free meals to anyone. In one small glass enclosure a Sikh 'priest' was continuously reading from their holy book – the 'Guru Granth Sahib'. This reading goes on 24 hours a day and Sikhs around the world are comforted by knowing that any time of day or night someone is praying for them.

Being the major religion in India there were plenty of Hindu temples in Amritsar as well. We went to a large temple and out the back we saw a number of concrete slabs. Our kids asked what they were for and we explained that in the Hindu religion when people died their bodies were burnt, not buried. As if on cue a trolley was wheeled in with a dead beggar lying on it. The attendants gently lowered his body onto the slab, covered him with wood and incense, cracked his skull and then lit the funeral pyre. We didn't take any photos – we just stood there transfixed at what was going on. We had wanted to expose Zoe and Charles to different cultures and religions, and this trip was certainly providing them with some unique experiences.

Another road trip was up the Swat Valley in Pakistan, past 'Churchill's Picket'. This was where the young Lieutenant Winston Churchill was posted during the late 1800s, when the British were fighting for control of the Malakand Pass. We also stayed in the charming hill town of Mingora, which achieved infamy in October 2012 when the Pakistani Taliban shot Malala Yousafzai on her way to school. Malala was not even born at the time of our visit, but having visited Mingora when our daughter Zoe was the same age as when Malala was shot made her story even more compelling for us. We were all pleased when Malala was awarded the Nobel Peace Prize in 2014, because we thought she was a brave young girl and could understand what a remarkable journey life had taken her on.

Another visit would have an even more dramatic follow-up. Each year the Pakistan military academy would invite a United Nations official to attend the graduation of young cadets into army officers. In 1993 I was invited to attend the ceremony, so Margaret and I drove the 110 kilometres from Islamabad to the military academy, situated in the splendid hill station town of Abbottabad. Almost 20 years later in May 2011, Abbottabad gained worldwide attention when US President Barack Obama announced that Osama bin Laden had been killed in his compound in the city.

Exiting the army

Around that time I had decided that it was time to leave the Australian Army. I had received a call from my career adviser in mid-1993 telling me that while I was still competitive for promotion, because I had been away from Australia so long, I was unlikely to be promoted any higher. This didn't surprise or bother me, and as I wanted to stay working for the United Nations in Afghanistan, I submitted my resignation. I stretched out all my leave and did not officially leave the army until 4 July 1994 – but in my mind I had long gone. I had enjoyed my time in the army and had no regrets. However, the irony was not lost on me that in my 23 years of service in the army I had never been in combat. Now, after a short time working in 'the service of peace' for the United Nations, I had been bombed, shot at, had a rifle held to my head and seen more dead bodies and injured people than I cared to remember.

The middle of 1993 also saw Australia withdraw the final Mine Clearance Training Team and by the end of the year, the last three remaining technical advisers had also left. Since 1989 Australia had provided 10 teams of trainers and from 1991 had been the sole country providing experts to the Afghanistan mine clearance program. Over 90 officers and non-commissioned officers had served with UNOCHA in Pakistan and Afghanistan, and had provided outstanding training and advice to all the Afghan demining NGOs.

The reasons given by the Australian Defence department to end the commitment included the deteriorating security situation, the fact that the initial reasons for the deployment had been achieved, and that Afghanistan was outside Australia's area of primary strategic interest. A Defence intelligence estimate at the time concluded that the 'security risk to foreigners engaged on humanitarian work and relief activities is assessed as high in Afghanistan and medium in Pakistan'.

The decision to withdraw the team was criticised in the Australian national press. A journalist from the Brisbane *Courier Mail* wrote: 'The politicians should visit a town like Herat where Afghan families are literally moving back into homes the moment the deminers announce that an area has been cleared of mines and live ordnance. Perhaps they (the politicians) should see the almost demigod status given to the Aussie deminers when they arrive in a town; a status they have earned through long hours in the blazing sun of summer and freezing plains of winter.'

Despite such wonderful rhetoric, the decision to withdraw the Australian training team was not changed and a remarkable, if little known chapter of Australian military history ended.

Campaigning to ban landmines

By 1993 there was increasing concern being expressed at the global level about the indiscriminate nature of anti-personnel landmines and the suffering they caused, particularly to civilians. In post-conflict situations like Angola, Cambodia, Mozambique and of course, Afghanistan, it was found that most civilian casualties were being caused by landmines. A group of six Western NGOs had formed a coalition called the International Campaign to Ban Landmines, or ICBL, which had the ambitious goal of banning landmines completely. This campaign was met with some scepticism in the early days, even from ex-military people working to clear landmines. Most of them agreed landmines were bad, but many still saw landmines as legitimate weapons for self-defence.

The campaign was initially driven by Bobby Mueller from the Vietnam Veterans of America Foundation (VVAF) and Tomas Gerbauer from Medico International in Germany. One of the first things they did was to hire a coordinator for the campaign – an American woman named Jody Williams – who went on to win the Nobel Peace Prize in 1997 for her part in leading the campaign.

I first came in contact with Jody when VVAF commissioned a study in 1993 to try to quantify the extent of the landmine problem around the world. This was a comprehensive survey of the global landmine situation and they undertook field visits and interviewed people in households in Afghanistan, Angola, Bosnia-Herzegovina, Cambodia and Mozambique. The resulting report was titled 'After the Guns Fall Silent – The Enduring Legacy of Landmines'. The title alluded to the fact that even after wars and conflicts had ended, people were still being killed or injured by landmines for years afterwards.

While the report gathered a lot of information from different countries, it was a difficult to compare factors like clearance rates or cost of clearance because each country collected different data in different ways – it was a bit like trying to compare apples with oranges. However, the study was a good first attempt at quantifying the problem and it helped to reduce some of the exaggerated claims about the numbers of landmines in the world.

I do not recall when I decided that landmines were bad and should be banned. There was no 'hallelujah' moment. I think that the more I saw of the indiscriminate death and injury caused by landmines and a growing sense about the futility of war, the more my views just drifted this way. There started to be an increasing number of international meetings called to promote the call for a ban on landmines and I would often attend these meetings and speak from the mine clearance perspective. We would also send some of the Afghan NGO Directors as we found that appearing on the international stage, dressed in their national clothing and speaking in their accented English, they provided a powerful message to western nations.

The United Nations was slow to respond to the call to ban landmines. As a United Nations official I could not openly speak out or take a strong advocacy position when the United Nations had not yet elaborated one. To get around this I granted some money to Sayed Aqa's survey organisation, MCPA, to form the local chapter of the Afghan Campaign to Ban Landmines. Sayed subsequently went on to become one of the co-recipients of the Nobel Peace Prize.

The increasing number of international meetings helped us with the operational aspects of mine clearance. The chance to share experiences and ideas with people working in other mine-affected countries was invaluable. I recall that the first ever international technical meeting focussed on 'demining' was organised by the Scheibel mine detector company, and it was held in Vienna from 12–14 May 1993. There was a presentation about Kuwait that highlighted some valuable lessons. After the invasion by Saddam Hussein and subsequent First Gulf War, Kuwait had been left littered by landmines and unexploded ordnance. Being a small country with lots of money Kuwait decided to divide the country into seven sectors and let commercial contracts for their clearance. Each sector contract was reportedly worth US$100 million and within a couple of years Kuwait was cleared of landmines and unexploded ordnance.

The positive outcome of this was that the international community saw that mine clearance was not 'mission impossible', nor would it would take thousands of years to complete, like some sceptics were saying. It just took time or money, and Kuwait had the money. On the downside over 84 deminers were killed during the clean-up in Kuwait, partly because the seven commercial companies were not allowed to share the lessons they had learned among each other. Also the Kuwait government kept changing the clearance criteria and many organisations had to go over the same ground two or three times, until the government was satisfied that the area was cleared.

One of the commercial operators attending the meeting spoke about how they had 'surface cleared' a specified area and then the wind blew the sand away and uncovered more ordnance. The Kuwait government made the company go back and clear the area again, and this happened a third time. The American company representative lamented that this 'really cut into our profit dollars'. The need for an agreed depth of clearance and other related standards, set well in advance of any clearance work, was apparent. Due to its involvement with the start-up of a growing number of mine clearance programs around the world, developing agreed standards was one area where the United Nations came to play an important role.

One of the first political meetings of significance was a three-day landmines symposium organised by the International Committee of the Red Cross in Montreux, Switzerland in April 1993. We sent Kefayatullah from the Afghan program to represent us at this meeting, and he did extremely well in highlighting the practical difficulties involved with clearing landmines.

The first time the United Nations General Assembly debated the landmine issue was in October 1993 when it adopted Resolution 48/7 entitled 'Assistance in Mine Clearance' and the initial report by the United Nations Secretary-General was presented in 1994.

From 5–7 July 1995 the United Nations also held a major meeting in Geneva to discuss the landmine issue, which I attended. This meeting was a mix of political issues and working groups that addressed technical aspects of mine clearance and victim assistance. One of the key speakers was a young Cambodian girl, named Song Kosal. Kosal was only about eight years old and she had lost her leg in a landmine blast. Despite, or perhaps because of, her shy manner in such an overwhelming gathering, a very quietly spoken Kosal highlighted the plight of landmine victims. She later went on to become one of the key faces of the anti-landmine campaign.

Some of the other early meetings that were held were extremely lively and interesting, as all sorts of people attended. I remember one such meeting organised by the Swedish defence research agency. There were political advocates, military engineers, civilian mine clearers, research scientists, and landmine designers and producers all in the same room. The landmine makers would proudly talk about their new 'smart mines', while agitators like Rae McGrath from MAG would scream at them from across the room that they were immoral people, and ask how they slept at night knowing that they had been responsible for the death of children.

Another deminer showed a photo of a landmine and an earnest military officer jumped up and said, 'You cannot show that landmine; it is still classified as secret equipment!'

The deminer responded dryly, 'I dug up that mine last week with my own bare hands and I will show it to who I bloody well like.'

The commercial company representative from Kuwait got up and spoke again about his loss of 'profit dollars', which brought loud jeers from the crowd. After this meeting the mine action sector as it was now coming to be known, seemed to split into two; the advocacy organisations pursuing their political goal of a total ban on anti-personnel mines went their way, and the more operational organisations like our program in Afghanistan involved with the business of clearing landmines as fast and efficiently as possible, went ours.

The issue of landmines was also starting to get more attention in the international press. Journalists were frequent visitors to the Afghan program, and it was in our interests to support them whenever we could. Increased publicity helped us raise money from donors and also promoted the growing call for a ban on landmines.

US *Time* magazine published a feature story on the global landmine crisis in its 13 December 1993 edition. On Afghanistan it said: 'Although the ongoing conflict between mujahedeen factions is complicating clean-up efforts, a United Nations-sponsored mine removal program there has been hailed as the most successful in the world. In the past three years, 35 teams of 32 men each have succeeded in clearing some 25 million square metres around major cities like Kabul of 60,000 mines.'

STEPPING INTO A MINEFIELD

All of us involved in the Afghan mine clearance program were extremely proud when this article came out, and it helped to maintain the positive goal that we had set within the program; that we could clear priority areas of Afghanistan in years, not decades.

CHAPTER 9:
CHAOS IN KABUL

While the security situation in many of the provinces of Afghanistan during 1993 and 1994 was fairly stable, in Kabul it was continuously spiralling downhill. After the fall of the Najibullah Government in 1992, the proposed power-sharing arrangement among the major seven mujahedeen parties fell apart. President Burhanuddin Rabbani clung to power, primarily supported by the forces of Ahmed Shah Massoud and sometimes General Dostum in the north. These groups were Afghan, but mainly of Tajik and Uzbek backgrounds. This upset the historical domination of Kabul by the Pushtoon tribes and a bitter 'civil war' broke out in the city, with the main protagonist being Gulbuddin Heckmatyar of the Hezbi Islami party. His forces, along with some other minor parties, shelled the city mercilessly with artillery, rockets and tank fire. Fighting and shelling occurred in the suburbs, which quickly emptied of people. Front lines were along major roads and high ground was fought over to try to gain domination over parts of the city. Public buildings like schools, hospitals and government offices that had survived the Soviet occupation were destroyed.

Despite the obvious humanitarian catastrophe, the double tragedy from my perspective was that large numbers of new landmines were being laid throughout the city. These mined areas were not marked and as the front lines changed frequently, extra mines kept being laid. In addition, there was a growing problem with unexploded ordnance.

Ordnance is a general term used to cover all types of ammunition, including artillery shells, rockets, mortars, grenades, bullets and the like. Ammunition which has not been stored properly may deteriorate over time and fail to go off when fired. If it is not fired correctly it may also not detonate. For example, the round fired from the shoulder-held rocket-propelled grenade (RPG) launcher has to travel 20 metres before it arms itself. If it hits something before then it will not explode, or if it lands at a shallow angle it may also not detonate. Kabul was rapidly becoming a city of rubble, which was also littered with thousands of pieces of unexploded ordnance.

During the darkest days of this civil war the United Nations kept a small presence in Kabul, mainly to oversee the delivery of humanitarian assistance. Graeme Membrey remained as our demining representative in the city and among other things, he supervised a small mine awareness and safety project which we funded through the Afghan Red Crescent Society. Minefield survey teams and clearance teams worked on a small scale. HALO Trust also kept their office open although most of their mine clearance operations were in the north of the country.

I made a number of visits to Kabul during this period and was always shocked by the increasing destruction and loss of life. The Rabbani Government had kept the Department of Mine Clearance in existence, but it was only in name. I visited them one winter and there were two men sitting in an office with even less than they had before – if that was possible. They had a small stove in the centre of the office and were ripping up a cardboard box to burn to keep warm. When that ran out I started to burn pages from my notebook. Dr Gunter Mulack, the German donor representative had come with me on this trip. The interpreter had failed to arrive for the meeting, but we discovered one of the government officials had previously studied at the German high school in Kabul and spoke some German. So the VIP guest, Dr Mulack, sat there and kindly translated for me from English to German.

Gunter and I then went to meet the acting Foreign Minister at the time, Abdul Ghafoorzai. There was no electricity in any of the buildings and it was freezing. We sat in the dark in the Minister's office in our overcoats, with our gloves and woolly hats on. A telephone line came in from a broken window and ran to a fax machine sitting on his desk. He proudly told us this was the only external line working out of Kabul. It was in fact a single telephone line running to Pakistan and it was using a Peshawar number – this was the only means of communication the so-called Afghan Government had with the outside world.

Next minute a violent earthquake struck. We were all trying to be nonchalant and sat there talking while rocking quite noticeably on our chairs. This was a bizarre scene: three men in overcoats rocking around a desk with a fax machine sliding haphazardly on it.

The acting foreign minister was keeping detailed notes of our discussion in a notebook and he said he was going to write a book about the liberation of Afghanistan when things settled down. Tragically, he never got to write it, as he died in a plane crash in Bamyan province in 1997.

On another trip to Kabul I brought along my Afghan program officer, Mohammed Shakir. He still had relatives in the city so he was pleased to have the chance to see them. At these times the United Nations kept a strict limit on how many international staff could stay in the United Nations guesthouse – usually 10 – because that was one planeload of people to evacuate if needed. Shakir and I went to meet the head of the Afghan Red Crescent Society to discuss the landmine safety project. The reception area was full of women and kids waiting for medical appointments. Next moment there was a deafening roar. I immediately thought it was an incoming rocket, and Shakir and I both dived on the floor. It turned out to be an extremely low flying fighter jet; one of the few Rabbani could keep in the air. None of the women or children in the room had moved. Shakir and I, the two brave demining guys, got up, dusted ourselves off and looked suitably embarrassed.

At one critical stage in the military stand-off that had developed, the opposition mujahedeen leader Gulbuddin Heckmatyar issued an ultimatum that if a specified area was not handed over by 3 pm on a certain day he would attack. Being the senior United Nations person in Kabul at the time, but for reasons I still cannot explain, I said to Shakir, 'Let's go and have a look.' We drove in the white UN vehicle to the site on the edge of the city and we saw a line of about 20 Soviet style T72 tanks belonging to the government commander, Ahmed Shah Massoud. They were in battle order, hull down off the side of the road and in staggered formation. I was quite impressed as it looked organised and 'by the book' tank tactics.

We drove along the road at 3 pm and went around a blind corner. There staring at us were 20 of Heckmatyar's tanks, lined up in exactly the same battle formation. We waved furiously and turned around and quickly got out of there. Fortunately the attack did not go ahead and the ultimatum passed. Later I gave a live interview about what I had seen with Peter Greste from the BBC, which was transmitted from Kabul to London via his briefcase-sized satellite phone. I had met Peter a couple of times before, and he was easy to deal with being a fellow Australian. This was the same Peter Greste who was imprisoned by Egyptian officials in 2013, and released in 2015.

I avoided meeting the Afghan political leaders as much as possible, in order not to jeopardise the neutrality of the mine clearance program. However, sometimes it was unavoidable if we wanted access to an area or needed support. Kefayatullah knew President Rabbani reasonably well so he arranged for me to meet him in the President's Palace in Kabul. We went through numerous layers of security before we met the man himself. He was relaxed and friendly and we discussed the ongoing mine clearance work in the city and asked for certain guarantees of safe passage. Shakir looked fairly glum throughout the meeting and later when I said he didn't seemed very excited to meet his President he said, 'When Rabbani asked who I was, Kef said I was just an interpreter.' It was unusual for Kef to put any one down, and I do not think it was intentional as Kef and Shakir got on well together.

Mass exodus

The fall of Najibullah in April 1992 and the subsequent in-fighting between the mujahedeen caused a massive outflow of people from Kabul. These were mainly people who had supported the Soviets or the communist government and they understandably feared retribution from the mujahedeen. Unfortunately, they could only go in one direction – east towards Pakistan. Pakistan refused to allow them entry because of their links to the communists, so huge groups of people were stuck around Jalalabad.

The local shura allocated an area of desert where the people fleeing Kabul could go and the United Nations was asked to help. In United Nations speak, a person who is forced from their home but stays in their own country is classified as 'internally displaced'. A refugee is someone who has crossed a border. These poor people neither knew nor cared how the United Nations classified them; they just needed help. As a result, a massive effort was started by UNOCHA to provide food and shelter.

A number of unexploded bombs were found in the area where the tented camp was being established. We were quickly called in to make sure that this was not a disaster in the making, with internally displaced people being housed in a minefield. We found no evidence that buried mines had been used in the area and although the site was not a former battlefield, random unexploded ordnance was seen. This was a hazard that had to be removed quickly.

We decided to adopt a technique known as Battle Area Clearance, which was used in the bomb disposal world, but was new to demining. Kefayatullah from ATC brought most of his teams to the area and we trained them to line up shoulder to shoulder in groups of 30 and walk slowly over the area in a systematic way. If a deminer spotted a suspicious object on the ground, he raised his hand and the item was marked. A couple of metal detectors were on hand in case anything suspicious was seen, possibly suggesting buried devices. At the end of the day the supervisors would collect all the marked items, or blow them up in-situ, depending on what they were. Using this method we were able to very quickly check 10 square kilometres in a couple of days and the establishment of the camp went ahead.

The extent of this tented camp became staggering. It went for about 5 kilometres along the side of the main road, and stretched a few kilometres back from it. It was clearly visible from the air when you flew into Jalalabad. Supporting the tens of thousands of people in the camp with tents, food and water was a massive effort and maintaining law and order was difficult and stressful for all involved.

I remember a young Australian volunteer had been assigned by one of the United Nations agencies to work at the camp. He arrived in Pakistan, was briefed in Islamabad and flown into the camp, but the very next day he asked to be removed because he could not stand the intensity and pressure of the situation.

Another day we received a report that a mine had gone off in the camp and a child had been killed. This was disturbing to say the least as we had completely checked the area where the camp was located. As I was in Jalalabad at the time with a German television crew I went to investigate and I was shown the spot where the accident happened. There was no crater in the ground but there was evidence of fragmentation damage to the surrounding tents. The accident had clearly not been caused by a buried mine. Our local colleagues talked to various other kids and it transpired that the dead boy had found a hand grenade in a dry creek bed outside the camp boundary. He had brought it 'home' and it exploded when he was playing with it. We increased the number of mine awareness teams working in the camp as a result of this accident and thankfully no other explosions were reported.

Despair and desperation

Back in Kabul the situation was getting grimmer by the month. The blockade of the city by Gulbuddin Heckmatyar's forces meant that everything was in short supply – fuel, clothing and food in particular. On the humanitarian side, Martin Barber had implemented an excellent scheme. It had the uninspiring name of the 'Widows Bakery Project'. Widows were trained to cook the traditional Afghan flat bread that accompanied every meal, provided some money to set up a kitchen and then given flour to make the bread. They could work from home and kept what they earned, in what was a forerunner of the now popular micro-credit schemes. However, the scheme relied on a steady supply of flour and Heckmatyar regularly stopped relief convoys coming in from Pakistan.

One time I was in Kabul when Heckmatyar blocked a convoy of 20 trucks carrying the flour for the bakery project. The representative of the World Food Program at the time was a British man and he was staying in the United Nations guesthouse. His employment contract had run out and he was waiting for an extension. As a result he refused to leave the guesthouse. As a United Nations colleague and humanitarian worker I was appalled at his attitude, so I volunteered to go with the local staff to see Heckmatyar to try to get the trucks released.

We drove to Heckmatyar's base near the village of Charasyab, but on arrival we were told he was away. Next minute we see Heckmatyar walk past! Then we were told he was too busy to see us, even after we sat there for hours, determined not to go away empty handed. As it was getting dark we passed on our message and left. A day or two later the trucks were released. The World Food Program guy still would not leave the United Nations guesthouse, so I went out at midnight in the lightly falling snow and helped guide the trucks into the compound. I felt good that I had made a small, practical difference to a few women's lives.

My lasting impression of Kabul during this period was a scene of utter despair. In the winter of 1994, Heckmatyar opened a short window of opportunity for the trapped Kabulis to collect some food from one of his checkpoints on the outskirts of town. From a high point we could see thousands of people stretching back kilometres. They were pushing handcarts, dragging sacks of flour and cans of cooking oil in any manner they could along the wet, slippery muddy road. I will never forget their hollow eyes and the complete look of desperation on their faces. This was as bad as any movie I had seen depicting images from World War II. What was particularly galling to me was that the world news headlines were now all about the war in Bosnia; more people were dying each day in Kabul, but it never made the world news.

A tide of humanity floods back into Kabul

On the political side, the former President Najibullah was still being held in the compound where the United Nations political offices were located. I had seen him and his brother a few times in the garden, but made no attempt to talk to him. The United Nations was trying to broker various deals to have President Rabbani step down but without success. By now Graeme Membrey had left the mine clearance program and was working in Kabul as the security adviser to the United Nations. Graeme was excellent in this role and he ran a tight ship.

On 11 March 1995 he had to escort a political officer from United Nations headquarters in New York, named Charlie Santos, on a visit to Kabul. As they approached the United Nations office, rockets started to land and explode in the main street. They ran up the driveway of the compound towards the underground bunker, but then Santos turned and started to go towards a door Graeme knew to be locked. As the rockets were now falling extremely close to them, Graeme grabbed Santos by the neck, pulled him to the ground and dived on top of him to give protection. In the same split second a rocket exploded in the driveway. This sent a blast of heat and fragments over Graeme, causing injuries to his back and neck. They scrambled into the bunker and another 40 rockets fell in the general area.

It was a very close call and Mr Santos freely acknowledged that Graeme had saved his life. I subsequently nominated Graeme for an Australian bravery award and was very pleased when I heard in February 1998 that he had been awarded a 'Commendation for Brave Conduct' under the Australian honours system. Later the United Nations presented him with a similar commendation for brave conduct.

In the flux that was Afghanistan, in March 1995 the entire city of Kabul suddenly came under the control of the forces of President Rabbani and a level of peace and normalcy returned. As a result, displaced families within the city, as well as those people who had fled to other provinces, started returning to their homes. This led to a high number of civilian mine accidents caused by mines and unexploded ordnance.

Staff from the UN High Commissioner for Refugees (UNHCR) reported observing over 10,000 people returning to Kabul each week. Figures obtained from the Kabul hospital and the Red Cross indicated that there was an average of 10 new landmine victims and 40 unexploded ordnance casualties every day in late March and early April 1995. We quickly mobilised an emergency plan, which included intensive mine awareness and safety briefings throughout the city, survey teams going to all corners of Kabul to record and mark mined areas, and large numbers of demining teams redirected to the city to clear priority areas.

By June, ATC had over 500 deminers working in the city and HALO redeployed its four teams from Jebal Seraj into the city. Impressive clearance results were quickly obtained and fortunately civilian casualty numbers dropped dramatically. While still hard, living conditions in Kabul eased somewhat in the second half of 1995.

The Taliban appear on the scene

As things were calming down in Kabul, the situation was getting worse down south in Kandahar. The warlords were constantly fighting each other, everyone seemed to be armed, people were kidnapped or forced off their land, and infrastructure like telephone wires and poles, and machinery in factories was stolen and sold in Pakistan. The extensive system of irrigation canals and *kareezes* (wells) fell into disrepair and the once flourishing agriculture sector all but disappeared. Against the trend in the rest of the country, people were leaving Kandahar in Afghanistan and heading back to Quetta. Pakistani trucking companies were becoming increasingly frustrated by the numerous 'chains' they had to pass through, and the taxes they had to pay when travelling through the Kandahar region to Herat and on to Turkmenistan. Trade was suffering.

Then in late 1994 the Taliban seemed to appear out of nowhere. A group of mullahs who formed the basis of the Taliban had some minor victories fighting against alleged injustices caused by warlords. Following the capture of a significant weapons cache by the Taliban at Spin Boldak, the flood gates seemed to open. Thousands of young men who had been trained in the religious schools or madrassas in Quetta flocked back into Afghanistan to support the Taliban.

The word Talib means 'students of Islam' and they were motivated by religious fervour rather than the traditional tribal system of the past. In November 1994, the Taliban forces swept into Kandahar with amazing speed and they defeated the individual commanders. Many of the mujahedeen commanders' soldiers converted to the Taliban's ways, rather than fighting them. The Taliban managed to rid the region of some of the worst offenders of law and order by meting out immediate capital punishment. A number of commanders were hanged and left dangling for days on the decorative archway at the entrance to Kandahar airport.

On the positive side, they disarmed the militias, dismantled all the road blocks and brought some stability to the region. On the downside the Taliban implemented a strict version of Sharia law, banned all forms of entertainment and sports, closed down girls' schools, stopped women from leaving the house and ordered all men to grow long beards.

By early 1995 the United Nations saw the necessity to resume its humanitarian work in Kandahar, but did not want to extend any political recognition to the Taliban as a result of their takeover. It was decided to send a 'technical mission' to make contact and to see what the Taliban's intentions were. I volunteered to go as demining was an obvious choice of technical issues to discuss with them and the mine clearance NGOs were already back working in the area. One of the United Nations political officers, Andrew Tessoriore would come with me, but I was to lead the first United Nations missions to meet the new Taliban leadership.

We flew to Kandahar airport and the United Nations plane dropped us and left. We stood around the completely deserted airport waiting for our hosts to pick us up. Kandahar airport had been a major Soviet airbase and later during the height of the US invasion in the early 2000s was reported to be the busiest airport in the world. This day, there was not another plane or person in sight and the terminal building was dilapidated and forlorn. Eventually our hosts picked us up and we drove to the governor's mansion in Kandahar city.

We were motioned to a room with no chairs, so sat on the bare concrete floor. The leader of the Taliban, the one-eyed Mullah Omar, was apparently away in his home province of Uruzgan, so could not meet with us as planned. One of the other founders of the Taliban, Mullah Rabbani (no relation to President Rabbani), and his entourage entered the room and sat down without shaking hands. All were dressed in *shawal-kameeze*, wore plastic flip-flops on their feet and black turbans on their heads. They offered chai but just threw the sweets and sugar on the floor. The meeting began. Through our interpreter I explained the purpose of our mission and my part went well.

Mullah Rabbani started off by saying, 'The landmines are un-Islamic. Local people are suffering because of them. You can continue your work in the region.'

The rest of the meeting didn't go so well. In the military there is a dictum that says you should 'select and maintain your aim'. The Taliban had embraced this wholeheartedly. When we asked about their plan for the resumption of health services, education, trade and farming, Mullah Rabbani said that would come in due course. Their aim at present was to 'restore peace, disarm the local population and enforce Sharia law'. Full stop. Nothing else mattered to them at this time. Any amount of discussion and rationalising came to nothing – they just wanted to take over Afghanistan. We flew back to Islamabad and reported our findings.

Eventually the United Nations negotiated with the Taliban to resume humanitarian operations in Kandahar. We needed a compound and office space, so the Taliban offered up a girls' school. This caused enormous angst among UN staff. Some were pragmatic and said that the United Nations needed to get a foothold in the city and that the girls' school was not going to reopen anyway in the near future. Others said it was immoral and unacceptable. A popular expression among aid workers at the time was 'I am forced to choose between a bad decision and a worse one' and this was the classic. In the end the United Nations took the girls' school but UNICEF, the UN children's agency, refused to use it.

True to their word the Taliban allowed the demining agencies to resume work. When the Taliban forces captured rebel commanders' bases they found all sorts of 'spoils of war' and subsequently returned our five stolen vehicles (although most were just burned-out shells) and the general security situation was the best it had been for years.

As the Taliban brought peace and stability to Kandahar and its surrounding provinces, the United Nations and aid community were caught unprepared for what happened next. Somewhat surprisingly the Afghan refugees living in Quetta started to return in very large numbers. Villages and farms were reoccupied to ensure that family land ownership was maintained. This seemed a positive thing on the initial assessment, but then the monthly civilian landmine accidents rose sharply in the area to over 40 per month. Thanks to inputs from the Red Cross we were able to determine the location of accidents and assess the magnitude of the problem. Dave Edwards and his team reviewed the data and quickly realised that Daman and Dand districts were taking the brunt of the accidents.

These two districts surrounded the Kandahar airport which had been heavily mined and fought over. They were also some of the best grape-growing and agriculture areas in the province. The influx of civilians and their attempt to regenerate the irrigation and agricultural systems had resulted in a huge human cost. Our Kandahar demining office then set about immediately directing a large percentage of our resources into these two districts – OMA for mine awareness, MCPA survey teams to mark areas and warn people and the DAFA teams to start clearance. The effort saw some immediate dividends after two months of operations, when the civilian casualty rates for these two districts started to reduce dramatically down to 5-6 per month. This was a good result, but the loss of lives and injuries were still occurring despite our best efforts. The influx of returnees did not stop and mine risk education teams were set up on the border at Spin Boldak, to intercept the returnees and provide them with information on the risks and threats.

In early 1995 the Taliban continued their military expansion towards Herat and Kabul. Here they met more determined opposition and their expansion slowed. A major push westward was launched and finally in September 1995 the Taliban took control of Herat, which was major blow to the Rabbani government. In Herat, the Taliban were more like foreign invaders as they did not speak the local Persian language and they imposed an even stricter version of Sharia law. All sorts of restrictions were placed on people's lives, arbitrary punishments were administered and girls' schools were closed. Herat had been such a beacon of positive progress in my opinion and now it was going rapidly backwards.

Signs of things to come

During this period, two tragic incidents occurred, the full implications of which were not fully understood at the time. The first occurred on 1 February 1993. The overall United Nations relief efforts in Jalalabad were in full swing at that time and road travel from Peshawar into Jalalabad by vehicle was commonplace. Without warning, four United Nations workers were ambushed and killed on the main road not far from Jalalabad. The party was driving back towards Peshawar when a grey pick-up truck full of armed men overtook them, forced them to stop and opened fire. The dead included one British national, one Dutch and two Afghans. Another Dutch member of the party managed to escape by hiding in a ditch on the side of the road.

This incident shook the United Nations family to the core, as the presumed protection of 'neutrality' had been violated. It had always been rumoured that there were 'Arab camps' in Kunar province and also near Khost. The attacker's' vehicle was last seen heading south towards Khost, and although the killers were never found the 'Arabs' were the main suspects. This Arab camp must surely have been the birthplace of Al Qaeda.

The second incident was much closer to home. Margaret was sitting in her office at the UN club in Islamabad on 19 November 1995 when an enormous explosion nearly knocked her off her chair. She immediately telephoned the journalist Gerald Burke and told him something big must have happened. Armed men had stormed the Egyptian Embassy in Islamabad and detonated a huge bomb, which killed 16 people and injured 80 others.

A massive crater was left at the front of the embassy building and most of the building had collapsed. The nearby British and Japanese embassies had also been damaged, and the windows of the ANZ bank had been blown in. As if drawn to danger, Graeme Membrey happened to be in the bank when the bomb went off and he was able to give the authorities a good account of what happened.

Later it was revealed that Ayman al-Zawahiri planned the attack in 1994, shortly after aligning himself with Osama bin Laden and becoming his number two. Who could have imagined what an even more dreadful path these two men would later take on 11 September 2001?

The loss of Shakir

One Saturday afternoon in late 1995 the telephone rang at home and it was the UNOCHA radio room. They said they had received a message that Shakir, our program officer, was missing, presumed drowned. I couldn't believe what they were saying and asked them to get more information. They called back later and said that apparently he had been in Peshawar for the weekend with his family, and on the way home had stopped at Attock for a picnic. This was that magnificent spot near Attock Fort where the Indus and Kabul rivers met. It seems that when he was playing with his children he had fallen into the river, hit his head on a rock and drowned. As no-one in the vicinity could swim, his body had just floated away in the fast-flowing Indus River.

There were frantic calls all round and a plan emerged. The next day I would go with our logistic officer, Tariq Zuberi, to the Pakistani Army headquarters in Rawalpindi, where we would try to use his old army connections to get approval for an army helicopter to search for Shakir. Meanwhile, Mohammad Younus and some others from the office would go to Attock and see what they could do. We had been told that the Pakistani army commandos from the Attock Fort would provide some divers to help with the search. The next day Zuberi and I went to army headquarters and saw every major, colonel, brigadier and general that we could corner. None of them was prepared to authorise the release of a helicopter to search for a missing Afghan.

Not one to sit at home, Margaret asked Younus if she could come with them to Attock. When they arrived at the picnic area by the river there was no-one to be seen. They went to Attock Fort and met with a Pakistani army captain, who said nothing could be done.

Margaret responded by saying, 'My husband is a colonel in the army; I do not speak to captains. Go and get your commanding officer.' The poor chap obliged and then Margaret gave the commanding officer an earful about how badly they treated Afghans, and if it was a Pakistani national they would be out there looking. The commanding officer finally agreed that he would send some divers to search the area the next day. I went to the site the following day and divers were there searching, but there was no trace of Shakir.

A sad week went by with no news of Shakir. Then on the following Thursday I got a call from the radio room to say that a body had been found at a village about 15 kilometres downstream from Attock. I called Dr Aleem, picked him up and we raced down to Attock. We left the highway and navigated our way along narrow winding tracks until we came to the village. Younus and the others had arrived before us and Shakir's body had already been placed in a coffin. The coffin had a small perspex window and I looked in and saw the bloated but recognisable face of my colleague and good friend. I was devastated.

The vehicles all headed slowly back to the refugee camp in Peshawar where Shakir had previously lived. An enormous crowd of men had already built up and Shakir's coffin was taken off the pick-up truck and carried aloft by his friends. I got swept up in the surging crowd in the narrow mud-walled alleys and got separated from Dr Aleem. I had no idea what was happening but I followed along. Suddenly the crowd turned back and the coffin was placed on the pick-up and we all drove to the cemetery.

A site in the cemetery seemed to be selected at random among other headstones and men started to take turns in digging the grave. I said to Dr Aleem that I would like to take a turn at digging, but he said as a non-Muslim it would not be appropriate. A car then pulled up and a number of veiled women got out. It seems that earlier the men had taken Shakir's body to the family house for the women to pay their respects, but they could not get the coffin inside the door. Instead, the black-cloaked women had been brought to the cemetery.

Shakir's wife was overcome with grief and fainted. The women left and Aleem and I just sat and watched the digging. Then, on some unseen signal, all the hundreds of men quietly lined up on the road and prayed for the soul of Shakir. That was the signal to go, so Dr Aleem and I just drove in silence back to Islamabad. When I got home the events of the past week caught up with me emotionally, and I hugged Margaret and cried over the loss of my good friend. The next day at the office I led a short service for all the staff to celebrate his life and to remember him.

The insurance policy for the mine clearance program only covered deminers, but I privately convinced the company to pay the death benefit to Shakir's wife, Khadeeja. We set up a trust fund managed by some reliable people to ensure that Khadeeja and her four children would receive a regular income. Margaret and I met with her on a number of occasions and spoke to her through an interpreter to make sure she was well looked after. Some months later she married Shakir's nephew, Jamil. This was the Afghan way and it meant at least that she was looked after in her own society.

Time to take our leave from Afghanistan

Towards the end of 1995 I was starting to think it was time to move on. I had been in the job for over four-and-a-half years and I was getting tired. The same issues seemed to keep cropping up and the overall security situation in Afghanistan was still going downhill. The Taliban were threatening to take Kabul and I was very disappointed by the Taliban takeover of Herat, as that was the one place in Afghanistan where I had seen real progress under Governor Ismail Khan. While the mine clearance program was supported by the Taliban, the rest of their policies, including the strict imposition of Sharia law and their poor treatment of women were disheartening. The death of Shakir had also affected me, as I couldn't reconcile in my mind the death of such a wonderful young Afghan man while other lesser people flourished.

On a personal level our daughter Zoe had two years left at high school and Charles had three years to go. In fairness to them, we would need to stay another three years to finish their schooling and I wasn't sure I wanted to stay that long. At 16 years old Zoe was an attractive, blonde-haired young woman and it was becoming impossible for her to go out on the street or to the bazaars without being harassed by local men.

I started to look around for another job – both with the United Nations and back in Australia. The other main United Nations mine clearance programs at the time were Cambodia, Mozambique and Angola, but they all had program managers in place. As is usually the case, I had nothing for a while and then I got two job offers in the same week. One was a senior public service position with an Australian government security agency. The other was a United Nations job to be the adviser to the government in Laos to help set up an unexploded ordnance clearance project. The only drawback to this position was that there was no English language high school in Laos, and we would have to send Zoe and Charles to boarding school in Australia.

Margaret and I agonised over this for weeks, but in the end the kids were fantastic – they said that they would support me in whatever I chose to do and would be willing to go to boarding school. I knew absolutely nothing about Laos, but the challenge to set up a new program from scratch appealed to me, and because it was a peaceful Asian country I accepted the offer.

We spent a hectic few months getting a place for our kids at a boarding school in Canberra and arranging removals to Vientiane in Laos. I was sad to be leaving my good friends, the Afghan NGO directors. We had made tremendous progress in making the mine clearance program more efficient and effective. By this time the program consisted of eight organisations employing over 7000 staff, had an annual budget of US$20 million and we were clearing almost 30 square kilometres of minefields and 25 square kilometres of battle area per year.

To mark our departure, the NGO directors arranged a large farewell party for Margaret and me at the ill-fated Marriott Hotel in Islamabad. During the evening, the Director of DAFA, Engineer Sattar, came up to me and said, 'I hope you don't mind, but I have brought a friend of mine along to say farewell to you.' We duly exchanged pleasantries with an urbane, well-spoken man named Hamid Karzai, blissfully unaware that we were chatting with the future president of Afghanistan.

CHAPTER 10:
A CHANGE OF SCENE: JOINING THE UNDP TEAM IN LAOS

The first impression we gained when flying into Laos was that of water. After the dry and brown landscape of Pakistan, everything below us seemed so green and wet. As we approached Wattay airport in the Lao capital, Vientiane, we could see the mighty Mekong River snaking its way through the countryside, surrounded by green rice paddy fields and numerous lakes and dams. The Mekong forms the border between Thailand and Laos and the city of Vientiane was visible sprawling out along the northern side of the river.

We had just spent the New Year's holiday together as a family in Thailand, and then departed for Laos on 2 January 1996 to start my new job. Our children Zoe and Charles were coming to spend a couple of weeks with us in Vientiane, before heading home to Australia to start boarding school.

After the plane landed, we were full of anticipation about our new home as we walked across the tarmac to the dilapidated terminal building. I had been told that we would be met by a United Nations representative at the airport and they would have the authority for our visas. We waited in the immigration area while all the other passengers went through, until we were the only people left. Then the immigration officers left their counters. We could see our bags going around on the carousel in the arrivals hall so we wandered through and collected them. A local United Nations driver appeared who said that the official was delayed but we should come with him. We asked if he was sure and when he said he was we wandered into Laos – minus a visa. Big mistake!

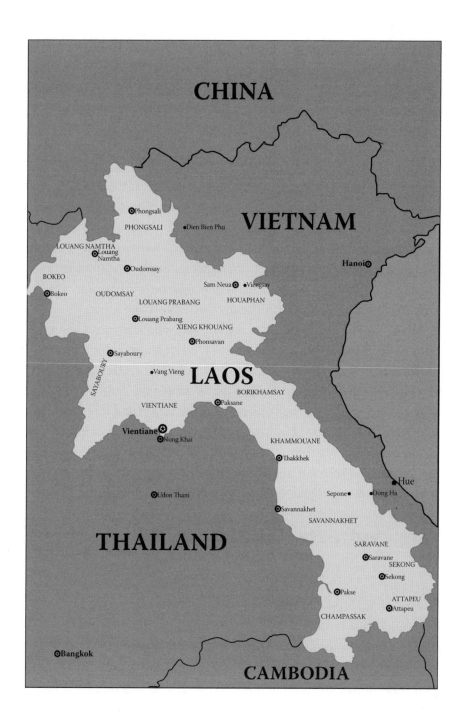

The road into town was sealed but very potholed and muddy because of the recent rain. All the traffic seemed to be going so slowly compared with the frenetic pace of Pakistan. The most common mode of transport was Honda moto-scooters – hundreds were being ridden by both men and women; again a situation that was so different to Pakistan. There were no high rise buildings and we learned later that there was only one elevator in the whole country. The driver dropped us at our hotel, the Parasol Blanc, which was close to the United Nations building and popular with the expatriate community, being one of the better hotels at that time.

The next day I met the head of the United Nations office, a quiet but extremely competent Swedish man about my age, Jan Mattsson. In Laos, the problem of unexploded bombs left over from the Vietnam War period was seen as a development issue, not a humanitarian one. As such the United Nations agency I would be working for was the United Nations Development Program or UNDP for short.

UNDP is one of the largest of the United Nations agencies and it has offices in over 140 countries. The head of UNDP is usually the most senior United Nations person in a country and in Laos the office had projects ranging from good governance through to sanitation. Jan Mattsson was most concerned that we hadn't been met at the airport and that we did not have visas. After 10 days of haggling with various government departments, including the very real threat of being expelled completely or having to leave the country and then enter again, we finally got six-month visas. This was despite the fact that my UNDP employment contract was for 12 months.

LAOS: THE BACKGROUND

The official name of Laos is the Lao People's Democratic Republic or Lao PDR. An old joke goes that any country with the word 'democratic' in its title probably isn't democratic, and Laos was no exception. At the time of our arrival in January 1996 it was one of only a handful of communist countries left in the world – along with China and Cuba. We discovered that among the foreigners working in Laos, it was generally considered that the 'PDR' could just as well stand for 'Please Don't Rush', as everything in Laos moved extremely slowly.

Laos also claims the dubious distinction of being the most heavily bombed country, per capita, in the world. During the Vietnam War period in the 1960s and early 1970s the US fought what was often termed a 'secret war' in Laos. On the ground it involved training and arming Hmong hill tribe people to fight against the communist forces. However, the major activity was aerial bombardment of the so-called Ho Chi Minh trail, which was the major supply route from North Vietnam into the south to support the Viet Cong forces. It was actually not one trail but rather a network of roads and tracks that crossed into Laos in many areas along the ill-defined border with Vietnam. The trail was bombed continuously during the war by all types of air dropped weapons, including cluster bombs. Infrastructure throughout the country was still poor, as were communications, but it was believed that many people living in villages along the border areas were killed or injured each year by unexploded ordnance, or UXO as they were called, left over from that time.

Laos became a 'closed' country after the war ended in 1975 and very few Western organisations were present, or welcome, in the country. A number of United Nations agencies had kept offices open in the post-war period, but they were very limited in what work they could do. Some countries maintained an embassy in Vientiane while others covered Laos with diplomatic representation from Bangkok or Hanoi. In the late-1980s the country slowly started to open up and some mineral exploration companies, logging operations and telecommunications agencies commenced activities. However, travel by foreigners outside the capital was strictly controlled and you had to have a permit entered in your passport to travel to the provinces.

In mid-1995, UNDP took advantage of the growing worldwide interest and concern about landmines when Jan Mattsson convinced the government to allow a donor visit to Xieng Khouang province. This was believed to be one of the worst affected areas in the country and a small pilot project to clear UXO was already underway in the province. The visit helped to raise awareness among the local donor representatives, although the extent of the UXO contamination throughout the rest of the country was still not known. A joint UNDP, UNICEF and Lao government Unexploded Ordnance Trust Fund was established, but very little donor money was initially contributed to the fund. It was also decided that the United Nations would assist the Lao government set up a national UXO clearance program, to help deal with the problem – which is where I came in. I was employed to advise the Lao government on setting up a mine and bomb clearance program and had the grand title of Program Management Adviser. At that time in January 1996, the National UXO Program consisted of me and a national counterpart, who had been assigned by the government to be the Program Director.

I met my Lao counterpart at the UNDP office. His name was Saykham and unusually for a Lao person, he only had one name, so I called him Mr Saykham. He was short even by Lao standards, well into his 60s and had grey hair – again unusual for a Lao man, as most of them dyed their hair black. He spoke perfect English and French and had worked for an international body, the Mekong River Commission, for much of his career. You could almost tell the age of a Lao person by the languages they spoke – the older ones spoke French from the colonial days, the middle-aged spoke Russian because of the communist connection and all the young people wanted to learn was English. Saykham had a high-pitched giggle and I came to learn that when confronted with a situation they were not sure about, Lao people often giggled.

The wife of a government vice-minister was also in the office at the same time and had been talking to Saykham in Lao.

I asked him, 'What was that all about?'

Saykham said, 'She asked me if she could become my deputy in the new UXO program.'

I replied, 'That could be a bit tricky. What advice will you give to our vice-minister about that request?'

Saykham giggled and said 'no advice'. I asked again, saying that surely he must have to say something to the vice-minister, and again he giggled and said 'no advice'. The alarm bells should have been going off in my head at that stage, but I was too new to know.

I later heard one of the common descriptions of the Lao communist system used by foreigners. It went like this. In the communist system, initiative and good ideas were not rewarded, but mistakes were punished. So what was a Lao government official to do to get ahead? Do nothing. If you didn't do anything you wouldn't make a mistake and thus would not be punished. This was, of course, a very simplistic analysis, but there were numerous examples where projects had taken months or years to get approved – and anything to do with the government took forever to get done – all because the Lao officials didn't want to make a mistake.

Setting up the UXO project

Within the government, the Ministry of Labour and Social Welfare was designated as the responsible ministry for the UXO problem. This was because the Lao mainly saw the issue as a social welfare problem to help the victims of accidents caused by unexploded ordnance. There had been little priority given to UXO clearance efforts. The Ministry was housed in a dreadful green, two-storey U-shaped building that had previously been the head office of a Chinese cigarette company. Our UXO project was assigned an old conference room and one small adjoining office.

So here I was, an ex-Australian Army officer reporting for work in the Ministry of a communist government, in a building that flew the red 'hammer and sickle' flag on certain national days. Officially, I was there to advise the Minister through Mr Saykham, but for day-to-day issues we worked with one of the vice-ministers, Mr Noy Indavong. Mr Noy was a short balding man who did not speak a word of English. For me this was all a big change. In Afghanistan I had been totally in charge of a large, multi-million dollar program, whereas here I was just an adviser. I fully accepted this and swallowed my pride when Saykham took the small office and I sat in the conference room with the secretary. The only consolation was that the squat toilet was off Saykham's office. Everyone had to go through his room to use the facilities and his room always stank.

We started to get some staff assigned to the project. I had no idea where they came from, but most seemed to be rejects from the Ministry. One of the first was Mr Thongphone, who was to be our operations officer. He was a cheerful chap who had no idea about anything, but he spoke English and was willing to learn. UNDP on the other hand, had arranged for a British UN volunteer, Jenni Rauch, to be our program officer and UNDP also assigned a Lao secretary.

Jenni turned out to be a godsend and she quickly became my right-hand person, trusted friend and confidant. Jenni had worked in Laos before as the supervisor of the United Nations volunteer program, and then became the first project supervisor for the Mines Advisory Group (MAG) project in Laos in July 1994. She spoke fluent Lao and had a healthy disregard for the military way of doing things. I once made a mildly disparaging remark about volunteers and Jenni chided me by saying, 'People become volunteers, not because they lacked the necessary skills, but because they were motivated to work for reasons other than money.' Point taken!

Making Laos home

On the home front we were moving at lightning speed by Lao standards. We had been told to check the noticeboard at the Australian Embassy social club to see if any houses were coming available for rent. We did this on our second day and saw an advert posted by an Australian family who were about to leave. We contacted them and found out that they had been the first tenants in this rather grand looking Thai style house. It seemed suitable to us so we took it. We later heard that some people had looked at 20 or more houses and taken months to decide.

We also needed a private car but there were a lot of government restrictions on buying a new car. By a stroke of luck a batch of new cars had just arrived and become available because of a temporary relaxation in government controls. Margaret went to the customs yard the next day and bought a green car, because it matched the shoes she was wearing at the time. Within a week we had a house and a car, which was unheard of in Laos at that time.

We had to wait a few weeks before moving in, so in that time we got to find our way around Vientiane. Some of the most interesting places were the many Buddhist temples (or *wats* as they were called) and large *stupas* – impressive onion-shaped monuments with pointy spires. I am not particularly religious, but in our time in Pakistan and South Asia we had learnt about the Muslims, Hindus and Sikhs, so now it was Buddha's turn. How the Lao had managed to combine the godless communist system with Buddhism was beyond me, but the two co-existed peacefully. On the surface we found Vientiane to be quiet and peaceful and the people extremely charming and friendly.

The Mekong River dominated the town and it flooded shortly after we arrived. Massive amounts of muddy brown water raced down-river and sandbag levees had been rapidly placed on the river banks. Due to the speed and power of the water there were no boats on the river at all. The first bridge across the Mekong had been built only a few years earlier with Australian assistance, but the Lao would not allow Thai vehicles into the country and the bridge was closed at night. The only other point of interest was a mini-replica of the Arc-de-Triumph, named the Phatuxay monument. It had been built years before at the centre of the main traffic roundabout. It was nicknamed the 'vertical runway' as the rumour went that concrete intended for a new runway at the airport had been misappropriated to build the monument. Around this area of town there was still a system of loudspeakers mounted on tall poles and each morning, loud martial music was played, the news was read and communist slogans chanted to remind the population of their patriotic duties.

To work ... but where were the mines?

Having settled in it was now time for Margaret to take Zoe and Charles back to Canberra to settle them into boarding school, and for me to get stuck into the job. My first thoughts were that I may have made a mistake coming to Laos. There was no evidence of bombs in Vientiane, no mine victims, no mention in the press about UXO, and little interest in the topic. Even Mr Noy, the Vice Minister in charge of the project, did not seem too bothered. I once asked him what had happened after the war with regards to UXO and he told me a story. He said that at one time all the people in his village were co-opted to work on a road project. They were all given a wicker basket and told to walk along the route and put any bombs they found into the basket and then later place them in a big hole.

I asked, 'Wasn't that dangerous?'

Mr Noy said, 'Oh, a few people were killed but it wasn't too bad.'

That was the common attitude among those who had lived through the war – bombs were around in the countryside, but that was part of life.

Although our program officer, Jenni Rauch, had provided me with detailed briefings on the UXO situation, I also needed to get out to the provinces to see for myself. The best place to go first was Xieng Khouang province, as that was widely reported to be the worst affected place in Laos. Also the Mines Advisory Group, better known as MAG, had a small project underway in the province. I went to the MAG office in Vientiane and met their country manager, Ben Lark. Ben was a friendly, jovial British man who was an ex-Hong Kong policeman and I knew straightaway that I would get on well with him. Ben explained that after Rae McGrath had completed the MAG survey in Afghanistan, he had gone to Cambodia where he had set up fully fledged mine clearance operations. Now MAG was expanding into other countries, such as Laos.

In Laos, during the post-1975 period, only a few foreign organisations had been authorised to work in the country and two of these were the religious groups the Mennonites and the Quakers. They had been welcomed because of their anti-Vietnam War stance. The Mennonites and the Quakers undertook agricultural projects in the provinces and were appalled at the number of Lao farmers being killed or injured by bombs. Some of the injuries were caused when ploughs pulled by oxen in the paddy fields hit a bomb, and others occurred when farmers were using a hoe or mattock to break the ground. The farmers used this tool by swinging it high over their head and then striking the ground. If the hoe hit a bomb it might go off, so both the Quakers and the Mennonites introduced the 'shovel' program. They felt that if a shovel was used to dig the ground, the amount of force used would be less and thus safer. As a result, they imported and distributed thousands of American made shovels throughout the country. However, this approach did not get rid of the bombs and as pacifist organisations they had no 'in-house' expertise in bomb disposal. For this reason they had invited MAG into the country to join them as a 'subcontractor', to carry out bomb disposal work in Xieng Khouang province.

The newly appointed national director, Mr Saykham, agreed that I could visit Xieng Khouang, but I had to get the necessary permits to travel within the country. One of the Lao staff would have to come with me, as foreigners always needed to be accompanied by a Lao official on a trip outside Vientiane. It was not possible to drive from Vientiane to the provincial capital, Phonsavan, even though the distance was relatively short. This was both because the road was basically non-existent and although it was never spoken about, there were allegedly bandits in some areas along the way that the government didn't quite control. So passport stamped, I boarded the Lao Aviation twin engine propeller plane for the short flight to Phonsavan. Mr Thongphone, our operations officer was assigned to come along and keep an eye on me.

As we approached Xieng Khouang, the landscape started to resemble the surface of the moon and the area all around the airport and the town was pock marked with large bomb craters. On arrival at the shed that served as the Phonsavan airport terminal we were met by Don MacDonald, the technical supervisor of the MAG project. As his name suggests Don was a Scotsman who was a highly qualified bomb disposal expert, formerly in the British Royal Air Force. There were no sealed roads in Phonsavan, so we bounced our way in an old Russian jeep that Don drove to the MAG offices on the outskirts of town.

BOMBS, BOMBLETS AND BOMBIES

At the MAG office they had arranged an impressive display of defused bombs. There were huge 500 pound aircraft bombs and then a variety of assorted bombs, rockets, mortars, grenades, pyrotechnics and other unidentified pieces of ordnance. One item of ordnance that needed to be treated with great care was white phosphorus rounds. These were usually artillery shells or mortars filled with white phosphorous. When the rounds landed and exploded, the white phosphorous would come into contact with the air and start to burn violently, and give off dense white smoke. These rounds were used to mark targets for aircraft bombers, or to produce a smoke screen to stop an enemy firing at you, or to cover a troop withdrawal.

However, by far the most prevalent and dangerous of the bombs left behind after the war were cluster bombs. There were a number of different types of cluster bombs used, but the most common cluster bombs found were called the CBU 24. The 'bomb' consisted of a large container about two metres long and they were filled with 670 small explosive bomblets, about the size of tennis balls. The bomblets had the bland military nomenclature of BLU 26 – standing for 'Bomb Live Unit'. These type of cluster bombs were delivered by an aircraft and when dropped the container would open in the air at a pre-determined altitude. The 670 bomblets would then spill out and hurl toward the ground and explode violently on impact. Depending on the height they were dropped, the hundreds of exploding bomblets could easily cover an area the size of a couple of football fields. I have never seen a live drop of a cluster bomb (because Australia has never held operational stocks of the weapon), but video footage of them going off is frightening.

Cluster bombs had been developed as early as World War II, but the Americans had refined them during the Korean War, as a way to try and break up massed infantry assaults. As an area weapon they were also useful against linear targets like roads or airfields, which are harder to hit with a single conventional bomb. The casing of each of the small bomblets was metal and embedded with ball bearings, while inside was 85 grams of high explosive and a fuse mechanism. On impact with the ground the bomblet would explode and send metal fragments flying out in all directions.

The problem with cluster bombs was that they had a high failure rate, which was due to a number of factors. The fuse mechanism inside the bomblet was intricate and it relied on the bomblet to spin in the air to align some parts of the fuse, to allow the striker to detonate the bomblet when it landed. This often failed. Also, if the bomblet landed in trees the leaves may slow it down enough to stop it exploding, or the same may happen if they landed in soft, wet paddy fields. If the bomb was dropped too low the container may not open at all in the air and when it crashed into the ground, it would spill unexploded bomblets all over the surrounding area. These bomblets were everywhere in Xieng Khouang and later I was to discover they were present in most of the eastern parts of the country. The locals had their own name for them – 'bombies', which they pronounced as 'bom-bees'.

The MAG project in Xieng Khouang was relatively small but well organised. Their workforce consisted of four expatriate bomb disposal experts and 50 Lao technical staff that they had trained. MAG had organised them into two roving teams and two clearance teams. The roving teams each consisted of one expatriate and five Lao technicians with a vehicle. Their role was to respond to a call-out if a village official reported finding a bomb. Otherwise they would go around the province in a systematic way, calling into villages checking to see if they had found any bombs that were visible on the surface of the ground.

This was an ongoing task, and inevitably if the team went back to a village a year later, more bombs would have been found. On average, the two roving teams were destroying 3000 items of general ordnance and 1500 bomblets or 'bombies' per year. The roving teams needed the expatriate supervisors, as it was important to accurately identify an item to determine if it could be safely moved or had to be destroyed in-situ.

The two clearance teams each contained 20 people and they were used to check specific areas of ground if some sort of digging or construction work was to be undertaken. These teams generally worked under a trained Lao supervisor, and unlike in Afghanistan, MAG was starting to recruit women to work as deminers. The site to be cleared was marked out with tape and then standard metal detectors were used to systematically check the area. Big air-dropped bombs that had failed to go off could possibly have penetrated the ground for several metres, so MAG also had some special deep search instruments for these tasks.

When Don took me to a clearance site people were walking all over the area marked with yellow safety tape. When I questioned him about this, he said it was not a minefield: 'We are looking for bombs that have not gone off and it's safe to walk over the ground. The tape is just there to show the extent of the area that has been checked.' This took a bit of getting used to after the strict minefield discipline of not straying outside a marked lane.

MAG also had another innovative program called 'community liaison', where they delivered safety messages to the local population, but also engaged with them in identifying the location of bombs and establishing their local priorities and needs. This involved both men and women, and was a vital part of their work in getting acceptance and cooperation.

One problem the community liaison teams tried to address was the question of the illegal scrap metal trade. Buyers from Vietnam would come into the country to buy scrap metal. As a result, some poor Lao villagers would go out deliberately looking for bombs and not report them. They would then try to crack the bombs open to get out the explosives for fishing and the metal shell casings to sell – often with disastrous consequences.

One good story that was often told is that the community liaison team went to a village and asked if they had any bombs. No, the people replied, the Vietnamese scrap metal dealer took them all last week. They went to another village and were told the same story. At the next village the team said to the people, 'I guess the Vietnamese scrap metal dealer got all your bombs?' 'No,' they replied, 'he is buried over there!'

Planning a national UXO program

After the field trip I was slightly more convinced about the problem of UXO in Laos and was starting to formulate a plan in my mind how to respond. Normally, to develop a project in the United Nations you would have an endless round of consultations and hold workshops with government partners, stakeholders, community groups and other interested parties. However, I could already see that government departments just followed the party line and there were very few 'partners' to talk to anyway. After my time in Afghanistan I felt that I knew what had to be done, so I decided to draft a plan first and then consult afterwards.

The Prime Minister of Laos had issued a decree in February 1995 authorising the creation of a steering committee to oversee a national UXO program. The decree was well written and nominated the Vice-Minister of Labour and Social Welfare to be the chairman of the steering committee and authorised the establishment of a national UXO program. The program would have the responsibility of coordinating all UXO-related work in the country. Also, with the help of UNDP and

UNICEF, the joint Trust Fund was established with the government which was to be used as the way to manage any funds raised.

With these two government decisions as a basis, I outlined a very simple plan. The aim was to reduce the number of civilian UXO casualties, and to increase the amount of safe land available for agricultural production and other development activities. I believed we needed to undertake a national survey to determine exactly which provinces and districts were affected by UXO. In addition, we had to establish a safety awareness campaign, strengthen our office and set up a database, establish a training centre to train Lao deminers, and then start clearance operations in other provinces. This would all be done on a phased basis as money became available.

I liked the model MAG had developed in Xieng Khouang with community liaison, roving teams and clearance teams, and thought we should replicate that in other provinces. To do that, we needed to identify some other technical partner organisations like MAG to come in and supervise work, until the Lao were able to do it themselves. I often described it as setting up something like a national fire brigade, except in this case the teams throughout the country would be responding to bombs, and not fires. This was a different model to the one we developed in Afghanistan, where the United Nations coordinated the work of the Afghan demining organisations, but here in Laos I could clearly see that nothing was going to get approved unless it was controlled by the government. In the draft plan, I set deadlines and targets to be achieved and estimated the cost for all the activities. We had about US$2.5 million in pledges in the Trust Fund and I calculated we needed about another US$2 million to do what I proposed in 1996.

The Prime Minister's decree had said that the new UXO program should coordinate all bomb clearance related work in the country. However, I advised Mr Saykham that we should avoid trying to get involved with anything the Lao Army may be doing at present. The Lao Army was highly secretive, so it was unlikely that we would get any cooperation from them, and in any case, most donor countries would not allow humanitarian funds to be used by military authorities.

There was also one Australian commercial bomb clearance company working in Laos, called Milsearch. They had a contract to check areas in advance of gold prospecting teams. Again, I advised Mr Saykham that until we were well established, we should not try to regulate commercial operators. On the technical side, I did not see a need for dogs or machines in Laos. All the bombs we were looking for were full of metal, so finding them using just metal detectors was not a problem. Given the hilly terrain, jungle vegetation and the nature of the UXO contamination in Laos, demining machines would be totally unsuitable.

One of the key elements of the plan was getting support from the United States. The US Ambassador was a seasoned diplomat name Victor Thomseth, who had been one of the diplomats held captive in the US Embassy in Tehran in the early 1980s. I told him that I had driven past the embassy during my visits to Tehran, which gave me some understanding of his plight. Victor was fully supportive of trying to get US involvement, but the Lao were making it difficult. The Lao refused an offer of US troops to come in and assist with UXO clearance. They also demanded that the US hand over all bombing records. The US had another program underway in Laos looking for the remains of US service personnel still listed as 'Missing in Action' and they were keen for this to continue.

Some limited UXO disposal work had been done in connection with this Missing in Action work. A number of draft documents had been developed by the US outlining various proposals to provide support, but these got nowhere. The US assigned Master Sergeant Mike Smith to work on the issue. I found this rather curious, because although he was a great guy and a qualified bomb disposal technician, he was way out of his comfort zone in dealing with senior government officials. As my plan was taking shape, we were starting to get a general sense that the Lao side would allow the US to send in some specialists to set up and run a training centre, plus assist with an awareness campaign.

Seeing the Cambodian program in action

I still had a feeling that my advice was not resonating with Mr Noy and Mr Saykham, or any of the other Lao officials involved. I spoke with Jan Mattsson at UNDP and got his approval to fund a study tour to Cambodia, in order to show the Lao side how that program was organised. I was also personally keen to go to Cambodia as I had never been there before. Aside from Afghanistan, it was the second longest running and next biggest mine clearance program in the world. Even though all the mine clearance programs at that time, like Cambodia, Mozambique and Angola, were receiving some form of United Nations support, each had been set up independently and in isolation from each other. I made all the arrangements and off we went to Phnom Penh, the capital of Cambodia.

The mine clearance program in Cambodia had been named the Cambodian Mine Action Centre or CMAC. The words 'mine action' did not mean anything in particular, but they conveyed a positive sense of taking action against landmines, and it was gaining common use around the world. Terms like 'demining' or 'humanitarian demining' were seen as being limited to just the actual clearance of mines, whereas the sector now included safety awareness and community liaison, surveys, training and the clearance of landmines and unexploded ordnance.

The Cambodian mine clearance program had been heavily influenced in its establishment by Canadian military advisers, and it had a much more military feel to it than the Afghan program. They called their teams 'platoons', wore uniforms, held parades, saluted people and so on. However, I was not there to judge them and I had learnt not to criticise actions when you were not involved, because you never knew what pressures and influences people were under at the time of doing things.

CMAC had arranged a comprehensive itinerary for our visit, and we were briefed at their headquarters in Phnom Penh by the director, a Cambodian national named Sam Sotha. We also visited the CMAC training centre, and visited clearance operations in the provinces of Kampot in the south and Siem Reap in the north. Thankfully, the penny finally dropped with my Lao colleagues – now they could see with their own eyes what I was proposing for Laos. They saw a Cambodian national program, being run by a Cambodian official through a network of provincial offices, and with Cambodians undertaking all the mine clearance tasks. There was still a very heavy presence of international military advisers, but there were plans to scale this down. In addition, there were a number of international NGOs working throughout the country. Unlike Afghanistan, one aspect about any visit to Cambodia is tragically the number of limbless landmine victims that you see on the streets. Because of the hot weather everyone wears shorts and t-shirts and amputees are painfully obvious.

The Cambodian officials were very formal and treated the visit of a Lao vice-minister with some importance. We were always well received at a high level and we were invited to a number of official dinners. I suggested rather firmly to Mr Noy that to complete the picture we should visit the offices of MAG and HALO Trust in Phnom Penh. At HALO we met with Tim Porter, who I knew from Afghanistan and got on fairly well with. Tim was dressed rather casually in shorts and T-shirt and spent half the meeting with his bare feet up on his desk. As we left Mr Noy rather tersely said to me, 'Why did you bring me to meet that rude man?'

From my side, I picked up on a few points of interest. The Cambodians lacked good survey data on the location of minefields. All they had were maps produced during the UNTAC peacekeeping period, with large circles drawn on them saying 'suspected mined areas'. CMAC clearance teams were tasked with clearing these areas and would spend weeks finding nothing. Clearly, they needed survey teams to be able to better identify mined areas. On the clearance side, in Siem Reap province there were three clearance operators working in the one province – CMAC, MAG and HALO Trust. This had come about because back in 1992 there was no strong central government, and the NGO operators had basically chosen where they were going to work themselves. To me this clearly led to some duplication of effort, and possibly other mine affected provinces missing out on clearance capacity. I was determined that in Laos we should only have one outside technical organisation per province to assist the Lao. As we were starting out in Laos with a national plan in place and had strong government control, I was confident that we could invite foreign organisations to work in Laos when and where we needed them.

UXO Lao: Establishing rules and standard procedures

After the visit to Cambodia, the program back in Laos started to gather some momentum. After months of enquiring about the progress of the Memorandum of Agreement with the Americans, Mr Saykham just walked in one day in late March and said that it had been signed. I was thrilled, as it finally meant we could get some activities started. By now we had about 10 people in the office, so I said, 'Let's all go for lunch to celebrate.'

We went to a reasonable Lao restaurant and had a pleasant lunch. When the bill came I looked and said that should be about 20,000 kip each – about $6. No-one made any move to get money. I looked at Jenni and she looked at me, and it became apparent the Lao were not expecting or intending to pay. She and I managed to settle the bill between us. I had been so used to the Afghan tradition of hospitality I had overlooked that for people in Laos, on a salary of $100 a month, $6 for lunch is a lot. It always annoyed me, though, that Saykham would never say anything in advance to help explain or clarify a local situation.

Another incident also highlighted the difference between Afghanistan and Laos, and caused some friction with Mr Saykham. When I was coming to Laos I made sure in my contract that I would be provided with a work vehicle. This was standard in Afghan projects and there were white four-wheel drive vehicles everywhere. After I had been in Laos for about one month, my brand new white Toyota Landcruiser arrived. It rather stood out in the Ministry building car park, where all the other vehicles were old government cars. I made it clear to Saykham that the vehicle was for general office use during the day, but he did not look happy.

Normally a project vehicle would get United Nations number plates, which I was keen on, as it gave me some diplomatic cover. Saykham insisted that the vehicle have government number plates, because when the project was over the vehicle should be given to the government. There was a stand-off for about three months where I had temporary plates on the car. In the end, the United Nations gave in and the vehicle got Lao government plates issued. The only silver lining was that in the United Nations system, if you use your work car for private use you have to pay a mileage charge. There was no such system in the Lao government and all those officials who had government cars regularly used them for private travel – so I did the same.

Now that we had a vehicle, Saykham and I started to look around for a site for the training centre we wanted to establish. Like Afghanistan and Cambodia, I had recommended that we set up a central training school for the whole country. This ensured that everyone was trained to the same standard and it was easier to manage. It also suited the Lao as they did not want the US instructors, who were coming to conduct the training, to travel out to the provinces. We looked at some dreadful buildings and compounds that would require substantial time and money to refurbish. Then we heard about an agricultural training centre located near a village called Nam Souang, about one hour north of Vientiane that may be available.

When we got there I could see that it was perfect. There was an administration block, classrooms, barrack rooms for students and five houses where the Americans could live. There was also plenty of land around to conduct UXO clearance training and set off explosives. The whole set-up was typical of many aid projects – it was built and then rarely used. The Ministry of Agriculture, who owned the training centre, said they only needed it for a couple of weeks a year and we could rent it for the rest of the time. That was the first element of the plan in place.

The next step was to set up a national survey, to try to establish the true extent of UXO contamination throughout the country. Mr Saykham said that our host, the Ministry of Labour and Social Welfare, had offices throughout the country and we could do the survey through them.

I disagreed with him and said, 'We could certainly draw on these offices for help, but it will be much better to use an external organisation to do the project. This way we can hold them to a deadline, and also write into the project that they have to establish a database unit in our office once the survey is complete.'

In the end he agreed and terms of reference were developed for the survey. The sum of US$400,000 was earmarked in the Trust

Fund to cover the cost of the first national UXO survey ever to be undertaken in Laos.

We could have asked MAG to undertake the survey, but I was keen to get another organisation into the country. Many people on the Lao side still saw MAG as the only element of the program, and MAG, with their 'can-do' approach to getting on with the job, often drew criticism from the government if anything went wrong. I felt that having another external group in town it would give some balance to the program. We invited a number of international NGOs to bid and as it was going to be under a United Nations contract, I arranged a bid assessment meeting to be held at the UNDP offices. Mr Noy came to chair the meeting and after due consideration Handicap International, or HI was selected. Handicap International was a French/Belgian organisation that was originally established to help landmine victims, but now was branching out into other aspects of mine action. As Mr Noy spoke fluent French, he was happy with the outcome and it added a new dimension to the program.

Our office continued to grow and we were allocated more space within the Ministry building. Part of the US support agreement was to provide assistance with developing a UXO safety awareness campaign. A small US army team, with the inappropriate name of the Psychological Warfare Unit arrived, headed by a captain. Their knowledge of how to develop a public safety campaign was limited, but they brought lots of equipment with them, which was the main benefit. We got computers, printers, plotters and screen printing equipment. We had also asked the Australian Government if they could send a bomb disposal expert to be the technical adviser to the program. They declined, but then New Zealand offered two officers on secondment – a major to advise on logistics and a captain who was a bomb disposal expert. By now we occupied about one-third of the Ministry building and had 10 computers. By comparison, the rest of the Ministry had just three computers.

As a lot was happening, I suggested to Mr Saykham that we hold monthly meetings with all our partners. He was not very comfortable with that idea, as the Lao normally sort things out privately and then a meeting is just a formal way of announcing the result. Dealing with all these foreigners would be unpredictable for him, and he didn't want to be put on the spot. We compromised by agreeing that he would chair more formal policy type meetings and I would chair 'technical working groups'. These working groups would involve the Lao staff as well as the international organisations. As a result of these meetings I would regularly draft correspondence for Saykham, but it would often just sit on his desk. He wouldn't sign it because he didn't want to make a mistake, or he felt it was outside his job description. Out of frustration, I said, 'How about we send the letters out unsigned, but marked as a draft?' He agreed, so I bought a big red stamp with the word 'Draft' on it and many documents went out of the office in this way. I would later telephone the foreigners and say that the letter is marked draft, but act on it anyway.

Other meetings had interesting cross-cultural outcomes. Our official title in the Prime Minister's decree was the Lao National Unexploded Ordnance Program. This was quite a mouthful, so we discussed a shorter title. Saykham liked Lao Mine Action Centre, or LMAC, based on what he had seen in Cambodia.

I said to him, 'We're mainly dealing with UXO so it could be confusing. Also, the US is going to be one of our major donors, but they're not backing the call to ban anti-personnel landmines'.

The US had made it clear that they could only fund or support activities in Laos related to clearing US ordnance from the Vietnam War period. Someone then thought of the name the Lao UXO program, or LUXO. The foreigners laughed, because I said Lux was a brand of soap, and we may not look too serious to the outside world with a name like that. I then had a thought. The local beer was called Beer Lao – why not turn the name around like that and call the program 'UXO Lao'. This was quickly agreed on.

I next suggested that we design a logo to put on our documents and also so that every staff member or organisation could wear it as a badge, to show that they were part of the national program – like we had done in Afghanistan. We had a local graphic artist produce some designs. The Lao flag has two horizontal red stripes – one at the top and one at the bottom of the flag and in between them there is a wider blue stripe. On this blue stripe there is a white circle. I suggested to the designer to turn this white circle into a stylised image of a bombie. Saykham said 'no'. I asked why but he just kept saying no. I later found out there was a law saying you couldn't alter the Lao flag, but why Saykham didn't just say this was beyond me. Anyway, we got three designs and the committee agreed on design number one and sent it to the Minister for approval. A note came back from the Minister saying he preferred design number two. I said to Mr Saykham, 'Are you going to see the Minister and tell him that the committee chose design number one'? A look of terror came across his face as if I were mad. The program duly adopted design number two as its logo!

We also spent some time on terminology, as I was keen to translate all our documents and letters into Lao language. We started to develop a Glossary of Technical Terms and set about getting agreed meanings and translations for them. A classic bad example was that one early translation used by MAG for the term 'UXO clearance' came out in Lao language like 'bomb gatherer' or 'bomb collector'. Not surprisingly, they had very few applicants for jobs until it was changed. At these terminology meetings we had an Australian, a New Zealander, a Scotsman, an American and two Brits – all allegedly speaking English. It must have been difficult enough for the translators to understand our accents, let alone describe the technical terms. It was in situations like this where our program officer, Jenni Rauch, was invaluable.

Jenni had a good understanding of the technical issues and with her Lao language skills was able to guide the translators in selecting the best words or phrases. One word that caused some issues was what to call our workers. I was keen to use the term 'deminer' to describe the people who cleared the bombs, as this was the most common, generic term in use around the world. MAG wanted to use 'technician', as this term was from the military and implied a higher level of training. We argued back and forth for about 10 minutes and then asked the translator what he thought. He smiled and said that they used the same Lao word for both titles.

While we were working hard in Laos to set up the program and establish rules of procedure and develop standard procedures, similar moves were being made at the international level. In June 1996 the

Government of Denmark, in conjunction with the United Nations, initiated and hosted a meeting with the aim of formulating a set of international standards for mine action. I convinced Saykham that this would be a valuable meeting for us to attend. He reluctantly agreed so we both set off to Copenhagen. The meeting brought together an interesting range of people from many different mine affected countries and a series of workshops were held discussing a range of topics – although Saykham did not say one word during the whole conference.

The result of the meeting was that the United Nations subsequently issued a set of International Standards for Humanitarian Mine Clearance Operations covering topics like safety, training, survey, minefield marking and clearance, medical and information management. The standards were not particularly useful in their original form, but they provided a good basis for future refinement and the development of more comprehensive standards some years later.

Reconnoitring in the provinces

By mid-year Mr Noy had approved the *UXO Lao National Workplan – 1996* that I had written some months earlier. We had it translated into Lao and printed in a dual-language booklet form. The document was then widely circulated among Lao government ministries and also to donors and other interested organisations. The foreigners who had been in Laos for a long time felt that my plan was too ambitious. However, I was getting more confident that we could achieve most of what we were setting out to do. The timetable I had set was slipping slightly, but overall we were on track.

I had also managed to get in some more trips to the provinces to try to build up my own picture of where the priorities lay. I went on one visit to the town of Sam Neua in Houaphan Province in the north of the country with Grant Curtis, a Canadian who was responsible for the project within UNDP. Travel to the north was often uncomfortable due to frequent bad weather and the fact that Lao Aviation used small, propeller-driven planes. Sam Neua was extremely remote with not much infrastructure. It had been the home of the Pathet Lao during the war and many of the current government ministers and party leaders came from the region. As a result, it had been bombed heavily and there was evidence of UXO in and around the town. Setting up a clearance operation in Houaphan Province was going to be difficult, though, due to the isolation and logistic difficulties.

Another trip I did was down south to Savannakhet with Mr Saykham. We drove for this trip and on the way we stopped at a village where some UXO had been reported. The village was actually a resettlement camp for people who had fled to Thailand during the war and a place where if they came back were offered land. Very few Lao people actually did return from Thailand. The reported UXO were just two M79 rifle grenades that had not been fired. I placed them in a hole under a tree for later disposal and marked the spot.

As we were leaving I said to Saykham, 'I think this is an isolated case. It is a pretty lousy piece of ground with no tactical significance and there is no evidence of any fighting having taken place here. We don't need to deploy any demining teams to the area. I'll arrange a roving team to come by and blow up the two grenades.'

We pushed on to Savannakhet where we met with the governor of the province. As Savannakhet province is one of the main crossing points into Vietnam and is adjacent to the 17th parallel which marked the border between North and South Vietnam, it had seen heavy fighting. After Mr Saykham explained the purpose of our visit, the governor said he wanted UXO Lao to buy him two bulldozers to do UXO clearance work. He said the bulldozers could push the dirt up in front and then people could pick out the bombies. Saykham didn't answer, so I said that I didn't think it was a good idea.

I politely said to the governor, 'The machines are very expensive and if we bought a couple of them it would use up our entire budget.' I continued on: 'From what I had heard in other countries where they tried this method, the results were not very good. The other problem is that if the area in front of the bulldozer is not thoroughly checked with a metal detector first and then the machine hits a big bomb, the bulldozer would be destroyed.'

I later learnt that the governor's brother owned a road building company, so it wasn't hard to guess what had motivated his request.

In Savannakhet we met up with US Master Sergeant Mike Smith, who had rented a helicopter so we could see more of the border area with Vietnam in a short time. Flying over the jungle along the Vietnamese border in a helicopter certainly evoked memories of the TV images that came out of the Vietnam War. We landed at an extremely remote village where it had been reported that the local people were suffering from the effects of the defoliant used during the war, named Agent Orange.

The huts in the village were of very basic construction and the people didn't appear to be in the best of health. There were large bomb craters filled with muddy water all throughout the village area. Agent Orange had reportedly been sprayed during the war (to kill the foliage in an attempt to deny the Viet Cong cover) and the people now claimed the ground water and the water in the craters were contaminated. The UXO Lao program did not have a mandate or the expertise to deal with Agent Orange but there certainly were people with deformities and birth defects in the group that we saw.

Our next stop was at one of the camps set up by the Missing in Action group, searching for the remains of US service personnel. The camp was in the middle of nowhere and consisted of 20 bright orange tents laid out in neat rows. This project team would search the records about US aircraft that had been shot down in the war, try to locate them and then search for any human remains. The project team consisted of anthropologists, archaeologists, military personnel and other support staff – including some explosive ordnance disposal staff. It was an amazing effort that was costing millions of dollars. I had mixed feelings about what I was seeing. As an ex-serviceman, I would have been pleased to know that my country was still interested in finding me long after a war had ended, but the cost of finding perhaps nothing more than just a tooth seemed very high. Being a US military 'base' the camp was alcohol free. However, the civilian helicopter crews supporting the project were New Zealanders and they had roped off their own 'base' so I went and joined them for a few beers. The next day we flew over some more battle sites and then back to Savannakhet town.

Getting Gunter and Gerbera on board

The last piece of my plan to put into place was to identify another UXO clearance organisation to start work in a new province. I felt that Savannakhet would be the next most affected province, but Saykham was adamant that it should be Houaphan province in the north. While we had some money left in the Trust Fund it was not enough to fund a new clearance operator. I had been in contact with donor embassies in Vientiane and Bangkok but was not getting much response. I visited the German embassy in Vientiane, but they told me there were no funds for Laos. I decided to contact my good friend Gunter Mulack in Berlin, and invited him to come to Laos and at least have a look at what we were trying to do. Gunter obliged and arranged to visit in mid-1996. I set up the usual meetings with Lao government officials and also organised a field visit to Xieng Khouang to see MAG at work. I then threw in a trip to the historic city of Luang Prabang just for good measure.

It was great to catch up with Gunter again and we shared many a story about our Afghan experiences over a Beer Lao, sitting at the Sunset Bar on the banks of the Mekong.

The meetings with government officials in Vientiane all went well and then we headed off to Phonsavan, in Xieng Khouang province, to see MAG's work. My wife Margaret also decided to come with us as she got on well with Gunter and she had not been to any of the provinces at that time. The MAG director, Ben Lark, had gone ahead and met us at the airport and provided the usual briefing back at the MAG office.

Later we went to visit the famous 'Plain of Jars' a few kilometres outside Phonsavan. The Plain of Jars contains huge stone jars which are scattered about in groups over a dozen different sites. The jars have been fashioned from solid rock and there are hundreds of them in varying sizes, with the biggest ones being almost two metres tall. The origin of the jars and their use is not fully known, with some theories suggesting they are over 2000 years old and that they were used for burial purposes, or for fermenting rice wine. During the war the *Plains Des Jars* as it was termed in French, or PDJ as it was nicknamed by the military, was a common navigational reference point for bomber aircraft on their way to Vietnam. After flying a mission to Vietnam, US planes were not allowed to land back in Thailand with any bombs on board. If a mission had been 'unsuccessful' and they could not find a target, the PDJ was a designated area where the planes could dump a load of bombs when returning to base.

It was arranged that the next day we would go out and visit a MAG roving team and a clearance team. We also included a visit to an infamous cave at Tham Piu, where hundreds of Lao had sheltered during the war, but were killed when an air delivered rocket attack made a direct hit on the cave entrance. There was little to see except a dark, blackened cave. The roving team visit went well and we saw lots of bombies on the ground which the roving team had decided to destroy in-situ. We then drove past a few villages to a site where a clearance team was working. It was about 2.30pm when we got there and the British supervisor announced that they had finished work for the day. I was annoyed given we had come to see the team at work, but he said that it was their policy that they stop work then, as it was the cut-off time if there was an accident for a helicopter to come from Vientiane, collect the casualty and return. I asked if MAG had a standing contract with the helicopter company, but they did not. I put this at the back of my mind to think about later.

We chatted with the team and then headed back towards Phonsavan. As we passed back through one of the small villages some local people flagged us down and the interpreter explained it appeared that there had been an accident. Ben went into a house and then the people motioned for Gunter and me to go in as well. Inside the hut, lying on bed was a boy about 10 years old, who was clearly dead. The people explained that he had been cutting bamboo with a machete and had hit a bombie, which exploded. The dead boy only had a few fragment wounds on his forehead and part of his upper arm had been blown away. There was a tin plate at the end of the bed where other villagers had placed some money for the family. I only had about $10 in local money on me so I placed it on the plate, feeling extremely frustrated that it was all I could contribute to honour a boy's life.

The incident naturally had an impact on all of us. An hour before when we drove through the village the boy had been alive. Now he was dead – killed by a weapon dropped 30 years ago in a war he knew nothing about, and probably of which his parents only had a vague memory. He was killed doing something he did every day without knowing the hazards that were waiting for him. This was not right. His death certainly changed my view that we were only dealing with some sort of benign problem and it added some urgency to getting on with the job. It also raised questions in my mind – had these people received any awareness training to understand the dangers of UXO? Also, as the boy would most likely be buried in the village that same day, was his death recorded anywhere? It made me think – how many untold stories of people being killed by UXO were occurring throughout the country? The need for the national survey to find this out was more necessary than ever.

The next day we finished up our visit to Xieng Khouang and then headed to Luang Prabang, which had been the ancient royal capital of Laos. Luang Prabang is World Heritage listed and was absolutely beautiful and charming. Old French colonial villas and numerous Buddhist *wats* were dotted along the tree-lined streets overlooking the river. We met some local officials who said that there had been reports of some bombs in the province, but there were none in the town.

Having seen the extent of the UXO contamination, Gunter was convinced that there was a need for support in Laos and all the stars seemed to align for me. After the reunification of Germany there were efforts underway to provide employment and incentives for companies from the former East Germany. Once such group, called Gerbera, had formed an explosive ordnance company and Gunter was looking for a project where he could fund them. Maybe they could come to Laos and oversee the clearance set-up in one of the provinces. The Lao were delighted with the idea. Being a former communist country, many Lao had studied in East Germany and they were comfortable with the idea of Gerbera coming to work in Laos. Privately, I asked Gunter for a big favour – would he include the purchase of a vehicle for Mr Saykham in the project funding if German support to UXO Lao were to be approved.

Settling in with Madame Sin

Throughout this period Margaret and I were settling into life in Vientiane. At the house we had kept on a delightful Lao woman named Sin as our housekeeper. The first time the phone rang she answered 'Mansfield residence, Madam Sin speaking'. We smiled to ourselves and explained to her that 'Madam Sin' may have some negative connotations to other Westerners, so perhaps just say hello. Unlike our staff in Pakistan, Sin was entirely trustworthy. We would give her the housekeeping money at the start of the month and she would look after everything. Despite Laos being a predominately Buddhist country Sin was a Christian; there were some small pockets in the country where the Catholic Church had gained a foothold during French colonial times.

One difference to some other cities in developing countries was that Vientiane did not have any particular suburb or area where all the foreigners lived. They just lived in houses dotted throughout the town. We lived on the edge of some rice paddy fields and early each morning small groups of saffron robed Buddhist monks would walk slowly by with their food bowls, receiving gifts of food from the local people. There were no house numbers or street names, so any invitation for a function was always accompanied by a map. There was no mail delivery and you had to go to the post office to collect mail. This small act highlighted one of the immense changes occurring in Laos. When you went to the post office you had to open all parcels, and if it was a book or video they were examined and you had to explain what they were about. At the same time we got permission to install a TV satellite dish and with the flick of a switch, we were getting unregulated 'foreign propaganda' from hundreds of channels. Although it was technically illegal, most Lao people in Vientiane watched Thai television and had Thai mobile phones.

On a personal level we were missing Zoe and Charles who were away at boarding school. They had settled in well and we telephoned them regularly. The school term was usually eight to ten weeks long and then they would fly up to us for holidays. The flights went from Canberra to Sydney to Bangkok where they had to overnight. We would arrange for them to stay the night in a transit room at Bangkok airport and then fly on to Laos the next day – quite an adventure for a 17-year-old and 15-year-old.

CHAPTER 11:

INITIATING A NATIONAL PLAN IN LAOS

By July 1996 we had been in Laos for six months and my visa had expired. I had submitted the request for an extension but there had been no progress. I mentioned this in passing to the head of UNDP, Jan Mattsson, and he raised it during a regular meeting he had with the Lao Foreign Minister. My visa was promptly renewed for nine months, through to 31 March 1997. Mr Saykham seemed surprised and somewhat annoyed when I told him about this, and he said next time I should go through the 'proper channels'.

Within the UNDP system there were a number of different ways that projects could be implemented. UNDP could undertake projects themselves with their own staff, or they could engage an NGO or a company to do the work. The third way was called 'national execution' and in this case the host government (usually through a relevant ministry) was responsible for implementing the project and achieving its targets. The United Nations could still provide technical advisers and buy equipment, but all activities required the agreement of the government. In the case of the national UXO program in Laos, the project had been set up in this latter way as 'national execution' through the Ministry of Labour and Social Welfare.

In principle, this approach was very good as the host government had to take ownership of the project and be committed to it. For the UXO problem in Laos this was exactly the way it should be. From the United Nations side, they were seen as trusting the government and helping with building national capacity. However, the effect on me was that everything to do with the program had to be cleared by the government, including the project budget, contract extensions, visas, travel requests and so on. The United Nations salary rates are published and even though I was on a standard United Nations employment contract, my salary figure in a budget always stood out, especially to the Lao counterparts who were earning much less.

Across all sectors and different projects you always heard the complaint from government officials that foreigners were too expensive and that the locals could do the job themselves. The counter to this, of course, was if the locals could do it, why hadn't they done so already? I also believed with my experience I was saving money by not making expensive mistakes, and although it was never stated openly, most donors were happy that there was some involvement of international staff in the projects they were funding.

The Trust Fund that had been set up was a joint UNDP–government arrangement. UNDP undertook the financial management of the fund, such as accounting and auditing, but the release of money required agreement from both parties. At that time the Mines Advisory Group raised their own funds from donor governments and other private sources. I suggested to Mr Saykham that we should encourage the donors to MAG to put the funds through the Trust Fund, and then we would engage MAG.

I tried to convince Mr Saykham by saying, 'From my experience, if you control the flow of the money, then you are able to exert more control over the recipient than you can if you are just a coordinating body.'

Saykham said 'no'. He said, 'The Trust Fund was only set up to fund Lao activities and MAG should get their own money.' No amount of persuasion would make him change his mind.

It was around this time that I decided in my own mind that I was here to give advice and I would do that openly and honestly. If the Lao chose not to accept my suggestions then so be it, as there were many underlying political and cultural issues I did not understand. The UXO problem was theirs to solve and I would be long gone before it was cleaned up. I decided I would only take a stand on three issues: corruption, safety or any attacks on my personal integrity.

NAVIGATING CULTURAL LANDMINES

A useful little book had been produced by UNDP called *Working with your Lao Partner*. I read it and nearly everything it said mirrored my own experience so far.

One piece of advice went like this: 'As a foreigner with years of training and experience you may arrive in the Lao PDR confident in your abilities and determined to pass them on to your new colleagues. However, if you are sensitive to your new environment, and take the time to observe and learn, you will discover that no expertise, regardless of how well it worked at home, can be transferred unaltered in a new cultural environment.' I understood that.

The book also went on to say: 'Officially, Westerners are perceived as a possible threat, a potential source of "spiritual pollution" leading to moral decadence. This attitude sometimes restricts contact between Lao people and foreigners. Understand that there may be official constraints and limitations for senior government officials which may limit your relationship with these individuals.' I was certainly encountering this with Mr Noy and Mr Saykham.

Other aspects outlined in the book covered the influence of Buddhism and its precept of acceptance of things as they are – why would you wish to try to change the inevitable? One popular Lao expression that came from this attitude was 'bo pen yang', which meant 'no problem' or 'never mind', and this was often heard during meetings or discussions. In the Lao work environment, bureaucratic organisations were very hierarchical and authority was not delegated. Directions from superiors were never questioned. Decisions may be made and agreed to, but your partner may take no action to implement them. A common answer by Lao officials would be to say that they were taking a 'step-by-step' approach to things.

The other big issue was not 'losing face' or suffering some embarrassment. One thing I had already discovered was described in the book – 'The Lao may hesitate to put something on paper that may come back to haunt them later'.

Finally, the book cautioned that information will not be volunteered by your counterpart and then gave this wonderful example on communications: 'yes' and 'no' have a variety of meanings. 'Yes' may indicate that the message has been heard and understood, but not necessarily agreed to. 'Yes' may mean 'no' when it is impolite to say 'no' directly. 'No' often means 'yes' when the other person does not want to let on that they know something. It was clear to me that the most difficult aspect of my job was not the technical issues, but negotiating the 'minefield' that was dealing with the Lao Government. So, armed with this knowledge and my own experience so far, we started to implement the national UXO Lao program.

Training kicks off in Nam Souang

The first element of the national plan to be initiated was to start to run courses at the training centre we had rented. The agreement that had been signed with the United States stated that they would provide military instructors to work at the training camp at Nam Souang. The Americans arrived in style. A huge US Air Force C17 Globemaster transport plane landed at Wattay airport, the first US military aircraft to land there since the end of the Vietnam war. The plane brought the team of 10 Special Forces soldiers who would conduct the training, along with boxes full of metal detectors, training aids, demining tool kits, medical stores and other assorted equipment. It also had on board hundreds of kilograms of TNT explosives and thousands of detonators.

The training was going to involve the students becoming qualified in setting up explosive charges next to bombies and setting them off. The Americans were only authorised to use explosives of US origin, so they had brought their own. This had required some difficult negotiation and the Lao military were on hand at the airport to take control of the explosives, and move them to a temporary store at the training camp.

In conjunction with MAG staff and the American instructors we designed a range of training courses, such as a community awareness course, a basic bomb disposal course, a team leader's course and a medic's course. MAG agreed to send some of their senior Lao staff down to help instruct on the courses. It was also agreed that the first

37 students for the basic course would come from Xieng Khouang and then be recruited by MAG when they completed their training.

The training of basic deminers or bomb disposal technicians is relatively straightforward and can normally be taught within four to five weeks. The course we designed for Laos lasted for seven weeks, as it included additional subjects such as first aid, map reading, report writing and the like. One problem that had occurred in many other demining programs around the world was that large numbers of local people were quickly trained, but then had no job to go to. I was determined to make sure that this did not happen in Laos, and that people would only attend a training course when there was a guarantee of employment at the end of it.

I would regularly visit the training centre while the first course was underway. The Lao had appointed a retired military officer as the camp commandant. He was not very effective as he did not speak any English and had no experience in training. He was probably the communist party official assigned to keep an eye on the Americans and the explosives.

On one visit Mr Saykham came as well and a US television crew had been given permission to film the training. During the day when working outside the students normally wore the conical woven straw hats common in South-East Asia. When we arrived the students all were wearing baseball caps.

I said to Mr Saykham, 'I think it would look more authentic if the trainees wore the straw hats for the filming, rather than the American style baseball caps.'

Saykham said 'no'. I asked again but as usual there was no answer or explanation. I am sure that Saykham didn't want the deminers portrayed as 'peasant farmers' but he never said anything.

The US instructors also indicated that one student was not doing very well and he should be failed. Saykham said 'no' – I assumed because this would involve 'loss of face'. This was a bit more serious.

Later when we were on our own I said quite firmly to Mr Saykham, 'We're not going to graduate students who have not passed the course and are potentially unsafe.'

The matter was left unresolved at the time, but fortunately the student was given extra training and eventually passed his exams and field tests, so the issue did not come to a head.

A training course for community awareness instructors was also underway at the same time. This was a smaller group of five men and five women from a number of different provinces. We had been fortunate to get an Australian volunteer named Amanda assigned to the program. Amanda was a journalist by training and specialised in public awareness campaigns. Along with the US Psychological Warfare specialists, she had designed an interesting training package that covered public speaking and the use of other media like video, puppet shows, child-to-child education and songs to get the safety messages across. The students were also trained in interview techniques so that they could get reliable and relevant information from villagers about the presence of UXO and the effect they were having on their lives.

The two courses ended and on 21 August 1996 we held the first graduation ceremony at Nam Souang. We invited a large number of guests and the ambassadors from Australia, Sweden and the US attended, along with representatives from the Netherlands, Norway, New Zealand and the United Kingdom. Jan Mattsson from UNDP was there along with Anne Sutherland, the UNICEF representative. The Lao side was represented by Mr Noy and a number of the members of the national steering committee. The students gave a demonstration of the skills they had been taught and a number of explosions were set off. The medic training was particularly impressive, as the US had provided state of the art training aids and equipment.

At the ceremony one of the students from Xieng Khouang province, Ms Lay, aged 22, spoke on behalf of the students. She said, 'Before attending the course I hated and feared the unexploded bombs while working in the field for our daily sustenance, but now I can face them with confidence. I will return home to find the UXOs and destroy them.' This positive attitude from a young Lao woman was extremely well received and overall the day was very successful. Mr Saykham was happy and we had achieved the first milestone in the program.

After the collapse of the Najibullah regime in April 1992, many Afghan officials from the communist government remained at their posts for some time. Here the former army commander in Herat is briefing Sayed Aqa and me on the location of the minefields surrounding Herat. (Photo: Ian Mansfield)

As the senior United Nations official in Herat during one visit, I was taken to see a mass grave that had been discovered on the outskirts of town. The circumstances surrounding the incident were not clear, but it was believed to have happened before the Soviet invasion. (Photo: Ian Mansfield)

Mines were laid everywhere. This photo shows a deminer pointing to a landmine found in the bottom of a dry irrigation canal near Kandahar. The sediment had to be regularly dug out of the canals, but when they were mined they could not be cleaned, thus the water stopped flowing. (Photo: Ian Mansfield)

On a visit to Kandahar an old man presented me with a bunch of flowers, in gratitude for the deminers clearing his land. This was one of the best gifts I have ever received. Sayed Aqa (left) and Engineer Sattar (both in white) look on. (Photo: Ian Mansfield)

In Kabul, unexploded ordnance was as a much a problem as landmines. Here a deminer points to a mortar round that has landed and failed to explode in the rubble of a building. (Photo: Ian Mansfield)

A huge 'refugee' camp near Jalalabad which was set up by the United Nations for people fleeing the fighting in Kabul in 1992. This whole area had to be quickly checked for unexploded ordnance before the camp could be established. (Photo: Ian Mansfield)

A monthly demining meeting held in Kabul in early 1993. Nearly everyone who was involved with the management of mine clearance in Afghanistan at the time is in this photo. (Photo: Ian Mansfield)

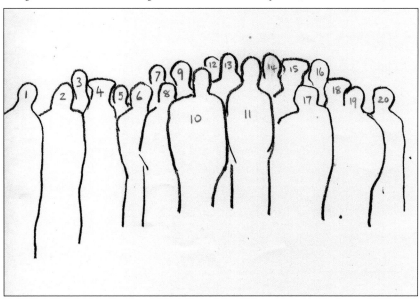

Attendees at a monthly meeting in Kabul 1993. 1. Abdul Samai (DMC) 2. Hamayun Amadi (DMC) 3. Rosadin (MCPA) 4. Haji Zarbat (MDC) 5. Mohammed Younus (MCPA) 6. Graeme Membrey (UNOCHA Kabul) 7. Tim Porter (Country Director HALO Trust) 8. Tariq Zuberi (UNOCHA) 9. Shohab Hakimi (Director MDC) 10. Ian Mansfield (Mine Clearance Program Manager - UNOCHA) 11. Martin Barber (United Nations Humanitarian Coordinator) 12. Unknown 13. Engineer Abdul Sattar (Director DAFA) 14. Fazel Karim (Director OMA) 15. Sayed Aqa (Director MCPA) 16. Mr Peter (ATC) 17. Sakhidad Fayez (Director Afghan Red Cross) 18. Kefayatullah (Director ATC) 19. Ian Bullpitt (UNOCHA Peshawar) 20. Engineer Ismail (MDC)

In March 1995 a relative calm descended on Kabul and large numbers of demining teams were moved into the capital to tackle the huge problem of landmines and unexploded ordnance. Here mine clearance teams from ATC line up on parade before commencing work. (Photo: Ian Mansfield)

A large collection of unexploded ordnance collected by bomb disposal teams from the Mines Advisory Group (MAG) in Laos. The ordnance ranges from large air dropped bombs to artillery shells and mortars, down to hand grenades. The yellow coloured munitions are one type of cluster bomblets. (Photo: Ian Mansfield)

A cluster munition bomb in Xieng Khouang in Laos. These cluster bomb containers held 670 smaller bomblets about the size of a tennis ball, and when dropped from the air they spread out and covered large areas. Many of the bomblets failed to detonate when they hit the ground. (Photo: Ian Mansfield)

The first UXO clearance plan for Laos, which I wrote in 1996. The cover includes the logo for the new UXO LAO organisation and shows a photo of a Lao farmer and his wife pointing out the cluster munition bomblets they had picked up on their land. (Photo: Ian Mansfield)

In early 1996 I flew by helicopter to this remote village in Savannakhet province, close to the Lao-Vietnam border. The village was located on the so-called "Ho Chi Minh trail', made famous during the Vietnam War. The people said that their village had been sprayed by the defoliant Agent Orange during the war. (Photo: Ian Mansfield)

The area around the Plain of Jars in Xieng Khouang province had been bombed heavily during the war. Fortunately most of the stone jars survived, but their origin still remains a mystery. (Photo: Ian Mansfield)

A United States Air Force Globemaster aircraft bringing US instructors, equipment and explosives to help set up the UXO training centre in Laos. This was the first US military aircraft to land in Laos since the end of the Vietnam War. Lined up to receive the aircraft are from left; unknown, Ben Lark (MAG), me (UXO Lao adviser), Mr Saykham (UXO Lao national director), Ambassador Victor Thomseth (USA), Dr Kempet (Lao Ministry of Public Health), Jan Mattsson (UNDP Resident Representative), Jenni Rauch (UXO Lao program officer), Master Sergeant Mike Smith (US army), unknown. (Photo: Ian Mansfield)

Standing outside damaged apartment buildings in Sarajevo in early 1998. All these buildings had to be checked for mines or booby traps before any reconstruction could start. (Photo: Ian Mansfield)

By 1997 a set of international standards had been produced by the United Nations to help regulate the humanitarian demining sector. Procedures for marking minefields, clearing mines and the use of protective equipment, for example, had been agreed. This deminer from Norwegian People Aid in Bosnia is wearing protective clothing and a helmet while working in a well laid out demining site. (Photo: Ian Mansfield)

New procedures had to be developed in places like Bosnia and Angola on how to deal safely and respectfully with human remains found in minefields. (Photo: Copyright Sean Sutton, 1995, Angola)

On 17 August 1997, just weeks before her tragic death, Princess Diana visited the Mine Action Centre in Sarajevo. Her visit was a huge success and her work helped to promote the campaign to ban anti-personnel landmines. (Photo: JJ van der Merwe)

A farewell gift from the office when I left Bosnia – a map of Sarajevo - where the red dots represent minefields in and around the city. (Photo: Ian Mansfield)

Outside the United Nations headquarters in New York. I worked in New York for four years, including at the time of the terrible September 11 attacks on the World Trade Center. (Photo: Ian Mansfield)

I met ex-Beatle Paul McCartney and Heather Mills a number of times in New York and Los Angeles, in connection with the Adopt-A-Minefield program. (Photo: Ian Mansfield)

Each year a major international meeting is held in the context of the Anti-Personnel Mine Ban Convention. Here I am in Bangkok in 2003 with (from left) Liz Bernstein (International Campaign to Ban Landmines), Jody Williams (Nobel Peace Prize winner 1997) and Steve Goose (Human Rights Watch). (Photo: Ian Mansfield)

At Government House in Canberra in September 2010, being made a Member of the Order of Australia by the Governor-General, Dame Quentin Bryce (Photo: Government House)

An abandoned anti-aircraft missile in the suburbs of Baghdad in July 2003, only a few blocks away from the United Nations offices at the Canal Hotel. (Photo: Ian Mansfield)

Meeting Kofi Annan, the former United Nations Secretary-General, in Geneva in 2011. (Photo: Ian Mansfield)

In Jordan, female deminers employed by Norwegian Peoples Aid, prepare their safety equipment before starting mine clearance work on the border between Jordan and Syria in 2011. (Photo: Ian Mansfield)

During World War II huge numbers of mines were laid in Egypt by both sides. Here I am at El Alamein in 2009 standing at the marker near the forward edge of the Axis minefields. (Photo: Ian Mansfield)

Setting up Gerbera in Houaphan

The next step was to start the clearance operations in a second province. The week after the first graduation from the training centre, the German Government announced a package of assistance totalling US$1.3 million for the program. This would be used to fund the former East German company Gerbera to set up the UXO clearance operations in Houaphan Province in the north of the country. The project included the provision of vehicles and equipment, advanced training and the cost of Lao staff salaries and operating costs.

Gerbera arrived with an elderly project manager named Klaus and three ex-army bomb disposal experts. Klaus had been a former East German diplomat who had been posted to Vietnam a number of times. He was happy to be back in the region, although Houaphan was much more isolated than what he had been used to in Hanoi.

We sent Jenni Rauch to the provincial capital Sam Neua to help with the selection of new recruits to undergo training at the training centre. Fortunately, the Lao trusted Jenni and were happy for her to represent UXO Lao and travel without a government minder. Jenni also spoke German, so she was able to assist the Gerbera team by translating from Lao to German. In the middle of the interviews Klaus became seriously ill and a local doctor said he needed to be evacuated immediately. There were only four commercial flights per week to Sam Neua and there was none due that day. A Lao military helicopter arrived but refused to fly Klaus to Vientiane.

Jenni tried calling the commercial helicopter company in Vientiane but they had no aircraft available. After Jenni called Mr Saykham and he questioned the need for an evacuation, she called me in desperation. After convincing Saykham of the seriousness of the situation and much wrangling at the airport, I was able to charter a civilian aircraft to fly to Sam Neua and evacuate Klaus, right on the cut-off time for a flight to get back to Vientiane before dark. Klaus was then transferred to Thailand where he was found to have a bleeding stomach ulcer, which almost certainly would have been fatal had he not been evacuated.

Due to the isolation of Houaphan there were many logistical difficulties in getting Gerbera established. However, within a few months they were set up and had received their newly trained students back from the training camp (and a new, young project manager from Germany) and they started UXO clearance operations. Soon after, Gunter Mulack flew out from Berlin to check on how the project was going.

One of his first tasks in Vientiane was to hand over the keys of a brand new Toyota Landcruiser to Mr Saykham, for his use as National Program Director. I had made sure Saykham got a better model than my vehicle, but also made sure it had a ridiculously large sticker on the side saying 'Donated by the German Government'.

Next we all flew up to Houaphan to see how the Gerbera-supervised teams were going. The visit went well and the UXO clearance work appeared to be being conducted professionally and safely.

During the visit Mr Saykham and I were looking around at different areas when we came across a rather remote spot that contained about 50 large concrete slabs set out in rows. It looked like it may have been a military base or some sort of barracks. I asked Saykham what it had been, but he said nothing and I thought no more of it.

The provincial capital of Sam Neua was in a very mountainous area and many of the valleys contained huge limestone karsts or rock columns. These were dotted with caves and during the war many of the senior Pathet Lao leaders lived in the caves. We saw the cave previously occupied by the head of the communist party and first Prime Minister, Mr Kaysone Phomvihane. It was equipped with concrete blast walls that could be sealed against poison gas attacks. As we drove around, Saykham would point out that one minister had lived in this cave, another minister lived in that cave and so on. It must have been a difficult life living in a cave for nearly nine years, sheltering during the day due to the threat of bombing and then working in the rice fields at night.

The weather turned bad and for two days there were no flights in or out of Houaphan. We finally decided to drive back to Phonsavan (in Xieng Khouang province) and then catch a flight to Vientiane. The distance was only 250 kilometres but the unsealed road was in very poor condition, so we left early as the journey would take all day. It was fascinating to drive through rural Laos and we came across many remote villages with local people living under very basic conditions. Along the road, whenever there was an embankment or a cutting along the side of a hill, we could see lots of small round holes dug into the embankments. The holes were about one metre in diameter and went into the embankment about two metres. I asked what they were and was told that during the war if a road convoy carrying supplies was attacked, the drivers would all jump out of their trucks and take cover in the small holes. It was a low-tech and simple solution to what would have been a big problem. We made Phonsavan that night after a long and slow drive, and were able to fly back to Vientiane the following day.

On my return to Vientiane I called a meeting of one of the technical working groups to discuss medical evacuation arrangements. I recalled the visit to MAG when they said they stopped work in Xieng Khouang at 14.30 hours because that was the last time a helicopter could make it up from Vientiane – yet there were no helicopters in Vientiane. The incident with Klaus also highlighted the difficulties in evacuating casualties from remote provinces.

The cost of hiring helicopters to sit on the tarmac on stand-by was prohibitive, so we had to have a realistic and more flexible system. The evacuation plans we developed were based on each clearance team having their own medic and vehicle. Then, depending on the province, the medevac plan would consist of driving the casualty to the nearest large town or hospital, and then using a commercial flight to Vientiane the next day. If the accident had happened in a border area then taking the casualty into Thailand or Vietnam was also an option. Although not a brilliant plan, it was practical and realistic, and much better than what most Lao villagers would have had access to.

Handicap International starts the survey

The contract to undertake the survey had been finalised with the French/Belgian NGO, Handicap International, and their team started to arrive. The project leader was a French man named Julien Temple. He did not have a military background, but he had experience working in the region and he was very calm and patient in his approach. His

English was very good, which helped us, and he got on well with Mr Noy and Mr Saykham by speaking French with them. Handicap International suffered the normal Lao bureaucratic delays in getting their agreements signed, renting an office and hiring local staff, but eventually they got underway.

Their team included three other foreign staff, including an American, Michael Sheinkman, who was responsible for the database. Michael was what you would call a 'computer geek', but I liked him as he was one of the few highly skilled technical people that I have met who could give a plain language description of what he was doing, or what needed to be done.

The type of survey we were doing has been given many names over the years, but it was basically a general or non-technical survey. It did not involve people with metal detectors searching suspicious areas of land. Rather, it involved gathering information through interviews, research and checking war data. Laos has 18 provinces and after an initial enquiry at the provincial level, it was found that 15 of them had significant problems with UXO.

Handicap International then recruited people from these 15 provinces and trained them in interview techniques and data gathering processes. The interviewers were then sent back home to start gathering information about the presence of UXO in districts and villages, along with determining the types of bombs found and the number of casualties they had caused. Due to the poor roads and infrastructure within the country, it was going to take well over six months to get all the data back, entered into the database and analysed.

Handling delicate staff situations

In September 1996 our kids came to visit during their school term break and we went away for a week's holiday in northern Thailand. When I got back Mr Saykham showed me a letter that had been sent to him by the head of MAG, Ben Lark. The letter raised a number of general points, but at the end Ben complained that MAG had some equipment stuck in customs and that UXO Lao staff had not been helpful in trying to get it released. Saykham was angry as this involved criticism and loss of face. I tried to calm him down and said that this was just the Western way, and it said more about the impatience of Ben than about any perceived failings of UXO Lao. I was also privately annoyed that Ben had not waited until I had returned from holiday, as I would have advised him to take a different course of action.

I pleaded with Mr Saykham, 'Please let me handle this, or at least draft a letter of reply for you,' as I could see that the situation may not end well. Saykham said 'no'.

Subsequently, a letter signed by Mr Noy was sent back to Ben. The letter outlined responses to the various points Ben had raised, but finished with an ominous sentence. I do not remember the exact words but it went something like 'We notice that your visa is due to expire on 30 November and any request for a visa renewal will be given due consideration at that time'. Ben got the message. He had recently married a French woman who worked at UNDP and they were expecting their first child, so at the end of November 1996 Ben left Laos and went to work for UNICEF in Geneva.

Sometime later we had a similar incident in the office. Our community awareness adviser, Amanda, had been provided to us by Australian Volunteers Abroad. Amanda was young and single and after some time in country she had started a relationship with one of the Lao men in the office. This was a fairly unusual situation. There were many Western men who had Lao wives or girlfriends, but I only knew of one other case of a Western woman marrying a Lao man. There almost seemed to be a prejudice amongst the Lao about this type of relationship. It was also a little bit messy in that Amanda was the man's supervisor, and he was also a recent widower with two children. Their relationship was not apparent in the office and Amanda was always extremely professional in her work. However, Jenni let me know that a whispering campaign had started in the office among the Lao against Amanda.

The situation came to head one day when Mr Thongdeng, the head of our administration, came to me with a draft letter and asked if I would check the English. It was addressed to the Australian Embassy and it went along the lines that Amanda was not doing a good job and she was disruptive in the office, and then the letter listed a number of alleged misdeeds she had committed. It concluded by requesting that Amanda be removed. None of the allegations were true, so I thought about it for a minute and then told Mr Thongdeng that there must be a misunderstanding.

I said, 'Australia is one of our largest donors and it would not be a good idea to upset them with an issue like this. Rejecting one of the staff that Australia had provided for free would be an insult.' I also listed the achievements Amanda had made while in charge of the community awareness project. Fortuitously, I had just received a copy of the Australian Volunteers magazine and it featured an article about Amanda. I exaggerated slightly and said that Amanda had just been named 'Australian Volunteer of the Year', so it would look a bit odd if we tried to dismiss her. Mr Thongdeng looked a bit dejected as he had clearly been instructed to get rid of Amanda.

About an hour later Mr Thongdeng came back and quite unashamedly gave me another letter. This one said that Amanda had done an outstanding job, and that because she had trained all her Lao counterparts to such a high level she could now leave, as UXO Lao no longer needed to have a foreign technical adviser. I couldn't believe the complete about face, but obviously for Mr Thongdeng this was a case of the end justifies the means. I had seen this situation coming and I had talked with Amanda about her status a number of times.

Within the broader United Nations system UNICEF had assumed the role of dealing with landmine and UXO safety awareness, so we had approached the local UNICEF office to see if they would be interested in getting more involved with supporting UXO Lao. They were, and it was agreed that Amanda would be reassigned to UNICEF and move to work in their offices. The Lao side were happy with this new arrangement and it worked out much better for Amanda in the long run, as she was hired as an international staff member by UNICEF. Amanda subsequently married her Lao partner and some years later she was posted to the Bangkok office of UNICEF.

Keeping up the clearing momentum

The last part of the plan for 1996 was to start UXO clearance in a third province and this was to be Savannakhet in the south. We selected a local Lao person as the Provincial Coordinator for UXO Lao and decided that we would use Handicap International to be the implementing partner in Savannakhet. Handicap hired an ex-engineer officer from the New Zealand army, Tony West, to be the technical adviser and they then helped establish a small provincial office for UXO Lao. Operations in Savannakhet province were going to be slightly easier due to the fact that you could fly or drive on a good road to the provincial capital, also called Savannakhet. There were more supplies available in town and good medical facilities existed across the Mekong River in the town of Mukdahan in Thailand.

The Lao way was step by step, which we were doing, but they were big steps and coming very quickly by local standards. A nice tension had developed that even Saykham could not stop. The training centre had been established at Nam Souang and we had the US instructors in place to conduct training. There was pressure coming from the Americans to keep the instructors fully occupied, otherwise they may be told by their own authorities to pack up and come home. Saykham certainly did not want to lose face by not having students in the pipeline ready to train. He had no choice other than to go to the provincial authorities and say that everything was ready and they had to hurry up and recruit potential deminers. By the end of the year 20 deminers and eight community awareness staff from Savannakhet had been trained, and another 40 were in the pipeline to be trained in early 1997.

By the end of 1996 I was pleased with myself because we had achieved all of the major targets in the 'ambitious' national UXO plan that I had written 10 months earlier, based on very little knowledge or understanding of the country. We had started community awareness training in Xieng Khouang and Houaphan, started the national UXO survey, established the national training centre and trained a total of 155 students from the three provinces, enhanced MAG's clearance work in

Xieng Khouang, had started operations in Houaphan with Gerbera and were all set to go in Savannakhet.

Also, the national UXO Committee was meeting regularly and functioning well. I was initially disappointed that representatives from other ministries on the committee were at a low level (for example the Lao army sent a captain), but in fact it kept us under the political radar. Because we were not drawing too much attention, activities had kept progressing.

On the all-important money side, we had received US$2.8 million in the Trust Fund and the in-kind contributions totalled US$3.8 million. This latter figure was an estimation of the dollar value of the US contribution, the direct funding by Germany to Gerbera for the Houaphan project and the funding that MAG raised themselves.

All in all a good year's work with solid plans set for 1997. What could possibly go wrong?

Growing global awareness of landmines

At the global level, the campaign against landmines was hotting up. In mid-1996 there had been some meetings at the United Nations in Geneva in the context of the traditional disarmament processes. Some existing conventions recognised the right of countries to self-defence and usually only placed limits on the use of certain weapons. There was already an international convention that restricted the use of landmines, but it did not ban them. For example, the convention stated that emplaced landmines should be mapped and marked, that they should be detectable by containing metal, and that they should be cleaned up after the conflict ends.

The International Campaign to Ban Landmines, headed by Jody Williams, tried to get countries to strengthen this existing convention and change it to a complete ban on anti-personnel landmines. They did not succeed, which frustrated the campaign as well as a number of mid-ranking world powers, notably Norway and Canada. The International Committee of the Red Cross, led by its President Dr Cornelio Sommaruga, also took the unusual and bold step of publicly calling for a total ban on anti-personnel landmines.

An increasing number of international meetings were held by the campaign or hosted by interested countries during the latter part of 1996, trying to drum up support for a total ban on anti-personnel landmines. They were also searching for a way to achieve this. The answer came in December 1996 when Canada hosted a meeting of like-minded states to discuss the matter. Quite unexpectedly, Canadian Foreign Minister Lloyd Axworthy issued a brave challenge on the last day of the meeting, calling on all concerned countries to return to Ottawa in one year's time to sign to sign a convention totally banning anti-personnel landmines. The campaign now had a clear focus and the political and advocacy activities went into high gear.

Unfortunately, I was not able to attend many of the meetings because Mr Saykham would not approve any travel for me out of the Trust Fund. He kept saying that the fund was only for Lao activities, and in any case Laos had no interest in signing the convention. But by now I had a good network of colleagues around the world, so if an important meeting came up I would organise a personal invitation and get UNDP to pay for travel, or arrange sponsorship. Throughout the second half of 1996 and 1997 we had a lot of high level visitors come to Vientiane, many of them trying to convince the Lao to join the call for a ban on landmines. Unfortunately they did not succeed.

From the United Nations perspective, the situation was clearer as the UN General Assembly now held an annual debate on the question of landmines and the Secretary-General, Kofi Annan, had issued a statement supporting the call for a ban. Emboldened by this, one day when I was talking to Mr Noy I said that Laos should consider joining the convention.

I said to him, 'Vice-Minister, from what I understand Laos does not produce anti-personnel landmines, does not appear to have any in stock with the army, and also Laos does not use landmines. As a mine- and UXO-affected country, it would be in your national interests to join this new convention.'

Mr Noy looked at me with disdain and said, 'I make government policy, Mr Ian, not you. Please leave my office.' I left and didn't formally raise the issue again.

STEPPING INTO A MINEFIELD

Quite unrelated to the efforts to ban landmines, the United Nations was becoming increasingly involved in helping countries affected by landmines to set up programs to clear them. By now programs that were supported by the United Nations were underway in countries like Angola, Afghanistan, Bosnia, Cambodia, Mozambique, Somalia and Yemen. However, the UN response was quite ad hoc. At the headquarters level in New York two UN departments oversaw mine action activities – the Department of Humanitarian Affairs and the Department of Peacekeeping. Both departments had appointed focal points – an ex-General from Canada, John McGuiness and a retired British Brigadier, Paddy Blagden – respectively. The Department of Peacekeeping was involved because the mine clearance programs in Angola, Bosnia and Mozambique were part of the peacekeeping missions.

Setting up any sort of program in a war-torn country is difficult and the United Nations was often criticised for delays and slow progress with their mine action work. In response, the Department of Humanitarian Affairs commissioned a four-country study to look at lessons learned and recommend the best way ahead. My old friend Bob Eaton was selected to lead a small team to undertake the study. It was a very comprehensive study and it took many months to complete the field work in Afghanistan, Angola, Cambodia and Mozambique.

A review conference for the draft study was organised to be held in Jalalabad, Afghanistan in December 1996. I arranged for Saykham and me to be invited. I was very keen to get back to Afghanistan to see my former colleagues and I thought it might help Saykham understand my experience and background a little better. We flew to Jalalabad via Pakistan and had a few very productive days interacting with people representing mine action programs from all around the world. I was also very pleased because the study found that the way that Martin Barber and I had set up and run the Afghan demining program was the best 'model', and that the United Nations should adopt this strategy in future programs.

Although the Taliban had taken over most of Afghanistan by this time, the Afghan mine clearance program was still operating effectively and Jalalabad was safe to visit. However, when we got back to Laos, Saykham told some people that I had put his life in danger by taking him there.

Mr Saykham says 'no' — again

On Friday, 4 January 1997 I was at work in my office at the Ministry of Labour and Social Welfare. Late in the afternoon Saykham came by and said rather tersely, 'Meeting with Mr Noy at 9 am tomorrow morning.'

He didn't say what it was about but I guessed it had something to do with my role. The Lao had only agreed to a three-month extension to my employment contract (to bring it in line with my visa expiry on 31 March 1997) and my relationship with Mr Saykham was difficult. I had been quietly complaining to UNDP and other interested parties about his attitude and approach, and he clearly didn't like me. A number of times I had gone to see him, closed the door and tried to discuss issues, but he never opened up. I only wished he would say to me, 'That is a good idea but it won't work here for this reason or that.' He never did, he just said 'no'.

I duly reported to the Ministry at 9 am on Saturday morning. On the Lao side of the table it was Mr Noy, Mr Saykham, Mr Thongdeng, our head of administration, and finally the assistant to the Minister. On my side it was only me. Mr Noy, whose English by now was very good, started by saying that he believed there were some 'misunderstandings' between Mr Saykham and me, and he wanted to review the 'management' of UXO Lao over the last year. He asked if I wanted to say anything, but I said it was more appropriate for Mr Saykham to go first. Saykham opened his notebook and I could see from over the table he had a list of about 15 points. In good Lao fashion he said that I had good points and weak points. The good points were that we had started the program and developed rules of procedures, I had developed the workplan and that UXO Lao had received sufficient funds in 1996. He said that the first five months of 1996 had gone well as a trial period.

Then he started on the 'weak' points. He said that I had given bad advice by saying that we should fund MAG through the Trust Fund. The fund was only for Lao activities, and in any case MAG had raised their own money, so I was wrong.

The second point was that while visiting the Governor of Savannakhet I 'ironically and categorically opposed the governor's views and suggestion for using bulldozers to fill up the bomb craters and clear UXO on the ground'. I had repeatedly said that this type of mechanical clearance has never been successful in the world, leading to unconstructive discussions instead of saying that 'we would further investigate the matter'.

Next he said that when we stopped at the refugee resettlement village to look at the two unexploded grenades, I had criticised the Lao Government by saying 'that refugees were being settled on poor land' (which was not my duty to comment on).

I never lose my temper but by this stage I was fuming inside, not so much by what Saykham was saying, which I thought were silly comments, but by the fact that he was giving precise dates and times for every point. Saykham had obviously been keeping detailed notes on everything I had ever said or done over the past 12 months. I did not interrupt and I did not show any emotion as he kept on going with his list of 'weak points'.

He said I had criticised the Lao Government on the rules and regulations for visas, travel restrictions to provinces and other issues, by saying 'the Lao system is too complicated and centralised and how are you going to get on when you join ASEAN'?

Next, I had criticised Mr Noy when I questioned why he had authorised the Saysomboun special zone to clear their own mines, as I had said this was 'contrary to the UXO regulations'. It seems I had always questioned why documents had to go to the Minister for approval and said instead that the UXO Committee 'should be the highest decision-making body'.

I recall one day I had come to work and asked Saykham to ask Mr Noy to sign something. Saykham replied that Mr Noy had gone away for five weeks. I had said to Saykham that it would be good if we could see Mr Noy's calendar in advance, as this long absence was going to cause lots of delays to the program. According to Mr Saykhams notes I was unhappy and 'demanded to know why I wasn't informed about this'.

Through my system of 'draft letters' I had arranged travel and requests for visas for some of the US personnel without proper authority. I had arranged personal invitations to meetings which was not correct procedure.

Saykham kept on going with some other minor points and then concluded by saying he was responsible to the government for the program, and that he would be the first to be criticised and punished if any mistakes had been made. He finished by saying that he had openly and frankly reported to the meeting, and wished that I would only play my advisory role for the rest of my assignment in Laos, which would end in three months in March.

Mr Noy then asked if I wanted to respond.

I took a deep breath and then replied as calmly as I could. I said, 'I was only informed about this meeting yesterday. As I was not told the purpose of the meeting I had not prepared anything, but it seems Mr Saykham had prepared what to say today. I'm pleased that Mr Saykham has spoken frankly, but I just wish that he had done this sooner to avoid this misunderstanding.'

I stressed that I had not criticised the Lao Government; I had just expressed my personal view to Saykham or given him my honest opinion on matters. I had never challenged Mr Saykham's authority, and I understood that he was the National Director and I was just the adviser. With Saykham's knowledge of government procedures and my knowledge of mine action, I believed that we formed a good team and that we had achieved a lot during the year.

Finally, I said, ' I feel that in order to finish the set-up of UXO Lao in all the affected provinces I will need to stay another year or two.'

Mr Noy concluded by saying that they would write minutes of the meeting and that the matter should be kept internal.

I went home and ranted a bit to Margaret and then called the head of UNDP, Jan Mattsson, at his home. I explained what had happened and he said he would look into it. I turned up at work on Monday and went on as if nothing had happened. True to form Mr Thongdeng came into my office a few days later and said that he had been tasked to write the minutes of the meeting and would I check the English. I thought that this was a bit like asking a convicted criminal to check his own death sentence, but it gave me the chance to alter a few things in my favour. The note obviously did the rounds within the Ministry because I did not get to sign the final version of the minutes until 14 February, almost six weeks later.

By now the UXO Lao office was getting quite large with 21 local staff and six expatriate advisers, so in February we moved from the Ministry building to our own separate premises. The compound was a few blocks away from the Ministry and consisted of a large house and a number of annexes. This seemed to help the office environment and all the Lao staff were more relaxed, and we did not get caught up in Ministry meetings and other distractions. On a personal level, I was getting excellent support from UNDP and a number of the key donors and I was determined not to leave. I do not know what happened behind the scenes, but in March I received a five-month contract and visa extension. With that sorted out, I started to focus on implementing our even more ambitious workplan for 1997.

Daily life in Vientiane

On a personal level life in Vientiane was quiet and fairly uneventful. Our social life revolved around travel and activities with other foreigners. In the whole time we lived in Laos we were never invited to a Lao person's home, and this was the case with most expatriates. Senior Lao officials were not allowed to have foreigners in their house, but we were invited to a number of local weddings held in hotels or function centres. Margaret got a job as the manager of the Australian Embassy social club. The club was in a fabulous location on the banks of the Mekong River and had a bar, restaurant and swimming pool. It was primarily intended for embassy staff, but historically it had been open to guests and for many years in the past was one of the few places Westerners could socialise. The club was a bit moribund when Margaret took over, but she quickly revitalised it and the regular weekly functions soon had over 100 people attending.

Shopping in Vientiane was fairly limited so we would often drive to Nong Khai, just across the Mekong River, or one hour further on to

Udon Thani in Thailand. Udon was quite a large city and had an air-conditioned shopping mall, complete with fast food restaurants and a Robinsons department store. The two challenges involved with going to Thailand were the long delays with the Lao immigration and customs at the Friendship Bridge, and driving. In Laos they drove on the right side of the road, but in Thailand it was on the left. It was always fun driving on the 'wrong' side of the road when we entered Thailand, dodging tuk tuks, buffaloes and motorbikes, with the passenger having to shout out instructions when it was safe to pass.

On one trip Margaret informed me that as our children had gone off to boarding school we needed a dog, so she rescued a scruffy little black poodle from a pet shop come puppy factory. We called him Pindi (after Rawalpindi in Pakistan) and he quickly settled in. I was initially too embarrassed to tell anyone we had a poodle and would only walk him at night. He was a great little dog and in the end he lived with us in four different countries.

Our housekeeper, Sin, continued to look after us and she became a good friend. Like most Lao people Sin had never been out of Laos, even though they looked across the Mekong River at Thailand every day. Margaret decided to take Sin with her to Thailand on a shopping trip. It took some months for Sin to get her passport and exit visa to leave Laos, but the big day came and they drove to Udon Thani. Margaret said that watching Sin's expression as she rode in an elevator and on an escalator for the first time was priceless.

Another time Margaret needed a minor operation in Bangkok so decided to take Sin with her. During a sightseeing visit they went to the temple containing the huge reclining Buddha statue. Next minute, Sin is praying and sticking gold leaf on the statue. Margaret said, 'Sin, what are you doing? You're a Christian!' to which Sin replied, 'Ah, but Margaret, you never know who is going to be right at the end.'

We also had a night guard named Bounmi. Security was fine in Vientiane, but it was almost expected that you took someone on to provide employment. Bounmi was probably 50 years old and he was in very good physical shape. He had been in the Lao air force during the time of the previous regime and had even gone to the USA for training.

He spoke basic English but was always very quiet and subdued. After the trip I did up north to Houaphan I told him where I had been. He replied that it was a bad place and when I coaxed it out of him he said 're-education camps'.

Then it dawned on me – the concrete slabs I had seen on my visit were the remains of a re-education camp that had been set up by the communists after they came to power. These camps had been used to 'instruct' members of the losing side of the war in the errors of their ways and indoctrinate them with new thinking. Bounmi had been through these camps and it was clear that while people like him were tolerated in society by the government, he was never going to be able to get a proper job.

Donors see the reality of UXO in Laos

The core of the UXO Lao workplan for 1997 was to finish the national survey, continue training new deminers, and to start community awareness and clearance operations in five new provinces. Preliminary results of the survey were starting to come in and it found that ten provinces were highly impacted by UXO and five provinces had moderate impact. Three provinces were unaffected. The provinces were ranked in order of severity of impact and Houaphan province, the home of the communist party and the one Saykham had insisted the previous year should be the second province we start work in, was actually ranked seventh. It didn't really matter and we drew up plans to start clearance work in Saravane, Champassak, Sekong, Attapeu and Khammouane provinces.

The Saysomboun special zone that Mr Noy had mentioned in our meeting was a special 'province' that the central government controlled directly from Vientiane, because of security concerns. Somewhat surprisingly, we had been able to survey it and it came in as the eighth worst UXO affected area. However, the government made it clear that UXO Lao should have no role in clearing mines in Saysomboun and that the Lao Army would be responsible.

The survey also found that 2861 villages reported UXO in or near their village, and this figure represented a quarter of all villages in Laos.

Data on nearly 10,649 UXO-related accidents which had occurred since 1973 was also collected. Although many of these accidents took place in the five years immediately after the war, UXO accidents were still continuing at the rate of 200 per year, and the accidents often caused multiple victims.

In discussion with Jan Mattsson at UNDP it was decided that we would host some donor visits to the provinces to raise awareness of the program. The first visit involved 10 donor representatives from Vientiane and Bangkok, and we took them to Xieng Khouang province. As always MAG did a good job with the arrangements and the itinerary, which included a visit to the local hospital. When we were standing in the car park of the hospital waiting to be met, we heard an explosion and then saw a thin plume of black smoke rising from a distant hill. We thought no more of it and started our tour of the hospital.

About 20 minutes later we were in the operating theatre when a man was brought in suffering wounds to his abdomen and genitals. We were told that he had been ploughing his field when he hit a bombie and it had exploded. This, of course, was the same explosion we had seen and heard while waiting outside. The doctors removed the woman who was on the operating table and placed her on the floor, and then lifted the UXO casualty onto the operating table. We decided it was time to move on and let the man be treated in private. This was certainly one group of donors who went home convinced about the reality of the UXO problem in Laos.

The next donor trip was much more ambitious. Work had started in the province of Savannakhet and operations were based around the town of Sepone, close to the Vietnamese border. We decided that we would take the members of the National UXO Committee, plus government representatives from the five new provinces where we wanted to start work, plus some donors for an overnight trip to Sepone. Gunter Mulack had come out from Germany and we had other donor representatives from Bangkok and Hanoi. Tony West, the New Zealander working for Handicap International, was tasked with arranging the visit. At our end we organised a Lao military helicopter to fly everyone from Vientiane direct to Sepone.

The big day arrived and a total of about 25 Lao officials and foreigners boarded a large, ageing Soviet-era Mi-8 helicopter. Because of the distance we were travelling it had been fitted with a long range fuel tank, which was just a large drum strapped down on the floor of the helicopter. The aircraft stank of aviation fuel and there were a few apprehensive looks as we took off.

Jenni had prepared a briefing paper for the visitors in both Lao and English, and it was interesting to observe the reaction. All the Westerners were reading the brief whereas not one of the Lao people was. They were still very much a society reliant on the spoken word.

We flew south and soon we were flying along narrow valleys covered with heavy jungle. The weather closed in so the pilot was forced to land in a clearing in the middle of nowhere. As we wandered around waiting for the cloud to lift, people started spotting unexploded bombs all around the clearing. It was a powerful message that you could randomly pull up anywhere in rural Laos and you would find bombs.

After about an hour we continued on and the helicopter landed on a school soccer field at the village of Sepone. Tony West had set up an excellent display of equipment and deminers were ready to demonstrate their techniques and procedures. However, just before the briefing was due to start, Saykham came and told me the Lao side had to have a meeting. Something had obviously gone wrong and they needed to discuss certain issues before the main meeting with donors the next day. I was annoyed because the whole purpose of the visit was to give the officials from the next five provinces a look at what they were going to be doing. Due to time constraints, we could not reschedule so the demonstration went ahead just for the donors. We stayed overnight in another disused agricultural college complex and the meeting with donors went well the next day.

When it came time to leave Sepone we headed back to the school oval to get on the helicopter. When we got on board and the pilot tried to start the aircraft, it just made a slow electrical whirring noise like a flat battery – which it was. It transpired that the pilots had repositioned the helicopter using only the batteries and had drained them of power in the process. We all got out of the aircraft and milled around. Out of the corner of my eye I saw Mr Saykham speak to the pilot then usher Gunter Mulack into his vehicle and take off. I asked Jenni to check and the pilots confirmed they could not fly today, and also that Saykham had left to drive back to Vientiane.

For the second time in two days I was annoyed with him. I gathered everyone around, explained the situation and then I allocated people to vehicles and sent them off on the seven-hour drive from Sepone back to Vientiane. The only consolation was that I later learned that Saykham's driver did not know the area well and had turned the wrong way when they left Sepone. They drove an hour in the wrong direction and didn't realise it until they hit the Vietnamese border (and subsequently got back to Vientiane two hours later than everyone else).

The next day back at the office I asked Saykham, 'Why did you just drive off and leave everyone behind at Sepone?' He looked embarrassed and said rather lamely, 'I had to get Dr Mulack back to Vientiane in time to catch a flight.'

It wasn't long before Tony West was in the spotlight again. He called me one day and said that he had evidence of corrupt practices. He said that each pay day our Lao Provincial UXO Coordinator in Savannakhet was standing around the back of the building and demanding that the deminers give him money, in return for being selected for their job. I knew I had to handle this carefully. I went in and told Mr Saykham about it and left it at that. Then the accusations started against Tony. A report came back that he was spying (because he had taken a photo of a bridge and walked up a hill) and that he was seeing local women (which he wasn't). Next month Tony called and said that the corruption was continuing. I went back in to see Saykham and said that corruption was unacceptable to UNDP and that if it continued I would have to report it. Mr Saykham never discussed the incident with me again, but within a week the Lao provincial coordinator had been sacked and replaced by another person.

Soon after the donor visit the UXO program suffered its first workplace accident. The normal procedure for destroying inert bombs was to dig a large hole, position the items of UXO neatly in it, place a large quantity of explosives on top and then cover it with sandbags.

Everyone would back off and then the explosives would be remotely detonated causing the bombs to blow up as well. After the explosion it was necessary to wait a specified time to make sure that nothing was slowly cooking off. One of the British supervisors at MAG had done this correctly, but when he approached the pit to check the completeness of the demolition a white phosphorous round popped off. He heard it and turned and ran away, but some pieces of burning phosphorous landed on his back causing some nasty burns. Strangely, Mr Saykham found this extremely amusing when he heard about it. He subsequently took great delight in telling everyone that the only accident UXO Lao had suffered involved one of the foreign experts.

Signing of the Anti-Personnel Mine Ban Convention

The anti-landmine campaign had a huge year in 1997. Although not a member of any formal campaign organisation, the visits by Princess Diana to Angola in January and Bosnia in mid-August 1997 made world headlines and provided great exposure to the landmine issue. Even her death at the end of August provided an extra reason for many to carry on with the cause. Canada, Norway and the International Campaign to Ban Landmines were tireless in their efforts to encourage countries to sign the convention in December, and meetings and rallies were held all over the world.

On 12 October 1997 Jody Williams and the International Campaign were awarded the Nobel Peace Prize for their efforts to ban landmines. Jody had always inspired me with her dedication to the cause and her outstanding oratory. Margaret and I were also pleased, as our good friend and the head of the Afghan survey organisation, Sayed Aqa, had become heavily involved with the campaign and was one of the co-recipients of the Peace Prize.

As the Lao Government was not going to join the Anti-Personnel Mine Ban Convention, I just kept on with my work throughout this period. After my last encounter with Mr Noy I decided not to push the matter of the Convention too hard. Then, on 3 December 1997, I went home, turned on the TV and quite by chance watched live coverage on CNN of world leaders gathered in Ottawa to sign the Anti-Personnel

Mine Ban Convention. I sat there transfixed, seeing all the mine action people I knew and watching diplomats or politicians take their turn to sign the Convention.

A mix of emotions went through me, ranging from happiness and satisfaction that the Mine Ban Convention had become a reality, combined with frustration that Laos did not join and that I was not in Ottawa to witness the event first hand. A total of 133 countries signed the Convention on that day and many more were to join in afterwards.

The beginning of the end of our time in Laos

At work, Mr Saykham was becoming erratic and started saying strange things in meetings with UNDP or other organisations. This was being noticed and I was hoping that people could see that I wasn't the problem in the relationship. One time he burst into my office saying, 'Who said? Who said?'

I was puzzled and asked, 'Who said what?' Saykham responded by asking, 'Who said that three million tons of bombs had been dropped on Laos during the war?' Obviously he had been challenged at a government meeting and didn't have the right answer. A lot of information had been obtained by the Mennonites from US Congressional records on US weapons expenditures during the war and from bombing records, so I did a quick bit of research and provided him with a one-page memo with all the facts.

A more worrying incident occurred as we were finalising the results of the survey. I regularly briefed Saykham on the survey results as they came in, and I had spent quite a lot of time with the Handicap International team writing up the conclusions and recommendations from the survey. I had shared all this with Saykham and said to him one day that we were ready to send the report to the printers. He said 'no'; instead we must send it out to all the provincial governors to see if they wanted to change any of the figures. I replied rather tersely that we had just spent over $400,000 on getting the correct figures and the strength of the survey was its independence.

The next day I started sending out draft copies of the report to various individuals and organisations. The report got printed in its unaltered form and Saykham was clearly not happy the day that Handicap International put on a function to launch the report.

Contract-wise I was still hanging in there. At the end of August, Jan Mattsson managed to arrange a four-month contract extension which would take me up until the end of the 1997. Around this time Saykham suffered a mild heart attack. I went to visit him in hospital and the medical conditions were very basic, to say the least. He was in a dirty room with only a saline drip in his arm. I actually felt sorry for him.

Laos was undergoing rapid change and the UXO Lao program had become quite big in a very short time frame. Saykham was an old-school communist and he had got to where he had in the government by not taking risks or making mistakes. I think it had all become too much for him. Saykham recovered and came back to work, but by the end of November 1997 he was retired by the government. I had outlasted him.

However, the constant tension at work and the ongoing hassles over getting short-term contract and visa extensions were wearing me down as well. I wanted to stay working for the United Nations and I also wanted to stay in mine action, so I had started to look around for an assignment in another country.

The Ministry appointed Mr Bounpone as the new national director for UXO Lao. He was like a breath of fresh air after Saykham. Mr Bounpone was easy going, open to discussion and willing to explain the Lao way to me. He was a pleasure to work with. I wondered what life might have been like if he had been the director from the start of the program. I almost thought about staying on in Laos for a few more years.

In early February 1998, the newly created United Nations Mine Action Service (UNMAS) arranged the first ever meeting of 'National Mine Action Directors and UN Advisers' in Geneva. Mr Bounpone and I attended on behalf of Laos. About 15 other mine-affected countries were represented and the meeting provided a valuable opportunity for the exchange of organisational and technical information between mine action programs. The meeting was also a great introduction for Mr Bounpone to the sector, and a chance for him to see that Laos was not alone in dealing with their legacy of war.

When we got back to Vientiane I drafted our annual report for 1997 for Mr Bounpone and the results were impressive. We had trained 327 students at the training centre during the year, and all of them had been employed by either the three provinces with existing UXO clearance teams, or the five new ones we had established during the year. Another international NGO, Norwegian People's Aid, had been invited to oversee work in Sekong and Attapeu provinces in the far south of the country. The national UXO survey had been completed and the results were being used to plan our future work. We had managed to raise another US$2.5 million in the Trust Fund and US$13 million as in-kind or direct bi-lateral contributions.

Mr Bounpone also oversaw the production of our workplan for 1998 and it included two more provinces to come on-line (which would then have the top 10 high-priority UXO affected provinces covered) and undertaking a period of consolidation.

In January 1998 my contract had been renewed for another six months, but by then I had received an offer to go as the United Nations manager of the mine action program in Bosnia, based in Sarajevo. The war in Bosnia had ended when the Dayton Accords were signed on 14 December 1995 in Paris. Since then the United Nations mission in Bosnia had been responsible for overseeing civilian landmine clearance activities, but this was about to be transferred to UNDP. The only drawback was that due to the tense security situation in Bosnia, it was an unaccompanied posting. Margaret would either have to return to Australia or live in nearby Zagreb in Croatia.

In mid-February I flew to Sarajevo for a job interview and I was offered the job on the spot. While I was there, I discovered that although it was an unaccompanied duty station, United Nations officials could apply for their spouses to visit if the security situation allowed. On the surface it looked safe enough to me so I immediately applied for Margaret to visit when I took up the post. I then flew back to Laos and started preparations to move to Sarajevo.

In a complete about face the Lao side then tried to make it hard for me to leave. They said they needed time to find a replacement and Mr Bounpone needed time to settle in. My post was advertised and Phil

Bean was selected as the next UNDP adviser to UXO Lao. I had first met Phil when he undertook a number of evaluations in Afghanistan and then later at many of the international meetings that had been held over the past few years. Phil had also done some evaluations in Laos so he had a good understanding of the situation. We got on well together and I was pleased that he was selected, because he was a qualified bomb disposal officer and he could bring a new set of skills to the job.

All the arrangements were made and Margaret and I were booked to depart Laos on 13 March 1998. The Minister of Labour and Social Welfare hosted a Lao-style farewell for me at the Ministry and presented me with the standard certificate of appreciation. I found it rather disappointing when the best the Minister could bring himself to say about my work over the past two years was that 'this project became much bigger than I thought it was going to be'.

CHAPTER 12:
DEALING WITH POLITICAL DYNAMITE IN SARAJEVO

I must admit that I never completely understood the reasons for the collapse of Yugoslavia, or what the Bosnian War was all about, until I arrived in Sarajevo and started to read more about it. The war in Bosnia took place from 1992 until October 1995, which is when I was working in Afghanistan and at the time I was just focussed on the job at hand. I found all the references to 'Bosnian Serbs', 'Bosnian Croats' and 'Bosnian Muslims' confusing to say the least. The only things I associated with the former Yugoslavia were the assassination of Archduke Franz Ferdinand of Austria in Sarajevo in 1914 (which was the precursor to World War I), the reign of Marshal Tito over Yugoslavia after World War II and the Winter Olympics of 1984.

WHAT REALLY DID HAPPEN TO YUGOSLAVIA?

Yugoslavia was formed in 1943 and consisted of six 'republics' – Serbia, Croatia, Slovenia, Macedonia, Montenegro and Bosnia Herzegovina. It was governed by Marshal Tito who ruled with an iron fist and who ruthlessly quashed any opposition and suppressed ethnic grievances. While Yugoslavia was a communist country, it was not part of the Soviet Union and Tito was able to play the Soviets and the West to his advantage. With the death of Tito in 1980 and the collapse of the Soviet Union in 1989, things started to unravel in Yugoslavia. Slobodan Milosevic had started to fuel Serb nationalism which alarmed the other republics.

In June 1991, Slovenia broke from Yugoslavia and declared itself an independent country. A short 10-day 'TV war' against the Yugoslav army followed, but soon after Slovenia's independence was confirmed. Croatia followed suit and also declared its independence in June 1991, but this was followed by almost four years of sporadic but intense fighting. At the time Serbia managed to keep its hold over its own territory (including the troublesome province of Kosovo) as well as Macedonia and Montenegro. This grouping was often referred to as the 'rump of Yugoslavia'.

Unfortunately, Bosnia Herzegovina was caught up in the middle of all these changes. After a referendum Bosnia declared its independence, which received international recognition on 6 April 1992, but this immediately led to open warfare and three-and-a-half years of continuous fighting.

Bosnia Herzegovina is situated at the very centre of the Balkans region, at the crossroads between Europe and the Middle East. It had always been a mixed community, rich in culture and history and populated by Muslims, Croats and Serbs. Bosnia is almost landlocked except for 20 kilometres of coastline on the Adriatic Sea. The centre of the country is mountainous levelling out to flat farm land in the north east. Sarajevo is the capital city and largest population centre.

When the break-up of Yugoslavia started, it was always rumoured that the leaders of Serbia and Croatia had made a secret deal to divide up Bosnia between them, each claiming the Bosnian territory where their own ethnic groups lived. Of course this took no account of the Muslims living in Bosnia, who made up about 40 per cent of the population and the majority group in Sarajevo. The deal didn't work and bitter fighting broke out between the different ethnic groups.

While the causes for the war and what happened are extremely complicated, the Bosnian Serbs encircled Sarajevo and imposed a blockade, while in towns and villages throughout the country 'ethnic cleansing' operations were undertaken by all sides.

Landmines were used extensively throughout the conflict, as one of the aims of the fighting was to drive people out of their homes and keep them away. Landmines were good at doing that against unarmed civilians. Large 'front line' areas also developed along the boundaries between the different ethnic groups, and again, landmines were laid in vast numbers to protect these lines.

The Yugoslav Army had been well trained and at first the minefields that were laid were mapped and marked, but as the war went on the mapping became less reliable, if undertaken at all. As with any armed conflict, a large quantity of unexploded ordnance was also left scattered around the countryside. During the period of fighting it was difficult to estimate the numbers of people being killed or injured by landmines or UXO.

STEPPING INTO A MINEFIELD

The war in Bosnia played out on television screens on a daily basis in Europe, but due to a lack of decisive intervention from Western countries, it continued to go on. It was not until the USA intervened that any real moves to end the fighting looked like succeeding. The USA hosted peace talks with all parties in Dayton, Ohio in November 1995 and after protracted wrangling a peace deal was struck.

The Dayton Accords were subsequently signed in Paris on 14 December 1995. The primary aim of Dayton, which it achieved, was to stop the fighting and to prevent a resumption of hostilities. In the broader sense, the goal was to promote peace and stability and to endorse a regional balance in and around the former Yugoslavia.

As a result of the Dayton Accords Bosnia was to remain one country; however, it was divided into two 'Entities'. One entity was called the 'Republika Srpska' and it consisted of districts mainly in the east of the country, bordering Serbia. The ethnic make-up of people in this entity was 90 per cent Serbian. The second entity was called the 'Muslim–Croat Federation' and it covered the rest of the country. The ethnic grouping in the Federation was 53 per cent Muslim, 41 per cent Croat and 6 per cent others. Apparently the country was not divided into three groups because it was feared two groups may gang up on a third. Also, the districts containing Muslims and Bosnian Croats were much more intertwined and it would not have been feasible to separate them. The critics of Dayton said that this outcome had legitimised the 'ethnic cleansing' that had just taken place.

The country was to be governed by a Council of Ministers, consisting of one representative each from the Muslims, Bosnian Croats and Bosnian Serbs, and they would share the office of President on a rotating basis. Elections were to be held to elect a parliament. Words were carefully chosen and the dividing line between the two Entities was not to be called a 'border', but rather the Inter-Entity Boundary Line, or IEBL. The Boundary Line was over 1000 kilometres long and a two-kilometre exclusion zone was declared either side of it. Each Entity was allowed to keep its own army, but a large international military force led by the Americans, subsequently called the 'Stabilization Force', or SFOR, was deployed throughout the country to enforce the peace.

By the time I got to Bosnia the response of the international community was comprehensive to the point of being bewildering. The main civilian body was called the Office of the High Representative. The High Representative was the ultimate civilian authority in all of Bosnia. To avoid the implementation of the Dayton agreement being delayed or obstructed by local nationalist politicians, the High Representative had the power to adopt binding decisions and to remove Bosnian public officials from office if they violated legal commitments. This had the advantage of decisions being made and things getting done, but it did not really help strengthen the government. The Bosnian Council of Ministers would avoid making tough decisions because they knew the High Representative would step in and make them.

The United Nations was present with a Personal Representative of the Secretary General and the United Nations Mission was responsible for demining and civilian police training. A whole range of other United Nations specialised agencies were present, like the refugee agency UNHCR and the children's organisation UNICEF. The Organisation for Security and Cooperation in Europe (OSCE) was present to oversee elections. The Red Cross did impressive work with tracking missing persons and dealing with prisoners of war.

However, the list of international organisations, NGOs, and commercial companies present in Bosnia just went on and on, and many of them had overlapping or conflicting mandates. There were more High Representatives, Personal Representatives, Excellencies, Ambassadors and so on all trying to be important and carve out their own patch.

On top of all that there were about 12 different national militaries in SFOR, and army generals were a dime a dozen. After being in Laos, which was largely ignored or forgotten by most of the world, this was a dramatic change for me. I know that Bosnia was in the international spotlight at the time, but the amount of effort being spent to coordinate the work of the different international bodies and avoid duplication seemed almost counter-productive.

Moving in with the formidable Fatima

On Sunday, 15 March 1998, Margaret and I took the final leg of our journey from Laos, with a short flight from Vienna to Sarajevo in order to start my new assignment. Pindi, our little black poodle came with us and survived the journey. We were met by one of the office staff and our one-year multi-entry visas were granted on the spot. It seemed far too easy after all the wrangling over visas in Laos. The English language news came on the car radio as we were driving into the city, and the lead story was that a 'Mr Ian Mansfield was arriving in Sarajevo to take over as the new head of the United Nations Mine Action Program'. The newsreader then went on to outline all the challenges I would be facing. I was both flattered by such 'recognition', but also cautious because the United Nations seemed to be being blamed for the lack of progress in clearing mines in Bosnia.

Sarajevo is situated in a valley that starts out quite broad where the airport is located, but then narrows down near the city centre. The surrounding mountains get quite steep and the valley ends with cliffs and high rock walls. From the airport there is only one road leading into the city and it is flanked by a tram track. All along the route high rise office buildings and Soviet-style apartment blocks were badly damaged and unoccupied. Traffic lights were not working and at some of the major road intersections, headstones indicated that people had been buried in the grassy traffic islands. As we got closer to the city the buildings were even more damaged.

Margaret had seen a lot of poverty in the developing world, but she was quite shocked by the extent of the destruction in this 'European' city, less than an hour's flight from Austria. Even though it was two years after the fighting had stopped, there was little evidence of any major repair or refurbishment underway.

When I had come to Sarajevo in February I had stayed in a 'bed and breakfast' house run by a local Muslim family, as not many of the hotels were operating properly. When I knew that I would be coming back, I had arranged to rent the top floor of the same house, which consisted of two bedrooms, a small kitchen/dining area, a small lounge and a bathroom. It was modest but it had running water and electricity for most of the day. Many of the damaged high rise apartment buildings had neither. The house was also well located as it was only about 500 metres up a steep hill from the city centre. From our tiny balcony we had a view of the main mosque in the old town, and we could even see the Latin Bridge over the Miljacka River where Archduke Franz Ferdinand had been shot back in 1914. The house itself was riddled with bullet holes, as were most of the houses in the narrow street.

Our landlady was named Fatima and she had stayed in Sarajevo throughout the war. Her husband was hugely overweight and not well. During the war he had 'escaped' from Sarajevo with his daughter through the tunnel under the main airport runway and gone to Germany to live. Fatima's daughter said to us, 'My mother is worth three men', and we had no reason to doubt her.

Fatima was a taxi driver and during the war she had specialised in driving journalists up and down the main road that was nicknamed 'sniper alley'. Her car was also full of bullet holes. Fatima said that her best fare was US$100 to take a journalist the one kilometre from the famous yellow-coloured Holiday Inn hotel to the United Nations office – while coming under fire. Later when we were watching a video documentary about the war we saw Fatima in the background, so we were sure her stories were true.

Around the corner from her house there was an embankment beside the road and sticking out of the stone wall, there was a pipe that was always running with spring water. Fatima said that during the war there was no electricity or water, and at night, under the cover of darkness, up to a thousand people would line up quietly and fill containers with drinking water from the pipe.

It snowed quite heavily soon after we arrived and Margaret and I went out on the roof top to admire the city lights twinkling on the snow. Next minute some gunfire erupted and we could see tracer rounds piercing the night sky. We called down to Fatima to ask what was happening and she said it was 'happy gunfire' from a wedding celebration. We watched for a while, but then I remembered Graeme

Membrey's story from Kabul when rounds from similar celebratory fire started to land around him, so Margaret and I moved back in under cover to watch the rest of the 'show'.

Being briefed at the United Nations Mine Action Centre

On Friday I had left work in Laos and now three days later on Monday I was turning up for work in Bosnia. The change could not have been more dramatic in every way. The weather was cold and miserable, the city was badly damaged and the people were all dressed in dark clothes and looked grim. The United Nations Mine Action Centre was located inside Marshall Tito barracks near the centre of Sarajevo and was housed in a combination of demountable buildings and one wing of the barracks. The barracks had previously been the headquarters of the Yugoslav army in Bosnia, but now was occupied by a variety of foreign military units belonging to SFOR and the demining centre.

The first thing I did was meet all the staff who consisted of United Nations employees, local staff and seconded military personnel from a variety of countries. I was replacing a South African chap who had been acting as the program manager for the past eight months – Johannes Jacobus van der Merwe, who was better known to everyone as 'JJ'. I had not met JJ before and discovered that he had been involved in a landmine accident in the past when serving in the South African military. A vehicle he had been travelling in had hit a mine and JJ had suffered severe burns on his neck and back. This had not deterred him from working in the landmine sector and I found JJ to be an extremely capable and competent person. He was leaving Bosnia to take up a mine action position with UNDP in New York.

JJ had arranged a briefing for me on the landmine situation in Bosnia. The majority of the known minefields in Bosnia were located along the 1000-kilometre long Inter-Entity Boundary Line. The Mine Action Centre had obtained the records of over 18,000 minefields and entered them into a database, but JJ reiterated that towards the end of the war many mines were laid without being recorded. It was estimated that these maps represented only 50 to 60 per cent of the minefields in the country. The Centre had produced a map of Bosnia with a red dot representing each known minefield. The map was just a sea of red dots and you could see clearly where lines of minefields demarcated different ethnic areas all over the country.

It was estimated at the time that there may be up to one million landmines laid in Bosnia and an unknown number of UXO waiting to be cleared. It was believed that 80% of the mines were anti-personnel mines, with remainder being the larger anti-tank variety. With very few exceptions all the mines used were of types manufactured in the former Yugoslavia. Although they had local names, the landmines were copies of Soviet mines and they fell into the two general categories of blast mines or fragmentation mines. It was difficult to get accurate casualty figures, but there seemed general agreement that since the end of the war there had consistently been about 50 civilians killed or injured by landmines or UXO every month.

Aside from the overall statistics, some of the local stories were chilling. One of the favoured methods to destroy someone's house when they had been run out of a village for being of the wrong ethnic group was to use an anti-tank mine. The mine would be placed inside the house and then fired electrically. This would blow off the roof and flatten all the internal walls making the house unliveable. Just for good measure, some anti-personnel mines would then be laid in the front and backyards.

Unlike the huge minefield belts surrounding towns in Afghanistan or along the borders of Cambodia, Bosnia seemed to be full of lots of little minefields. In my second week in the job a report came in that two old people were killed while collecting mushrooms about 500 metres further up the hill from where we were living in Sarajevo.

Another good example of the scale of the problem became evident when SFOR launched Operation Harvest in March 1998. The aim of the operation was to declare an amnesty and gather illegal and unregistered weapons from local people, as well as any other explosive ordnance. The program was extremely successful with thousands of weapons being handed in, along with a huge number of UXO and also hundreds of landmines. Why did civilians have landmines stored in their basements? We could only speculate that they were going to use them to protect their own property, or kept them in waiting to use against people of a different ethnic background.

In addition to the designated collection points, local people knew about the mine action centre in Marshall Tito barracks and often we would arrive at work in the morning to be greeted by a pile of UXO or other explosives neatly stacked at the front gate. Operation Harvest was so effective that it was repeated many times over the next few years.

I discovered that the international response to the landmine issue in Bosnia was just as diverse and duplicative as the overall political and humanitarian response. The Dayton Accords had specified that all former warring factions should give up their minefields records and called for the 'marking, removal and destruction' of all mines and UXO within 30 days'. The first requirement had been met but the second was completely unrealistic and impractical.

In January 1996, the fledgling Bosnian government had requested the United Nations to assist with setting up a mine action program. The responsibility had gone to the United Nations Mission in Bosnia Herzegovina, which had the unpronounceable acronym of UNMIBH, and they established the United Nations Mine Action Centre in June 1996. One stroke of good fortune was that the deputy head of UNMIBH was my old boss and colleague from Afghanistan, Martin Barber. When I arrived UNMIBH was scaling down and Martin was actually finishing up, but it was good to see him again and to get his wise counsel on the way ahead for mine action. The responsibility for the mine action program was meant to transfer from UNMIBH to the government on 1 January 1998, but as the government was not ready, UNDP was taking over the interim responsibility. I was employed by UNDP to be the program manager until the conditions were right to transfer the program to the government.

The first United Nations program manager had been a Canadian named Georges Focsaneanu, who had previously been instrumental in setting up the Cambodian Mine Action Centre. Georges had started to set up an organisation in Bosnia similar to Cambodia where the one central mine action centre would both provide the coordination for all the mine clearance work and manage its own mine clearance teams.

Georges only lasted about one year and then left in frustration at the slow pace of progress. However, as part of the transition to national ownership, a rather complex set of organisational changes had been agreed between the Council of Ministers and the United Nations in October 1997. Now in early 1998 these changes were about to be made.

The UN Mine Action Centre would become the Bosnia Herzegovina Mine Action Centre (BHMAC) and its responsibility would be to manage all the records in a central database, set priorities and issue tasking orders, oversee the quality management or standards of work being done and to raise funds. The two Entities, the Republika Srpska and the Federation, would set up their own offices to supervise and undertake mine clearance.

It took me some time to get my head around all this and until national counterparts could be identified and trained, UNDP would continue to fill the posts with international staff. I met with the head of UNDP and my new boss, Mr Hans Bruntjes, and he was keen for the transition to the government to take place. As I had heard on the car radio, the government was always conveniently blaming the United Nations for the slow progress of mine clearance. The only problem was that within the Mine Action Centre there were only one or two Bosnians who had been identified as suitable to take over management roles.

One step the government had taken was to set up a Demining Commission. Its role was to keep the Council of Ministers informed on the progress of demining in the country, to approve national mine action plans and standards, and to oversee the work of the BHMAC. The Demining Commission consisted of three members – Mr Enes Cengic representing the Muslims, Mr Bersislav Pusic of the Bosnian Croats and Mr Radislav Ilic from the Bosnian Serbs. I made a point of going to meet them all.

The Muslim representative, Enes Cengic spoke very good English and I found him easy and approachable to deal with. I then travelled to Mostar to meet the Croat, Mr Pusic. Pusic was a tough looking character and he just glared at me. He said that he was happy with JJ and did not know why the United Nations was replacing him. I thought I can play this game, so stared back at him and said that this is what the United Nations wanted to do.

Finally I went to the town of Pale just outside Sarajevo. Pale had been the centre of the Serb war effort and home of the leaders Radislav Karadzic and General Ratko Mladic. I found the Bosnian Serb representative, Mr Ilic, to be very pleasant, but as he did not speak English our conversations always had to be translated. My initial impression of the Demining Commission members was that I could work with them, but unfortunately I was soon hearing allegations of nepotism, favouritism and corruption against all of them.

As I mentioned, the UNDP mine clearance program I was now heading up was not the only show in town. In 1997 the World Bank made funds available to the Entity Governments to finance mine clearance operations by international commercial companies, all of whom had established subcontracts or joint venture arrangements with local commercial mine clearance companies. The World Bank established offices called Project Implementation Units to oversee the contracts and they were staffed with locals and some international advisers. This was the first time the World Bank had funded mine clearance work and it was not without its difficulties. Over US$10 million had been made available and because it was all to be awarded to commercial companies, it had led to about 40 local companies suddenly springing up – many of dubious quality.

Fourteen contracts had been let but most of the money went through two international companies. These were a Zimbabwean company called MineTech and the US Company RONCO. Both of these were reputable companies and they had established partnerships with some Bosnian companies – one for each of the three ethnic groups. However, when I arrived MineTech was pulling out of Bosnia and due to a disagreement with the World Bank, the USA had withdrawn its funds and given the money directly to RONCO.

This was my first real experience with commercial mine clearance on a large scale. Although I had no responsibility for the World Bank program, there was clearly a duplication of effort and I felt that it had to be more closely associated with the national program. Also, with a weak central government the possibility for corruption existed, so I could see that setting national standards and instituting proper accreditation procedures for all demining operators was essential.

Quite a heated debate was ongoing about the merits of using commercial companies for mine clearance, versus not-for-profit organisations, like NGOs or government agencies. The pro-commercial argument was that commercial companies were more efficient because they were in a competitive environment. The counter-argument was that commercial companies only took on easy tasks and it was alleged that the local Bosnian companies cut corners and compromised on safety to keep their costs down. On the other hand, the NGOs said that they focussed on house clearance which was very slow but a priority in Bosnia, as refugees needed to be able to return home. Various figures were produced by different commercial or NGO groups estimating the clearance costs per square metre, but to me none were very accurate or convincing one way or the other.

In the former Yugoslavia, a government body called the Civil Protection Organisation, or CPO, had existed to deal with natural emergencies like fire and floods, and they also had the responsibility for civilian bomb disposal. The CPO still existed in Bosnia but in a much weakened state. It would have been the ideal organisation to give the responsibility for mine clearance in the country except that it came under the Ministry of Defence, which made it difficult for the United Nations and World Bank to deal with them. However, in 1997 the European Union (EU) decided it would support the Civil Protection Organisation. The EU had funded the training and provision of equipment and vehicles for 12 mine clearance teams and nine bomb disposal teams. In the urgency to get things moving in Bosnia, little thought had been given to sustainability of projects. When I arrived the CPO could not afford to take on the teams who had been trained. As a result, hundreds of deminers were laid off and equipment was sitting idle while waiting for more funds to come from the European Union.

The United Nations refugee agency UNHCR had been frustrated at the slow pace of house clearance in Bosnia, so had decided to fund its own clearance teams. In 1997, a total of 240 deminers had been trained and equipped. This project was overseen by an ex-Royal Navy Clearance diver named Tim Horner. Tim was very capable and cooperative and

I quickly reached an agreement with him that the teams would work to UNHCR's priorities of house and apartment clearance in the two Entities, but that the project would come under the overall umbrella of the national program.

Since 1996 the Norwegian and Canadian Governments had both provided funds and technical advisers to the UN Mine Action Centre. Norway also funded the NGO Norwegian People's Aid, who was the first civilian organisation to undertake mine clearance in Bosnia. They had focussed on clearing damaged houses and apartments in support of refugee settlement programs in Sarajevo, as well as clearing important infrastructure projects and cultural heritage monuments. The German Government was funding the trial of two demining machines and a German bomb disposal school was training Bosnian refugees in Germany.

The Government of Belgium had unilaterally decided to fund two technical advisers to the Demining Commission. This had initially concerned me as it was part of my job description to advise the members of the Demining Commission, but once I had met the two individuals involved we were able to work out a good division of responsibilities and establish a sensible working relationship.

Both of the Belgium-funded advisers were ex-British army officers. Eddie Banks was a former bomb disposal officer who tended to focus on technical aspects, rather than the national level issues. Eddie was writing a specialised reference book about landmines, so he was a good source of information and he was often used to investigate landmine accidents.

The other adviser was a much more interesting character. Peter Isaacs had been in the British Army, joined the Australian Army and served in Vietnam and then joined the Sultan of Oman's army. During this latter tour one of Peter's soldiers stepped on a landmine and when Peter rushed in to help him, he subsequently stepped on a mine himself. Peter had lost a leg, severely damaged his arms and also lost an eye, with the result that he wore a distinctive black eye patch. Despite his 'disabilities' Peter drove a large Mercedes Benz car and he gave me a lift in it one day.

On the seat was a pair of binoculars so I asked him, 'What are they for?' His reply was not what I expected. He said, 'When I'm driving down the autobahns at a 130 kilometres per hour I can't see the road signs very clearly, so I need the binoculars to read the signs to know when to exit!'

Peter knew all the different mine action players in Bosnia and was one of the few people I came across who understood the big picture.

Because of the high number of donor countries involved in Bosnia a 'Board of Donors' had been established to advise and oversee mine clearance work. The board was co-chaired by Hans Bruntjes, the head of UNDP and the Military Assistant to the High Representative, a British Major General named John Drewienkiewicz. No-one could pronounce John's last name, so he was happily referred to by everyone as 'DZ'. Because of DZ's links with the High Representative, the Board of Donors virtually had veto power over the three demining Commissioners and it was an effective body in keeping an eye on things. I regularly attended the Board of Donors meetings and they were a great source of support for the changes I was pushing through.

Finally, under the Dayton Accords the two Entity Armies were required to undertake mine clearance work. This worked on a carrot and stick approach. Under the supervision of the international military contingents from SFOR, if the Entity Armies undertook certain tasks, like mine clearance, they earned 'credits' which allowed them access to funding, new weapons or certain training opportunities. I was told that the Entity Armies had previously undertaken what they called 'mine lifting' tasks. This involved getting a minefield map and then lifting only those mines marked on it. They did not check outside the mine lanes for any additional mines that may have subsequently been laid. As the work had been undertaken by recently conscripted troops, there had sadly been a high number of deaths and injuries to the soldiers undertaking the clearance. No central records were kept of this work and no-one was confident that the areas involved had actually been totally cleared. To me this seemed a waste of effort and the Entity Armies certainly had huge potential to speed up the national mine clearing effort.

Trying to get a handle on the big picture

So, although the National Demining Commission was notionally the government authority in charge of all mine action, in fact it only had varying influence over the seven different groups that I just outlined. The things in my favour were that UNDP were co-chair of the Board of Donors so could influence the donors, and in my job description I had the mandate to be the principal adviser to the National Demining Commission. However, I was certainly faced with some challenges in trying to draw these disparate groups together.

I had to quickly understand the bigger picture and the complex political situation in Bosnia, along with getting to know all the mine clearance projects and agencies. I had just spent two years in Laos adjusting to being an adviser to the government and now I was back in charge of the United Nations program – albeit one in transition to government control. In Laos there had been a strong central government and I had been able to help them formulate a national plan first, and then invite partners into the country as required. Here in Bosnia, there was a weak government and a whole range of significant mine clearance activities were already well underway without any coherent national plan in place. While I had been frustrated with the slow pace of getting things underway in Laos, I had grown used to the politeness and subtle, diplomatic way of working. While there was a sense of urgency in Bosnia, I found many people to be aggressive and argumentative in their approach.

A meeting of the Demining Commission was about to be held so I thought that this would throw some light on the way ahead. Unfortunately I was disappointed. The main item on the agenda was the transition plan from the UN Mine Action Centre to the nationally owned BHMAC. The Demining Commissioners spent most of the meeting arguing over the equipment lists, like how many desks and chairs each Entity would get. It got to the point when one of them said why are they getting seven computers and we are only getting six. The logistic officer said, 'One of theirs is broken, so if you like I will come and break one of yours.'

This was not a very uplifting meeting. At the end the chairman said something about not wasting time. I couldn't help myself, so I interrupted and said that although I was only new, I thought we had just wasted two valuable hours.

I said to the meeting, 'In the next few weeks we have the Foreign Ministers of Japan and Canada visiting, a number of key projects are up for renewal and we urgently need to develop a national plan and standards. At your level, you have much more important issues to deal with than computers and desks.'

The commissioners all looked a bit sheepish and they undertook to discuss bigger issues in the future.

The situation in the UN Mine Action Centre office was also a concern. The office was quite large with almost 50 staff. The key posts like operations, finance, logistics and database management were all filled by United Nations staff. While all of them were nice people and they knew their own jobs, they did not have a broader vision and there had been little effort to train national counterparts to take over. Other posts were filled by foreign military officers on attachment and they came and went quite quickly.

The shining light was an Indian army officer, Lieutenant Colonel Suresh Sharma, who had arrived at the same time as me and had been attached to be the operations officer. Suresh had never seen a computer before but within a couple of weeks he had taught himself database management and had overhauled the whole system of allocating demining tasks to operators. He was impressive to say the least and we quickly developed a high regard for each other. When I enquired about his selection he said that there had been 1500 army engineer officers in the bracket for consideration and that he had met all the selection criteria. India had certainly sent its best candidate to be the first officer they had ever attached to a United Nations mine action program.

In the subsequent weeks, each of the Demining Commissioners said to me that they did not think that the government could meet the date of 1 July for the transition from UN control of the mine action program to government control. I discussed this with my boss, Hans Bruntjes, at UNDP. We both agreed that in many ways the government was not ready but that politically it had to be done. Even in the short time I had been in country, there had been a number of reports in the press about civilian landmine accidents and criticism of the United Nations for slow progress. Hans Bruntjes was very sensitive to this criticism, as was

I. At the next meeting of the Demining Commission I announced that UNDP was firm and that the handover would take place as planned on 1 July 1998, and that there was no possibility for an extension.

Drafting a national clearance plan

My next task was to develop some sort of national plan. I had found in Afghanistan and Laos that presenting all aspects of the program in one published document was the most effective way to get all the involved partners, like the government, the mine action operators and the donors, focussed and agreed on the way ahead. I did not have enough information to develop a comprehensive plan and I also did not control the activities of the projects the World Bank and European Union were implementing. However, I managed to get broad agreement from them to cooperate and I drafted the 'Bosnia Herzegovina – National Mine Action Plan – 1998'.

The goals of the program were to reduce the number of civilian landmine and UXO casualties, clear houses for returning refugees and internally displaced persons, and to make land safe for agriculture, reconstruction and development activities. The key elements of the plan covered the transition to Government control and outlined what the United Nations components would do in detail. The rest of the plan really just described what the other projects would be doing, but at least they were all included in the one document for the first time. I also added up what funds were confirmed and what other pledges had been made for the year. The total came to a surprising US$18 million already in hand for 1998, plus another US$22 million requested – a grand total of US$40 million for the year. One of the main reasons for such large numbers was the salary costs for deminers. In Afghanistan or Laos deminers were paid US$100 per month. In Bosnia, because of its proximity to Europe, the going rate was around US$800 per month.

I presented the draft national plan to the next Demining Commissioners meeting and got it approved. I said that it was my intention to publish the document in English, but to also to translate it into the Serbo-Croat language. The spoken language between all the groups was roughly the same, but the Muslims and Croats used Latin script whereas the Serbs used Cyrillic script – so this would mean three lots of text in the booklet. After the meeting, each of the commissioners came to me privately and asked that I only publish the plan in English. Their reasoning was that if it was translated, they would all have to argue over the meaning of terms and place names. This went against what I had found to work well in other places, but in the end I agreed to just publish the National Mine Action Plan in English.

Everyday life in post-war Sarajevo

At home we found it surprisingly easy to settle into Sarajevo. Most international officials were unaccompanied, but Margaret found a couple of other English-speaking spouses and started to get involved with local activities. As spring was arriving, the pace of reconstruction seemed to pick up slightly. While daily life was still difficult, each week a repaired building was reopened, more traffic lights started working, the trams were more frequent and new shops opened up. It was an easy city to find your way around and the tram system was good.

Unemployment was still very high and the cafes were full of swarthy looking men in black leather coats just sitting around all day. Somewhat surprisingly local security was good and there was no evidence of petty crime. You got the impression that people were worn out after surviving a horrible war and that stealing a handbag wasn't worth the effort. However, the newspapers were full of stories about organised crime and criminal gangs that were into trafficking illegal drugs, smuggling goods and stealing cars. One local joke said that if there was ever to be a tourism campaign launched in Germany it should say, 'Germans, come and visit Bosnia – your car is already here'.

Every man and women in Bosnia smoked. The cafes, bars and restaurants were always thick with smoke and your clothes would stink after a night out. At work I had a bright young 20-year-old female assistant named Jasna, who smoked heavily. When I suggested that smoking was not good for her health, she just shrugged and said, 'Boss, when you have managed to live through a war, nothing else really matters.' I couldn't argue with that. I also discovered that cigarettes were a black market currency. One day our taxi driving landlady, Fatima, asked me if I could get her a carton of American Marlboro cigarettes.

I asked why. Fatima replied, 'I was driving my taxi when I was pulled over by a policeman for allegedly speeding. The policeman demanded a cash "fine" or I would lose my licence, or even be arrested. I told the policeman I had no money, but that I could get him American cigarettes.'

As Fatima's livelihood relied on driving her taxi I relented and bought her some cigarettes from the international Post Exchange shop. It was forbidden to sell duty free items, so I gave them to her as a gift and she managed to avoid arrest.

On another occasion Fatima asked if I would drive her to Srebrenica to visit some relatives. Srebrenica was the scene of the dreadful massacre of almost 8000 Muslim men and boys by Bosnian Serb forces during the final stages of the war in July 1995. Although Srebrenica was only 110 kilometres away, it would not be safe for Fatima to drive through the Republika Srpska in her own car fitted with Sarajevo number plates. I knew about the massacre but it was not often talked about locally and did not seem to come to world attention until the matter was raised at the International Criminal Tribunal at The Hague some years later. As I had no reason to visit Srebrenica and the United Nations had strict rules about not carrying unauthorised people in vehicles, I had to decline Fatima's request.

Even though the war had finished there were constant reminders of it everywhere. We visited the ice skating rink in downtown Sarajevo used during the 1984 Winter Olympics. This was the venue where the British skaters Torvill and Dean had obtained a perfect score and won the gold medal dancing to Revel's 'Bolero'. The stadium building had been damaged but we were told that during the war dead bodies had been laid out on the ice until relatives could come and claim them.

In the cobbled stoned alleyways of the old town there were hundreds of what the locals called 'the Sarajevo rose'. These were a distinctive marking in the stone footpaths formed when a mortar round had landed and violently exploded. In the centre was a round shallow crater surrounded by a circular pattern of 'petals' where metal fragments from the mortars had gouged out the stone. In some areas people had filled in the gouges with red paint to serve as a ghastly reminder of the war.

However, the most telling evidence of the war was the massive cemetery on the side of a large hill on the outskirts of town. The hill looked white from a distance due to the thousands of new headstones that had been placed there over the past few years.

A person's ethnic background could be easily distinguished by their car number plate, as each Entity was responsible for issuing the plates. There were a number of major intersections along ethnic dividing lines within Sarajevo, where taxis from one group would have to stop and let out passengers. The traveller would then have to walk across the road and get into a taxi with a different number plate to continue the journey. During our time in Bosnia the High Representative forced through a new system of issuing number plates throughout the country with randomly generated, non-identifying numbers on them.

Likewise the currency meant to be in use after Dayton was officially called the 'Konvertible Mark' or KM but the German 'Deutschemark' was widely used – except in the Croat part of the Bosnia where they used the Kuna from neighbouring Croatia. Again, while we were there the High Representative introduced new banknotes and forced through the widespread use of the Konvertible Mark.

On the home front, our daughter Zoe had followed in my footsteps and had entered the Royal Military College, Duntroon and our son Charles was finishing Year 12 at boarding school in Canberra. Holidays were coming up for both of them so we got permission for them to come to Sarajevo to visit.

I had a pass that allowed me to enter the secure areas within the airport, so I went into the immigration area to meet the kids. I got chatting to an official who told me that the visa on arrival system for Bosnia had been cancelled last week. I got rather anxious about this and pleaded with the official to grant my young, innocent 'school age' children a visa when they landed. Fortunately, he agreed and when I met the kids I whispered to them to say nothing and let me do the talking. While all this was playing out a strange activity was underway at the airport arrivals. About 50 young Eastern European looking men in their early 20s were lined up at another immigration counter. All wore jeans and a black leather jacket and held a new passport and a US$100 note in their hands. This was obviously some sort of people smuggling activity being conducted quite openly.

Having the kids visit provided a good opportunity to have a look around Sarajevo and beyond. During the siege of the city the only way in or out was through a 350-metre long tunnel that had been dug under the runway of the airport. We went and found the entrance to the tunnel (which I knew to be clear of landmines) and crawled along it for a short way. At its peak of operation the tunnel had electricity, an oil pipeline and even a rail track system – where sick or old people would pay money to be pushed through the tunnel on a trolley. We also went to the ski jump facilities for the Winter Olympic Games at Mount Igman. Part of this area was still heavily mined and it was sad to see that the Olympic Rings on the stage where the medals were presented had been all shot up and damaged.

We also drove to Mostar, which was the main city in the Croat part of Bosnia. Mostar is famous for a stone arch bridge called the Stari Most (Old Bridge) high over the Neretva River. The bridge was built in the 16th century and had survived for centuries. Sadly it was part of a front line during the war and it was deliberately destroyed. Fortunately, when we visited a temporary bridge had been erected over the river and various cultural agencies were funding the repair of the 'Old Bridge'.

We continued on down to the Adriatic coast and stayed in the historic city of Dubrovnik across the border in Croatia. Dubrovnik is a magnificent walled city and port dating back centuries. Tragically, it was shelled during the early stages of the war and it was estimated that half the buildings suffered some form of damage. Again, during our visit repair works were underway although damage was still evident in and around the town.

Visiting Bosnian villages

As the distances in Bosnia were not too great I was able to get around to most parts of the country to visit demining sites. The main roads were still in reasonable condition and although a lot of bridges had been destroyed during the war, SFOR troops had erected temporary military-style bridges over most rivers. By now the 'humanitarian demining' sector had been underway in many countries around the world for nearly 10 years and the release of the International Mine Action Standards meant that many of the technical arguments of the past were now solved. One of the few new issues we had to develop procedures for was if human remains were found during the demining process.

Most of the demining teams I visited were well trained and equipped and doing a good job under difficult conditions. House clearance was the hardest task as the metal detector was rendered useless because of all the steel reinforcing bars in the concrete floors and walls. Often deminers were forced to remove rubble by hand and carefully prod their way through houses. There was general agreement that mine detecting dogs would be useful in Bosnia for house clearance and fortunately the USA and Norway had just announced plans to establish a dog training centre.

I visited some villages along the Inter-Entity Boundary Line (IEBL), where the houses were still deserted because they were located within the two kilometre exclusion zones. The demining team supervisor showed us where his teams were working clearing houses along one side of a road.

I asked the supervisor, 'When will you start to clear the houses on the other side of the road?' I knew that we were in the area of the IEBL, but it surprised me when he replied, 'Those houses are in the other Entity, and it is not my job to clear them.' Although Dayton had stopped the shooting it had left some difficult situations to be dealt with. The supervisor then said he had seen three landmines in the front yard of a nearby house, so he would take us to see them.

We drove along a narrow sealed road towards a house when he stopped and pointed to a yard. I opened the car door and carefully put my foot on the edge of the sealed section of road. When I closed the car door and looked down, I saw that only centimetres in front of my foot were the three, fully armed landmines, lined up in the dirt along the edge of the road. Someone must have kindly placed them there for easy collection! As we had all been looking ahead into the yard we completely overlooked seeing them. This was certainly the closest I had ever knowingly come to stepping on a landmine and a long shiver went down my spine.

Further on we met an old lady who had recently moved back into her house. Some bomb disposal technicians in full protective clothing were checking the neighbouring houses. Through the interpreter she said, 'They needn't bother coming to my house as I got all the mines out myself.' It transpired that she had nowhere else to live, so when she had moved back home and saw two landmines in her backyard, she gently picked them up and placed them under a tree. Sure enough, when the technicians checked there were two anti-personnel blast mines under the tree. Fortunately the mines had not been fused or armed, but this incident certainly highlighted the difficulties people faced in returning home and the risks they had to take due to economic necessity.

The last site we visited was along an unsealed road where we came to a team of deminers digging up a roadside bomb. A hole about one metre deep had been dug in the centre of the road and they were gently lifting out the 20 kilograms of TNT that had been the main explosive charge of this improvised explosive device. I enquired through the interpreter how they had found about the location of the bomb and was rather shocked when some of the men said that they had laid it during the war. Once again I had mixed feelings about a situation like this. It was great that they were removing the bomb, but obviously a few years earlier they had no compunction about setting up the device which could have caused death and injury to many people.

Hosting dignitaries

As Bosnia was close to Europe and the implementation of the Dayton Accords was still a top international issue, we received many visitors who wanted to see the mine clearance work. The most famous visit had occurred a few months before I arrived, when Princess Diana visited the UN Mine Action Centre in Sarajevo in early August 1997, just weeks before her tragic death.

My predecessor, JJ van der Merwe, had hosted the visit when Diana came to the centre. The offices in Marshall Tito barracks had two courtyards and for the visit a display had been set up and all the staff were assembled in the second courtyard to meet her. When the driver arrived he mistakenly pulled up in the first courtyard. Princess

Diana got out of the car and wandered on her own through to the second courtyard where everyone was lined up facing the opposite way. Apparently Diana burst out laughing at the mix-up, which immediately started everyone else laughing as they turned around and saw her. Her personality and friendliness broke the ice and the visit was a huge success. The local staff were still talking about Diana's visit months later, and the lucky ones who had a photo taken with her still had them proudly displayed on their desks. The impact Princess Diana had on their morale in the office, and the global impact she had on publicising the landmine cause, was enormous.

The first visitor I hosted was Lloyd Axworthy, the Foreign Minister of Canada. After Dayton, the Bosnian Government had joined the Ottawa Treaty banning anti-personnel landmines that Axworthy had so boldly challenged the world to come and sign just a few months earlier. I admired Mr Axworthy immensely, so I was very pleased to get the chance to meet him. Many people felt that he should have been one of the co-recipients of the Nobel Peace Prize that had been awarded to the anti-landmine campaign. The visit went well and as he was obviously abreast of the landmine issue, he was able to see through the gloss of an organised visit and ask some penetrating questions. One of the Canadian army officers attached to our staff described some activity to Axworthy and when quizzed on how it would work, the officer said it relied on the goodwill of all parties. Axworthy just looked at him and said, 'In my experience, young man, you cannot rely on goodwill – everything needs to be agreed to and written down.'

The next visit was certainly entertaining if nothing else. I was advised by the Japanese Embassy in Austria that the Japanese Foreign Minister, Mr Keizo Obuchi, intended to visit and would like to see some mine clearance work. This was a major event for the Japanese and it was planned to the minutest detail. As Mr Obuchi, who shortly afterwards became the Japanese Prime Minister, was only going to be in Sarajevo for a couple of hours in total, I decided that we would meet and brief him at a demining site in the city. In the week before the visit, I must have received 10 phone calls from the embassy checking on details or advising me of a change to the plan such as: 'Mr Obuchi will not arrive at 14.05 hours, he will now arrive at 14.07 hours'. We were told how many people would be in his party and advised that 'a few' journalists would accompany him.

We chose an active mine clearance site close to the centre of town where some destroyed apartment blocks were being checked and quite a lot of mines had been found among the rubble. The site was well laid out and the yellow minefield marking tape clearly defined the safe areas and clearance lanes. Visits like these always run late so we were quite flexible and relaxed as we waited for his party to arrive. Eventually three black cars flying the Japanese flag pulled up in the narrow street, signalling that our visitors had arrived. However, we were slightly surprised when two 40-seater buses full of Japanese TV crews and journalists pulled up behind them.

I welcomed Mr Obuchi, and then handed the proceedings over to the team leader to brief him about the site and what the team were doing. We then offered Mr Obuchi the chance to put on a deminer's protective vest and helmet and go forward in the lane to look at a mine that had been found. He accepted, but this sent the media pack into a frenzy. Despite having been given a safety brief, photographers started to step over the yellow tapes marking the safe areas and clamber through the rubble to try to get the best photo. As this was a real minefield we had to halt proceedings and shout at all the photographers to get back before the visit could go on. We quickly restored order and fortunately the rest of the visit went without incident.

Coincidentally our next visitor was also Japanese, as the head of the United Nations refugee agency at the time was Mrs Sadako Ogata. It had been estimated that half the Bosnian population had been forced from their homes and were either internally displaced within Bosnia, or living as refugees in another country. UNHCR had a major operation underway to assist return and resettlement and the clearance of mines was an important precursor to this. I met and briefed Mrs Ogata on two occasions and I found her to be very focussed and compassionate about the plight of refugees – and fortunately there was a lot less fanfare meeting with her than there had been with the Japanese Foreign Minister (or some other senior United Nations officials).

Getting ready for the handover

At work I was keen to keep things moving along, due to the 1 July deadline for the handover of responsibility to the Government. Like we had done in Afghanistan and Laos, I decided that we should hold a technical meeting with all the various demining team leaders and supervisors. The International Mine Action Standards released by the United Nations were still relatively new and they needed to be adapted to the Bosnian setting. There was also some distrust and animosity between the commercial operators and the NGOs, so I saw some benefit in getting them all together to discuss a range of common issues.

I arranged a two-day workshop on 11–12 June 1998, to be held at Marshall Tito Barracks and over 100 demining supervisors from a variety of organisations from the two Entities attended. Getting people into Sarajevo from all over the country involved some detailed logistical planning and United Nations vehicles had to be despatched to ensure the safe passage for many of them.

The meeting went extremely well, with technical people sitting around discussing technical issues. The fact that most of them had been former combatants and had probably fought against each other was not lost on anyone, yet here they all were in the same room. There were a couple of misspoken words which brought sharp responses, but all in all it was a very successful meeting which helped clarify the way ahead for the national program. The mine action sector, because of its technical nature and obvious benefits to communities, had shown that it could be part of the 'peace building' efforts in Bosnia.

The other issue that I wanted to fix was the use of the Bosnian Entity armies in mine clearance. This was a huge resource that was not being fully utilised and had the capacity to provide clearance capacity well into the future. There was natural resistance from the military to take tasking orders from a civilian body, or to have their work checked upon by civilian inspectors. As the team leaders' meeting had involved some personnel from the Entity armies, they had gone away with a better understanding of what the national program was all about. Following some subsequent meetings with the Entity armies, SFOR representatives and donors, I was able to reach some significant agreements.

The international military contingents from SFOR agreed to train and equip the Entity army deminers according to the new international standards and the US announced that they would set up three training centres to do this. The Entity armies agreed to accept clearance tasks from the Mine Action Centre and to allow civilian inspectors to accredit army units and check their work. Due to sensitivities about the war, it was decided the military would focus on tasks like clearing around military bases, airfields and industrial sites, and not clear houses. The one sticking point was extra insurance cover for the army deminers, but fortunately Canada and Norway agreed to provide funds to cover the premiums for this. All of this would require numerous written agreements to be signed and these were all planned for 1 July.

In the midst of all this intense planning and quite out of the blue I received a call from UNDP headquarters in New York. The caller identified himself as Robert Piper and he said that UNDP were setting up a unit in New York to address the global landmine issue and they would like me to become the head of it. He said they were looking for someone who had the right field background but also the 'political savvy' to work at the headquarters level. I was flattered to say the least and as the United Nations in New York was getting more involved with mine action it was a great opportunity.

However, I said to Mr Piper, 'I appreciate your offer very much, but I have made a commitment to UNDP Bosnia and also there are a number of changes in the pipeline that I want to see through.'

About a week later he called again to say he had smoothed everything over with UNDP Bosnia and would I at least come to New York for an interview. I went home and discussed it with Margaret and decided that I would go for it. At that time I was the only person in the United Nations system who had managed three national mine action programs. I had also covered the spectrum of different types of organisations from a United Nations run program in Afghanistan, a program led by a national government in Laos, and now one in transition here in Bosnia. I felt that maybe I had something to offer on the international scene.

I flew to New York and was interviewed by the Deputy Head of UNDP, Mr Rafi Ahmed. As I sat in his corner office on the 21st floor of the UNDP building overlooking the iconic United Nations headquarters building, I had to pinch myself to believe this was happening. Here was I, the youngest of five children who grew up in a modest house on a dirt road in a small country town in Australia, being interviewed for a job at the United Nations in New York. Not in my wildest dreams had I ever imagined that this is where life would take me. The interview went very well and having managed mine clearance programs in the field for the past seven years, I was able to give sensible answers and advice on what UNDP should do. I was offered the job on the spot. As I had nothing to lose I said, 'I am very honoured and will accept the job, but because of the wide scope of responsibilities involved with it , I would like the level of the post raised one step to 'Director' level'.

To my surprise this was readily agreed. I was off to New York to take up a senior post with the United Nations.

Back in Sarajevo the pressure was now really on me to finalise the arrangements for the handover of the mine action centre to the Bosnian Government. We had identified local candidates to head the new BHMAC and the Entity centres, and some of the other key posts within the office. However, quite a few other positions would still have to be filled by United Nations staff. In some ways it was probably good that I was leaving, as my own post would also change from being the manager to that of an adviser. I could have made the change but for appearances sake it would be better to have a new person come in as the adviser. Due to his grasp of the issues in Bosnia, Peter Isaacs was selected to be the first United Nations adviser to the new BHMAC and he would start on 1 July 1998.

The big day came around and ceremonies were held to mark the handover of responsibility for mine action to the government. The new Bosnian managers were sworn in and took up their posts. The ceremony was meant to include the signing of the agreements with the Entity armies to come under the umbrella of the national program but at the last minute some alleged inequality was raised that halted proceedings. The signature of this agreement eventually took place on 6 July, but by then Margaret and I were on our way to New York.

CHAPTER 13:

FROM BOSNIA TO NEW YORK AND BEYOND

Arriving to work and live in New York reminded me of when I started at the Royal Military College, Duntroon. It was exciting, challenging and a wonderful opportunity, while at the same time it was confronting and overwhelming. The scale of everything in New York was big and the pace full-on. Fortunately, through a friend we had arranged in advance to sub-let an apartment in Manhattan, so we had somewhere to head to and get our bearings. It helped that our son Charles was with us as he had just finished high school, and Pindi the dog was about to settle in to his third country of residence. However, I hadn't learned from my last experience, because we left Bosnia on a Friday and I started to work at UNDP headquarters on the following Monday – another interesting culture shock.

Although as Australians we like to think we know about American life through the movies and TV, the reality of trying to settle in and live there is quite different. By now Margaret and I had been married for 25 years, and because of working for the army and the United Nations we had lived in 19 homes in seven different countries. We felt we knew what was involved, but moving to New York would prove to be the hardest move we had undertaken so far.

After seven years living in developing countries, we decided we wanted to live right in the centre of Manhattan and experience big city life to the full. Margaret took on the task of finding an apartment and contacted a real estate agent to assist. The agent said, 'I will meet you at the north-east corner of 3rd and 33rd', which we were meant to understand was a certain spot on the corner of 3rd Avenue and 33rd

Street East. Margaret asked, 'Aren't you going to pick me up in your car?' to which the agent replied in typical New York style, 'Lady, are you kidding me?'

New York was booming in the late-1990s and apartments were hard to find. Margaret saw a nice one advertised and so she went and saw the building manager in the morning. When she said that she would like to go away and discuss it with me, the manager said, 'Lady, it will be gone by noon.' So she just took it on the spot. The manager then asked, 'Are you or your husband a diplomat or a lawyer?' Apparently both were bad tenants – diplomats from certain countries had a habit of leaving without paying the rent and lawyers sued the building management if anything went wrong. Without a social security number it was difficult for us to open a bank account, get a credit card or get services connected to the apartment, but in the end we sorted things out and soon settled into life in New York.

Understanding the UN network

The United Nations in New York consists of many different parts and it took some time for me to fully understand what everyone did. The Security Council and the General Assembly are well known, and the members of these bodies are diplomats representing their own countries. The United Nations Secretariat is headed by the Secretary-General and has a number of Departments, like Political Affairs, Disarmament, Peacekeeping and so on. These departments are staffed by United Nations officials who are recruited from all around the world. A number of other specialised United Nations agencies also have their headquarters in New York, and UNDP was one of these.

Because of its role in assisting many mine-affected countries, the United Nations has played a leading role in the mine action sector, which involved everything from surveying and clearance, to conducting mine risk education and post-clearance development initiatives. Within the United Nations Secretariat the Department of Peacekeeping Operations was designated as the focal point and they established an office in late 1997 called the United Nations Mine Action Service, or UNMAS.

The tasks of UNMAS included coordinating the work of the 14 United Nations agencies that have some role to play in mine action, managing a global trust fund and also actually implementing mine action programs linked to peacekeeping missions.

Directing the UNDP mine clearance effort from headquarters

UNDP is one of the largest United Nations agencies and it has offices in over 140 countries. UNDP provides funding for a wide range of development issues, like good governance, poverty reduction, gender and the environment. I was assigned to work in what became the Bureau of Crisis Prevention and Recovery and it covered natural disasters, emergency relief in post conflict situations, small arms and landmines. As the landmine issue was now at its peak of international interest, UNDP saw the need to become more involved in helping affected countries, particularly as landmines were hindering recovery and reconstruction in these countries.

When I arrived in July 1998 UNDP had landmine assistance projects in just four countries. I established a small team consisting of only six people, but we had quite an impact once we got going. My deputy was a native New Yorker named Judy Grayson, who had good field experience and a sharp mind. There were not so many women working in mine action at that time, but Judy could hold her own and I had no doubts about sending her on difficult assignments. However, she did hesitate slightly about one mission and when I asked why she said, 'You do realise that as a woman, on every trip you send me on I have to spend the first day convincing the local authorities that I actually know something about landmines?' On one of her visits to the Ukraine, an army general actually asked Judy, 'Where's the man?' By the time I left UNDP four years later, our small team was supporting programs in almost 20 countries.

My work involved travelling to some of the poorest, war-torn countries on earth, like Angola, Cambodia, Chad, Lebanon, Mali, Mozambique, Sri Lanka and Sudan to advise them on setting up or improving their national landmine clearance program. I also helped raise money for these countries and provided technical advisers and equipment. The success of these programs varied considerably, because they depended heavily on the commitment and quality of national staff assigned by the respective governments, international financial support and the maintenance of peace.

The comprehensive four-country study previously undertaken for the United Nations by Bob Eaton had noted that the local management of mine action programs was weak. In response to this, I arranged a partnership with Cranfield University in the United Kingdom and set up a senior managers training course. National mine action directors were brought in from all over the world to attend a six week training course specifically tailored to suit their needs. Aside from the knowledge these courses imparted, they were extremely important in enabling officials from mine-affected countries to build up their own network of colleagues. These management courses are still continuing in a similar form today and hundreds of mine action managers have benefitted from attending them.

The management training courses, combined with the experience national officials in mine-affected countries were gaining, led to what is called south-south exchanges, where experts from one developing country can help those in another. I was able to secure some funding to set up what I called the Mine Action Exchange program, or MAX, to facilitate study tours and staff exchanges between mine action programs. If Jordan, for example, wanted to set up a mine detection dog program, then it made sense to send some Afghan experts to go and advise them, as they had 10 years of experience, were culturally aware and could communicate in local languages.

Another project I became involved with was called Adopt-A-Minefield and it was an eye opener in many ways. The project was overseen by a young American named Oren Schlein, who was working at the United Nations Association of the USA (UNA-USA), which is a not-for-profit organisation whose aim is to support the United Nations. The idea was that my team at UNDP would provide a list of 'interesting' minefields that needed to be cleared in affected countries, like schools, churches, temples, cultural sites, etc. UNA-USA would then use their fundraising network and have the minefields 'adopted'

– that is, get individuals or groups to pay for them to be cleared. We tried to arrange it that each minefield would cost about $50,000 to clear. It took a while for the program to get going, but it soon was raising a significant amount of money. The stock market was booming in the USA and it was unbelievable the amount of money that could be raised privately.

I was at my desk one day when the head of UNA-USA, a prominent New Yorker named Bill Luers, called me and asked if I would be available to meet for breakfast the next day. I said I was due to fly out to a meeting in Canada but asked, 'What's up?' He said that he was trying to convince Heather Mills and her new partner, Paul McCartney, to sign-up to the Adopt-A-Minefield campaign. I quickly assessed that meeting one of the Beatles was far more interesting than going to Canada, so I said, 'I'm in!

Heather Mills had lost the lower part of one of her legs when she had been hit by a police motorbike in London and she was now supporting efforts to help landmine victims, particularly amputees. Her developing relationship with Paul McCartney was certainly giving her cause some high level exposure.

The next morning I went to the prestigious University Club on 5th Avenue and discovered that there were just six of us for breakfast – Paul, Heather, Bill Luers, Ambassador Don Steinberg (the adviser to President Clinton on landmines), Oren Schlein and myself. The club had all sorts of stuffy rules about no books or documents in the dining room, or no taking of photographs, and you had the feeling that all the club members were very important people. However, I could see our table was drawing a lot of attention as other patrons were pointing and staring at us. I felt like a million dollars sitting there looking nonchalant and chatting with Paul, as if it were an everyday occurrence.

Heather and Paul agreed to support Adopt-A-Minefield and I got to meet them three more times. The most amazing night was a celebrity fundraiser held in Los Angeles which raised over $1 million from a room full of A-list celebrities. Margaret and I attended the function and the highlight was Paul McCartney playing live on stage with Paul Simon. Unfortunately Paul and Heather's marriage did not last and so after a few very supportive years they withdrew from the project.

In December 2009, after 10 years of activities, UNA-USA also decided that they had achieved their aim and closed the Adopt-A-Minefield program. In that time they had raised over $25 million, paid for the clearance of one thousand minefields in 14 countries, and assisted numerous survivors of landmine accidents.

For me personally the program had provided a tiny glimpse into the power of celebrity and it had also demonstrated different possibilities to market a good cause.

THE RESULTS OF THE OTTAWA TREATY

The Anti-Personnel Mine Ban Convention became a huge success. The rules governing the Convention stated that it would come into force six months after the 40th country had ratified it – which happened on 1 March 1999. Although the Convention had been negotiated outside the framework of the United Nations, it had been decided that the Convention would be lodged with the Department of Disarmament Affairs within the United Nations.

To mark the entry into force of the Convention, a ceremony was held outside the United Nations building on the morning of Monday 1 March 1999. With light snow falling, a small group of us watched as the UN Secretary-General Kofi Annan rang the Peace Bell to mark the occasion. Kofi Annan said the entry into force of the Convention was a result of the collective effort of the United Nations, governments, non-governmental organisations, individuals, and grassroots organisations. He stressed that the event symbolised the international community's determination not to let anti-personnel mines lie in wait 'to maim and kill innocent women and children long after the conflicts have ended'. As I had not been able to attend the signing ceremony in Ottawa back in December 1997 (because I was working in Laos), I was particularly pleased to be present now to witness the official start of the Convention.

The Ottawa Treaty, as the Convention is commonly referred to, is unique in many ways. It was the fastest international disarmament convention to come into force and, at the time, the only one to ban a complete weapon type. It has the dual aim of preventing future use of anti-personnel landmines, as well putting obligations on countries to clear all landmines from their territory and to provide support to landmine victims. Deadlines were set for destroying stockpiles of mines and clearing landmines from the ground.

The Convention provides the political framework and direction for many countries in the world when tackling the landmine issue, whether as an affected country or as a donor. To date 162 countries have joined the Convention and while a number of significant countries have not joined, the results have been impressive.

The sale of landmines has stopped (even by non-signatory countries) and the new use of mines in conflicts has virtually ended. Millions of landmines that were held in stockpiles have been destroyed and significant areas of mine-affected land have been cleared in countries around the world.

Over 60 member states to the Convention declared that they were affected by landmines and while there has been slow progress in some cases, to date 28 countries have now declared themselves to be mine-free.

The number of new landmine victims each month has dramatically decreased in countries like Afghanistan, Cambodia and Mozambique, and improved services are available to support landmine victims.

While challenges will always remain, the Convention has been instrumental in making huge steps in ridding the world of landmines.

September 11 in New York

My work with UNDP in New York involved a lot of travel and in early September 2001 I attended some meetings in Geneva and Brussels. I flew back to New York and landed at JFK airport on the afternoon of 10 September. By now, Margaret was working at the United Nations security office and so on the morning of Tuesday 11 September 2001 we were walking together to work along 3rd Avenue. We both noticed a low flying commercial airliner and actually stopped to look at it, commenting on how low it seemed.

The noise from the engines of the plane was also unusual because they were changing pitch all the time. We thought no more of it and went to our respective offices. Around 8.50 am Margaret called me to say that she had just seen on the TV in her office that a plane had hit the World Trade Center (WTC). As I worked on the 20th floor of the UNDP building I went to a window on the south side, and even though it was a couple of kilometres away, I could clearly see smoke billowing from one of the WTC towers. I ran back to my office and called Margaret and said that I would call our kids back in Australia, as I was sure this would be big news. I quickly rang Zoe and Charles and told them that a plane had hit the WTC but that Margaret and I were safe. I then went back to the window and saw that another plane had just hit the second tower.

Everyone in the office was becoming quite anxious because it was clear that two planes hitting buildings was not an accident, and it was also becoming clear that these were passenger jets involved and not light aircraft. We were also starting to hear about a third plane hitting the Pentagon in Washington. An attempt had been made to fire a rocket into the United Nations building some years earlier, so now we were starting to think that maybe we would be next. I saw the first tower collapse and then the word came to evacuate the building.

I ran around our floor and the one above to make sure everyone was out and then made my way 20 storeys down the crowded flight of stairs. I got Margaret from her office and we walked home to our apartment in mid-town Manhattan. People were rushing everywhere and there were endless sirens from police cars and fire trucks. We got home and like everyone else sat and watched events unfold on TV. The full horror and tragedy of the day started to sink in and we also realised that the low flying plane we saw must have been the first plane, American Airlines flight 11. We felt helpless and thought that we should be doing something, but on the TV the authorities were urging everyone to stay away from lower Manhattan and go home.

The next day was eerie, because except for the sirens it was so quiet. All the bridges and tunnels to Manhattan were closed and there were no aircraft in the air. We lived close to the Empire State Building and all the roads around it were cordoned off, so there was very little traffic. Later the wind changed direction and blew the smoke over Manhattan and we will never forget that smell of death and destruction. A temporary command centre was set up in a National Guard armoury a few blocks from our apartment and sadly a fire station in the next street lost many of its members.

Within hours of the attacks, notices and posters seeking information about missing people started to be stuck on every post or wall in the neighbourhood by concerned relatives. We didn't go down to the site for some weeks and even then the grey dust was still covering everything in sight and it was hard to imagine that almost 3000 people had lost their lives on that awful day. Margaret and I were never in any personal danger and we did not lose anyone close to us, but the events of that day will always be etched in our minds.

Only a week later the 'anthrax attacks' occurred when letters containing anthrax were sent to media outlets and two congressmen, killing five people. This caused a new round of anguish and turmoil for the people of New York. When it became evident that the perpetrators of the WTC attacks, the then little known group called al-Qaeda were based in Afghanistan, the US decided to invade. There were people cheering on the streets of New York when this started, but knowing something about Afghan history, I could only shake my head in disbelief at what was happening.

Just prior to 11 September I had hired one of my former colleagues from Afghanistan, Mohammad Younus, to work on my team at UNDP. His landlord started harassing him about being an Afghan, so I had to go and see the landlord to assure him that Younus was a United Nations official and not a terrorist.

Keeping in touch with past programs and people

Even though I was working at the international level, I still kept an interest in the events that were happening in the three countries where I had managed the mine clearance programs – Afghanistan, Laos and Bosnia. In Afghanistan the Taliban took control of Kabul city in September 1996. The former President Najibullah, who had been living in the United

Nations compound since 1992, was dragged outside, tortured and then hanged from a lamp post outside the Presidential Palace. The regional manager for the mine clearance program, Tahsin Disbudak, was one of the few United Nations staff still in the city at the time. Tahsin was stuck in a different office compound on the other side of the city and could not do anything, but he was the last person to speak to Najibullah over the radio before he was killed. The Taliban went on to control about 90 per cent of the country, but they were only ever recognised as a 'government' by Pakistan, Saudi Arabia and the United Arab Emirates.

Despite enormous difficulties the UNOCHA mine clearance program in Afghanistan continued to function under the Taliban. I had been replaced as the program manager by yet more Australian ex-army colleagues, first Bill van Ree and then later Ian Bullpitt. In May 2000 a Canadian, Dan Kelly, took over the program and he oversaw much of the mine clearance work involved with highway reconstruction tasks after the US invasion of Afghanistan. Logically the new Afghan government of President Hamid Karzai should have taken over responsibility for mine clearance throughout the country, but because the program was well established the government asked the United Nations to continue running it. Later program managers were Alan McDonald and Abigail Hartley.

The specialised Afghan NGOs and their directors are still the backbone of mine action efforts on the ground and all moved their head offices into Kabul around 2002. The mine clearance NGO, Afghan Technical Consultants, claims to be the oldest mine clearance NGO in the world.

I went back to Kabul in October 2009 as the guest of honour at their 20th anniversary celebration. My good friend Kefayatullah was still the director, despite an unfortunate incident in 2001. At that time Kef was kidnapped from his office in Peshawar by armed men and held in captivity for seven months. When he was finally released he was in very poor physical condition and could not walk. Fortunately he recovered and was able to return to work, although he has never set foot in Pakistan again.

The Mine Dog Centre relocated to Kabul in 2002 and it has expanded its role into providing drug detecting dogs and security dogs. The centre continued to be run by Shohab Hakimi, who was also the Afghan representative of the International Campaign to Ban Landmines. Engineer Sattar was still Director of the Demining Agency for Afghanistan based in Kandahar and Fazel Karim remained as Director of the Organisation for Mine Awareness. Fazel had also opened an impressive landmine museum in Kabul and runs a Pashtu language satellite television channel.

Finally, Sayed Aqa from the survey organisation MCPA replaced me at UNDP in New York when I left. Sayed later became a mainstream UNDP staff member and has headed up a number of their country offices in the Middle East. I admire all the Afghans who stayed and worked for their country during extremely difficult conditions, but I am equally proud of those who moved on and were successful in the international arena.

Although I was long gone from Afghanistan, in 2009 it was at the forefront of my mind again. After he had finished university, our son Charles had a decided on a career in the army. After graduating from Duntroon in 2004 as an engineer officer (exactly 30 years after me) he deployed as a captain to Tarin Kowt for 10 months as part of Operation Slipper – the Australian Defence Force operation in Afghanistan. I certainly had mixed emotions about this. As a former military officer I saw that it was his duty to deploy, but as a father with a good knowledge of the difficulties of operating in Afghanistan, I was deeply concerned for him at the time. I must admit I was relieved when his tour ended safely.

After having been a forgotten story for many years, Laos came to prominence in 2010 when it hosted the first meeting of a new convention banning cluster munitions. In the time since I had left the country, most of the Lao officials had changed. The Minister for Labour and Social Welfare had moved to a new ministry, Vice-Minister Noy had retired and my national counterpart Mr Saykham had passed away. Most of the other Lao staff had also retired or moved on. Mr Bounpone, who had replaced Saykham just as I was leaving Laos, remained in his post for over 10 years and he did a remarkable job.

I was replaced as the UNDP adviser by the very capable Phil Bean, and he was later succeeded by other people, including Tim

Horner who I knew from Bosnia and another friend, Tim Lardner. My good friend and colleague Jenni Rauch came and worked for me in New York for a couple of years and then moved to the mine action team at Cranfield University in the United Kingdom. She now works for another university in England, managing their foreign student program.

Following an independent review, the UXO Lao program was restructured by setting up a new office to deal with the regulatory aspects of UXO activities, such as tasking, coordination, standards and quality control, while UXO Lao focussed on actual UXO clearance work in the field. While this change was based on the successful organisational model used in Afghanistan, I personally felt that the way the program had been originally set up within the Lao government was still appropriate and adequate. UNDP continues to provide advisers to both organisations. Rather than phase out the number of foreign organisations working in Laos as I had foreseen, there has been an increase of them, partly because of the increased interest in Laos. Fortunately, the number of new civilian casualties has gone down significantly in Laos and most affected provinces now have a UXO response capability to safely deal with unexploded bombs.

In Bosnia the situation never got any easier. In 2000, the High Representative removed the three Demining Commissioners – Mr Cengic, Mr Pusic and Mr Ilic – from their posts due 'misuse of office and breach of public trust' and in 2004 Mr Pusic was indicted by the war crimes tribunal in The Hague. In 2001 I was asked to go to Bosnia to help with an investigation into the alleged misuse of demining equipment granted by the USA, but I found no evidence of corruption and that all the equipment had gone to the Bosnian organisations that the Americans had wanted it to go to.

The man with the eye patch, Peter Isaacs, who had replaced me, continued as the UNDP adviser for some years and was then replaced by another Australian, David Rowe. In an encouraging move, David was not replaced at the end of his tenure as it was felt that the Bosnians had sufficient management and technical capacity of their own. The Bosnian government passed a Demining Law which regulated all mine action activities in the country and the program has produced a number of multi-year national mine action plans.

One very positive step in the Balkans was the establishment of the International Trust Fund in Slovenia in late 1998. It was a unique and clever move by the Americans to set up the fund in Slovenia – a former state within Yugoslavia, but not mine affected itself. This ensured that the fund managers were knowledgeable about the situation in the region, but neutral in making decisions affecting funding support to Bosnia, Croatia and Serbia. The US initially provided $28 million to the fund, but with a caveat that money could only be released if it was matched dollar for dollar by another donor. This had the advantage of providing an incentive to other donors to contribute through the fund and thus centralise and coordinate most of the money going into the region.

The International Trust Fund set up transparent and open contracting procedures which helped 'clean-up' the mine action sector, particularly in Bosnia. This led to significant areas of land in the region being cleared of landmines and UXO. I was fortunate to serve as a member of the Advisory Board of the Fund for a number of years.

The Australian Army also deserves a mention at this stage. During the late 1980s and early 1990s, Australia provided a total of 66 engineer officers and 104 warrant officers/senior NCOs as advisers to United Nations mine clearance programs in Afghanistan, Cambodia, Mozambique, Eritrea and Bosnia. Afghanistan was by far the largest commitment with 94 people over a six year period, while in Cambodia a total of 45 advisers were deployed over a five year period. In all these countries the officers and NCOs acquitted themselves extremely well and were highly regarded for their professionalism and commitment to the job. They all endured hardship in the field and threats to their personal safety and security, while being unarmed. Fortunately, no-one was ever killed or seriously injured.

Many of the humanitarian demining techniques and procedures that were developed or adapted by the Australian Army instructors in these programs are still in use today. Of the total of 170 Australian Army advisers who worked in these programs, I estimate that over 30 of them (like me) left the army at some stage and worked in the mine action sector as a civilian for the United Nations, an NGO or a commercial company. Those who continued to serve in the Australian Army put their mine clearance knowledge and skills to good use when the army subsequently became busy with operational deployments to East Timor, Iraq and Afghanistan.

One 'loose end' from the Australian Army deployment to Afghanistan was that we were not eligible to receive the United Nations medal, because we had not come under a formal United Nations Security Council resolution. This irked us because we had represented the United Nations in a hazardous area and had contributed to the cause of peace. Numerous applications for the medal had been rejected by United Nations headquarters. Fortunately the situation was resolved in a rather unconventional way some years later.

In early 2000, the United Nations Secretary-General Kofi Annan visited Australia en route to East Timor. A parade was held in Sydney in his honour and many Australian soldiers who had served with various United Nations peacekeeping missions lined up and were addressed by Mr Annan. He thanked them for their commitment and asked if there was anything he could do for them. My army replacement in Afghanistan, Lieutenant Colonel Greg McDowall, put up his hand and explained our situation with regards to the United Nations medal. Mr Annan said he would look into it and true to his word, some months later we were advised that all the military demining advisers who had served with Operation Salam in Afghanistan would be eligible to wear the United Nations Special Service Medal – inscribed on the back with the words 'In the Service of Peace'.

An unexpected offer from Switzerland

At the peak of the international community's interest in landmines in 1998, the Swiss government had established an organisation titled the Geneva International Centre for Humanitarian Demining, better known as the GICHD. The role of the centre was to act as a practical 'think tank' or 'study centre' to support the mine action sector with research, training, publications and technical information. The centre was headed by a Swiss ambassador and because it was well resourced, it quickly assembled a team of experienced experts and established its presence with high quality work. The centre was also asked to house the secretariat for the Ottawa Treaty and be the repository for the International Mine Action Standards. These responsibilities involved hosting many international meetings in Geneva and led to the GICHD becoming something of a hub for the mine action community.

My work with UNDP in New York involved regular travel to the GICHD in Geneva to speak at these international meetings, and we also started to engage the Centre to undertake research for the United Nations. The director of the GICHD at the time, Ambassador Martin Dahinden, approached me during one of my visits and said that if I was ever interested, he would be happy to have me at the Centre as his deputy and the director of operations. I gave it some thought and discussed the prospect of another move with Margaret.

After four years in New York and a total of 11 years at the forefront of mine action, the slower pace of Geneva looked appealing. I was also impressed with the quality and the practical relevance of the work the Centre was producing. I was pleased with the results my small team had achieved at UNDP in New York, but decided in early 2002 to accept Martin Dahinden's offer to work at the GICHD. This time I took three months off between jobs and Margaret and I returned to Australia for the wedding of our daughter, Zoe, and to catch up with family and friends.

After our extended holiday, Margaret and I moved to Geneva in order for me to start work at the GICHD in July 2002. By now Zoe was married to Craig Rossiter, who also happened to be in the Australian Army, and they were posted to Townsville in the north of Australia. Charles had been accepted into university in Australia and was studying science. As both the kids were now adults and were pursuing their own careers, we felt a little easier about leaving them in Australia.

Geneva is a lovely city, set on the shores of Lac Leman and nestled in the foothills of the Swiss Alps. It is a very international city and the Centre for a lot of international trading. The result is that it is an extremely expensive place to live. I managed to find a reasonable apartment close to the city and within walking distance to work.

Although I was on a decent salary, by the time I had paid the rent and Swiss tax, about half my pay was already gone. Pindi, the dog also came with us and he saw out his days with us in Geneva.

The GICHD was involved with undertaking a wide range of research into a variety of mine action topics. The Centre published books which quickly became the standard references for mine action field operations, and we also conducted evaluations and ran training courses. My work still involved travel to mine-affected countries and to donor capitals. Unlike the United Nations, the GICHD did not get bogged down in global politics or broader security issues, and being Geneva based we could draw on the Swiss reputation of neutrality.

The Centre offered to host the annual meeting of national mine action programs started by UNMAS, so every year hundreds of mine action practitioners from all around the world would come to the Centre for a week to discuss a whole range of practical issues. By this time, I had an extensive network of United Nations and national colleagues in over 50 countries and it was always great to catch up with them at this meeting. While I would often get back to New York to attend other meetings at the United Nations, I did not miss living there.

One of the early trips that I undertook for the GICHD was to Baghdad for a week in early July 2003. The US invasion of Iraq had lasted from 19 March to 1 May 2003 and by July the situation had stabilised somewhat. UNMAS had demining staff on the ground overseeing battlefield clearance and they were also advising the Iraqi government. The purpose of my trip was to help Cranfield University run a training course for senior Iraqi government officials, who had been appointed to run a national landmine and UXO clearance program. I flew into Baghdad on a United Nations flight, feeling slightly comforted by hearing the Australian accents coming from the air traffic control tower as we approached Baghdad airport. All the passengers were bundled onto a bus with drawn curtains and then we made a high speed dash down the highway under armed escort to the United Nations headquarters at the Canal Hotel. I was met there by my partners and taken to the Al Rasheed Hotel, situated in the Green Zone, where I would be staying.

STEPPING INTO A MINEFIELD

The training course went well and I found the Iraqis we were dealing with to be committed and interested people. After the course finished my departure was delayed a few days due to security concerns with the United Nations flights. One evening in the hotel I saw the United Nations Special Representative, Sergio Vieira de Mello. I did not know him well, but I had met him twice before so we said a brief hello and shook hands. The next day I did some sightseeing, visiting one of Saddam Hussein's palaces and noting lots of abandoned anti-aircraft missiles on vacant lots. Finally the United Nations flights resumed and I repeated the process of getting back to Baghdad airport and then flew home to Geneva.

I was in my office in Geneva on 19 August 2003 when we started to hear reports of a truck bomb going off at the Canal Hotel in Baghdad. As the news filtered through we heard the tragic news that Sergio de Mello had been killed along with many others. UNMAS had arranged a mine action mission to Baghdad at that time and many of my friends were there. Martin Barber was holding a live TV press conference in the Canal Hotel when the bomb went off and he was injured. Mohammad Younus, who was there representing UNDP, was seriously injured and had to be evacuated to Germany for treatment. JJ van der Merwe, who I took over from in Bosnia, was also present and he did an outstanding job assisting the wounded. Another Australian colleague, Polly Brennan from the mine awareness team at UNICEF in New York, was also badly injured. I was devastated by the news and was deeply concerned for my friends.

I pieced together all the facts I could gather and sent out an open email to my mine action colleagues telling them what had happened. As I had been in the Canal Hotel just weeks before I also started to feel guilty that I was not there. If the training course had been on at that time, I know I would have gone to the press conference. If I had not left UNDP in New York, I most certainly would have been part of that mission to Baghdad. The 'what ifs' played on my mind for a while, but fortunately all my friends recovered and life slowly got back to normal for them.

The time passed quickly at the Centre and each year had its rhythm of regular international meetings, field trips, studies, training courses and general staff issues. I had never intended to stay very long at the Centre, but I found the work extremely rewarding. Some critics would say that 'everything has been studied in mine action', but each year some new topic or issue would arise that needed attention. A lot had been achieved in the mine action sector, but a lot remained to be done. The Centre also had a range of regular services that it provided, such as overseeing the international standards dealing with mine action, developing an information management system that had been provided to about 40 countries and supporting the various international conventions dealing with landmines, cluster munitions and other explosive remnants of war.

To maintain family contact, Margaret and I would get back to Australia most years to see Zoe and Charles, or they would come to us. As we all enjoyed skiing, it was not hard to convince them to come to Switzerland in the winter, as there were world class ski slopes on our doorstep. Zoe's husband, Craig, deployed with the Australian Army to East Timor and then Iraq, and on both occasions Zoe came and stayed with us. Charles had met a young lady, Rachel Davies, and they were married in 2009 in a castle near her home town of Chester in England. Being in Geneva was handy as we were able to fly to the UK quite easily to attend the ceremony and meet Rachel's family.

In early 2010, I was advised by the Australian Government that I was being considered for a civilian award in the Australian honours system, and asked if I would accept it. Naturally I said yes, and in the Queen's Birthday Honours List announced on 14 June 2010 I was appointed a Member of the Order of Australia. The citation for the award read 'For service to international humanitarian aid through the establishment of global landmine removal, safety and training programs'.

I was extremely pleased about receiving this national recognition, because although I had worked internationally for 20 years, I was still very much an Australian at heart. The inauguration was set for September and as I wanted to share the day with my family, I opted to receive the award at Government House in Canberra. Margaret and I travelled back to Australia for the ceremony, and Zoe and Charles were invited. It was the proudest day of my life when the Governor General of Australia, Dame Quentin Bryce, pinned the award on my chest in front of my family.

I ended up spending nine satisfying and rewarding years at the GICHD. In that time I had the pleasure to work with two other talented Swiss directors – Ambassadors Stephan Nellen and Stephan Husy. The Centre also had a good mix of experienced international staff who had worked all over the world, along with dedicated Swiss support staff. One of my more satisfying 'projects' was to set up an internship program where a young graduate from a mine-affected country was selected to come and work for me at the Centre to gain international exposure. When their year was up, they would return to work in the national mine action program in their own country. In most cases we chose young women, as their career opportunities were limited at home, and we had delightful young people from Eritrea, Albania, Iraq, Sri Lanka and Afghanistan come and work for us.

EPILOGUE

Finally, in 2011, Margaret said enough. Geneva was the longest we had ever lived in the one place in our married life and because we now had some grandchildren, she wanted to go home to Australia. As I was about to turn 60 years old, I also agreed it was time to slow down. When leaving Geneva in mid-2011, it was hard not to reflect on the remarkable 20 years that had just passed and the experiences that we had shared. We had left Australia in 1991 on a one-year army posting and now, 20 years later, we were finally going home. We still had furniture and effects in storage in Australia from when we first left and when we opened the boxes it was like a time warp – reel to reel tape recorders, records, VHS tapes, kids' clothes and bottles of wine (which sadly had gone off).

I had been given the privilege of commanding Australian troops in a hazardous environment on an overseas deployment in Pakistan and Afghanistan, and the officers and NCOs under my command had all done an outstanding job. By going to Afghanistan at that time, I was fortunate to be part of a significant transition that saw dealing with explosive remnants of war shift from being seen as purely a military activity to that of an essential humanitarian response.

While working for a communist government in Laos was extremely frustrating at the time, in retrospect, the setting up of a national UXO program in little over two years was perhaps one of my better achievements.

Working in Bosnia exposed me to the rawness of a bloody civil war, but also highlighted the possibilities of mine clearance to be used as a positive, peace-building measure.

Through my work I saw the aftermath of three wars at close hand. While not particularly unique or startling, the conclusion I came to is that no-one wins a war. The devastation and suffering caused to all sides did not seem to justify the original intentions. While as a former military officer I still believe in the right of a nation to defend itself, the use of force must be weighed against clear national objectives and used in accordance with international humanitarian law.

I was pleased to have played a small role in bringing about a total ban on anti-personnel landmines. Despite claims by certain militaries about the usefulness of landmines, the argument that the long term, indiscriminate impact of mines on civilians was totally unacceptable finally won the day. The same argument also saw a ban on the use of cluster munitions, another indiscriminate weapon.

On a personal level I have visited over 70 countries, many of them war torn and impoverished. While again not unique, I found that in most countries the ordinary citizen just wants to live in peace, have a job, raise a family and provide their children with an education. The extremists we see on television usually represent a small minority and as Kofi Annan once said, the biggest threat to mankind is ignorance, caused by lack of education.

I have been privileged to become friends with people of all races and religions and I still keep in touch with many of them today. I am always saddened when I hear about the loss of the brave men and women deminers who died in the service of their country clearing landmines and other explosive devices.

Coming from a very narrow and homogenous background like the Australian Army, I found it fascinating to work for the United Nations in the international arena and alongside national officials from many countries. Through this I met a diverse range of people of all nationalities, with widely differing skills and motivation, including some of the most talented, dedicated and skilled people you could hope to meet (and some not so).

Throughout every step of this journey I have had the total support of my wife, Margaret, and our two children, Zoe and Charles. Together, we hope we have made a tiny impact on making the world a better place for a few people.